States and statistics in the nineteenth century

Manchester University Press

This publication has been made possible with the financial support of the Netherlands Organization for Scientific Research (NWO)

Nosti hominum mores et vite nodos et laqueos rerum, quarum perplexitates nec arythmeticus numeret nec geometra mensuret nec rimetur astrologus; sentiunt autem qui inter eas apertis oculis gradiuntur.

Petrarch to Boccaccio, Letters of old age, VI, 2

You know the ways of men and the oddities and snares of life, whose intricacies neither an arithmetrician could count nor a geometrician measure nor an astronomer examine. But those who approach such things with their eyes open do perceive them.

States and statistics in the nineteenth century

Europe by numbers

Nico Randeraad

Translated from Dutch
by Debra Molnar

Manchester University Press
Manchester and New York

distributed in the United States exclusively
by Palgrave Macmillan

Originally published in Dutch as *Het onberekenbare Europa. Macht en getal in de negentiende eeuw*

The right of Nico Randeraad to be identified as the author of this work has been asserted by him in accordance with the Copyright, Designs and Patents Act 1988.

Published by Manchester University Press
Oxford Road, Manchester M13 9NR, UK
and Room 400, 175 Fifth Avenue, New York, NY 10010, USA
www.manchesteruniversitypress.co.uk

Distributed in the United States exclusively by
Palgrave Macmillan, 175 Fifth Avenue, New York,
NY 10010, USA

Distributed in Canada exclusively by
UBC Press, University of British Columbia, 2029 West Mall,
Vancouver, BC, Canada V6T 1Z2

British Library Cataloguing-in-Publication Data
A catalogue record for this book is available from the British Library

Library of Congress Cataloging-in-Publication Data applied for

ISBN 978 0 7190 8142 2 hardback

First published 2010

The publisher has no responsibility for the persistence or accuracy of URLs for any external or third-party internet websites referred to in this book, and does not guarantee that any content on such websites is, or will remain, accurate or appropriate.

Edited and typeset
by Frances Hackeson Freelance Publishing Services, Brinscall, Lancs
Printed in Great Britain
by CPI Antony Rowe Ltd, Chippenham, Wiltshire

Contents

Introduction

This book is a history of an illusion. It is also a history of the dream that preceded the illusion. The dream was of the progressive utility of statistical knowledge, and was shared by many a nineteenth-century statistician. Their dream would be fulfilled in three phases. First, data about society would be gathered in every country, employing uniform methods and categories. Then, the data would be compared and governments would base their policies on the knowledge thus acquired. And finally, all of humanity would experience greater happiness and prosperity. The belief in progress had no truer, more faithful or more ambitious proponent than the statistician. He calculated, classified and concluded, until every law that governed society seemed to materialise from the numbers spontaneously. As obvious as it is to us that this was an illusion, the statistician had no doubt that his ideal was achievable.

Statistics in the nineteenth century is a far cry from the science we know today. Power and numbers had not yet acquired the inextricable and obvious connection they would in the twentieth century. During the Enlightenment, an academic elite had already determined that knowledge was power, but although the notion of 'statistics' had cropped up here and there, it had not yet entered the mainstream. There was no consensus about the meaning of the concept in the eighteenth century.

In the Napoleonic Age, statistics became an established part of the administrative repertoire. Good government and statistics were practically synonymous. This applied not only in the states that had been absorbed into Napoleon's empire, but also in Prussia and Russia, where the institutional foundations were laid for government statistics in the first decade of the nineteenth century. Nineteenth-century governments clung to the idea that solutions to social problems could be derived from systematic, empirical observation of a quantitative and qualitative nature. How this idea was put into practice differed from state to state. In the same way that statistics did not develop linearly as a branch of knowledge, no uniform European model of statistics as a branch of government emerged.

A speaker at the third international congress on statistics held in Vienna in 1857 called statistics 'the science of the century'.[1] While not everyone would have shared that opinion, statisticians themselves were certain they were right and fully convinced of the necessity of their mission. They wrote books, established journals, organised congresses and, when called upon, were tireless servants of the state. In their fervour, however, they failed to unify their science. Statistics was a repository of various sciences and disciplines, which enjoyed short- or long-lived popularity. In the first half of the nineteenth century, the dividing lines between scientific disciplines were still vague, or positioned differently than we would expect today. The fate of statistics would be tied to political economics one day and geography or ethics the next. If statistics was not the science of the century, then at least it was the chameleonic manifestation of a procession of sciences that emerged and disappeared throughout the nineteenth century.

Statistics was a field with as many practitioners as definitions. Statisticians all shared a desire for factual knowledge, but there the similarities ended. At the universities, statistics initially found a home with the legal disciplines or political sciences. There was little interest in numbers or calculations. In the first half of the nineteenth century it was barely conceivable that statistics would end up as merely an auxiliary science. This development progressed through various stages and was unpredictable. After counting 62 definitions, Gustav Rümelin hypothesised in his *Zur Theorie der Statistik* (1863) that 'there had to be a hidden enticement and it brought to mind the suitors in Gozzi's fable who, undeterred by the bloodied heads of their unfortunate predecessors, sought to solve Turandot's riddles over and over again'.[2] Ernst Engel, director of the Prussian Office of Statistics, identified 180 definitions in 1869. In his view, this demonstrated that there was nothing to be gained from searching for a definition on which everyone could agree.[3]

The discord about the essence of statistics hindered the uniformisation of statistical research methods. Statistical laws were seldom formulas. Not all statisticians were searching for laws, however carefully formulated. Some even had a categorical and explicit aversion to them. Descriptive statistics, which stemmed from the work of seventeenth- and eighteenth-century German scholars such as Hermann Conring and Gottfried Achenwall, remained influential for a long time. They defined statistics as the description of *Staatsmerkwürdigkeiten*, a kind of political science without theory. From this tradition emerged considerable resistance to endless streams of numbers and the laws derived from them. This difference of opinion – particularly on the issue of whether these laws signified a negation of free will – was the subject of fierce debate until the end of the nineteenth century.

Nineteenth-century statisticians were inspired by a scholar who was not engaged in statistical research. The name of Alexander von Humboldt (1769–

1859), naturalist, explorer and cosmopolitan, appeared in numerous statistics journals. The fact that he was not a card-carrying statistician did not lessen his appeal to statisticians. Geography and statistics were disciplines that easily overflowed into one another. Humboldt's thirst for knowledge carried him from flowers to the stars, from Europe to South America, and – perhaps the most difficult feat of his day – from Berlin to Paris and back again. Like statisticians, he was mesmerised by the connection between the general and the specific. His goal was to find unity in diversity. Every discovery was the tendril of a new insight and a step towards a higher truth. Each natural law was a springboard to the discovery of another. Despite his tremendous faith in empirical observation and classification, science was also an emotional matter to Humboldt. His meticulous drawings of botanical diversity are the visible proof of his sensibility.

The same applied to statisticians. They would never openly admit to being motivated by sentiment, but their desire to expand the body of statistical knowledge was fuelled by more than reason alone. Though they were occupied with cold hard numbers and tables day and night, they believed that a perfect world lay beyond. Many intuited that society was governed by laws and those laws could be found only through patient observation and precise description. Without that desire and intuition the protagonists of this book – the giants of nineteenth-century statistics – would not have been half as interesting as they were.

Statistical laws were less fundamental than one might think. Many scholars spoke and wrote about them, but few actually put them into words. Statistical laws were neither natural nor legal laws, but constituted an assumed order. The mere fact that slightly more boys than girls were born was sufficient to suggest a law. Frequently, the wish was father to the statistical law. French and German statisticians, for example, fought hardest to formulate 'laws' that could explain the rate of population growth: the French in order to reason away the decline in their population, the Germans to embellish the importance of the growth of their population. Statistics was a desire for certainty in what seemed to be a rapidly changing world. Collecting, editing and publishing statistics were all part of the control offensive that preceded the nineteenth-century civilisation offensive.

Statisticians were particularly interested in social problems that, in their view, had a moral root. 'Statistical research,' wrote the Frenchman Alfred Legoyt in 1860, 'leads to the discovery of the laws of the moral world as sure as astronomical observations lead to the establishment of laws in the physical world.'[4] It was most remarkable, according to Legoyt, that all manner of phenomena which are believed to have arisen from deeply personal motives display a high degree of regularity at the aggregate level. It could not be coincidental that every year approximately the same number of crimes were committed, by the same number of people, of the same sex, same age, same profession etc. More salient still, in his view, was the annual regularity in the number of suicides and marriages (while one would assume these were the most personal of choices).

Generally speaking, statisticians were cautious about prescribing solutions to the problems they identified and quantified. It was not that they were bereft of ideas on the subject, but their ideas had to be deduced from reading between the lines. They tended to be concealed in the questions or categories on which the statistical research was founded. Statisticians encouraged each other to believe that the world could be changed. But the problem was, how? The 'lawgivers' and the 'lawless', those who believed in reverberating statistical laws and those who wanted nothing to do with laws, shared an unshakeable belief in perfectibility. Progress constituted perfection. And if the world could not be improved, at least statistics could. Legoyt's main priority was undoubtedly the declining birth rate in France. This notable fact, he emphasised, went hand in hand with an increase in the number of marriages and a rise in the general standard of living. In addition to putting a positive spin on a development that was not widely welcomed, Legoyt was ultimately able to establish a link between the birth rate and the questionable reliability of the census data. Sometimes the lack of reliability was due to the questions asked and to the instructions given by those in charge, more often it was the result of execution problems at local level, but the most pervasive problem was the uncooperative attitude of the people who saw the census-taker as a tax agent in disguise.[5] Legoyt stressed the necessity of good statistics, and particularly of the flawless execution of the census as such, and therefore of his own services.

Statistics was not only a disputed science but also a complicated administrative practice, steered by statistics offices, prefectures, ministerial departments and other government agencies. Sometimes private associations or individual researchers initiated statistical investigations. One can imagine how difficult it was to conduct statistical research in Europe before the communication revolution: telecommunication was rudimentary at best, transport was unreliable, adding machines were impractical, the typewriter had not yet been invented and illiteracy was widespread. In the second quarter of the nineteenth century Britain and Belgium had fledgling railway networks, but large parts of Europe were devoid of this kind of infrastructure. The national censuses that were carried out across Europe in the course of the nineteenth century were immense operations given the limited resources available at the time.

The first Italian census took place in the year of unification, 1861, and was coordinated from the city of Turin, the capital at the time, and covered the entire peninsula from Como to Agrigento. Every household was to receive a census form and every form would have to be returned, if not to Turin at least to the prefecture. Some forms were transported thousands of kilometres over land and sea because there were few railway connections. What was a colossal undertaking in Italy turned out to be completely unworkable in Russia. Nevertheless, statistics was a flourishing field there too. Like Gogol's Chichikov traversing the Russian countryside to gather 'dead souls', suffering all manner of deprivation along the way, the revisers – the Russian government's official census-takers – travelled the same barely negotiable roads to collect the desired information from the population. A difficult task indeed. The census-takers could not do their work from behind a desk. They had to 'go to the people'. So, statistics was not only hard work, it also frequently necessitated direct contact between census-takers and the people, which brought with it a range of disruptive influences. Precision was the goal, but tainted information was frequently the result.

Methodical to a fault, most statisticians tried to invent solutions for every potential problem in advance. The first phase of their dream involved collecting uniform data, by country and, if possible, for all of Europe. They exchanged information with each other, sharing the results of their research as well as their ideas about organising the science of statistics and its objects.

The Belgian Adolphe Quetelet was the initiator of the first international statistical congress, which was held in Brussels in 1853. Around that time, most countries had a statistics office. Some were more or less autonomous, while others were part of a government ministry. This institutional diversity hindered the exchange of data, which was a thorn in the flesh for Quetelet. Originated by learned societies and academies, which had existed for some time at local and national level, the scientific congress was a relatively new form of communication between researchers. As the permanent secretary of the Belgian Royal Academy of Arts and Sciences, Quetelet had contacts throughout Europe. To him, 'international' was synonymous with cosmopolitan and science was by definition international. This was true of his first academic love – astronomy – but equally true of statistics, the science that would bring him worldwide renown. He believed that the field needed a forum that would enable internationalism to flourish. During the Great Exhibition in London in 1851 he introduced the idea of an international congress that would make the dream a reality.

Like every other science, though, statistics did not become international automatically. The modern nation-state crystallised in the nineteenth century. Newly unified states like Italy and Germany emerged, and the great empires such as the Austro-Hungarian monarchy, Russia and Turkey began to crumble. The 'old' states of Europe were following a nationalist path. Politics, economics, social services and other aspects of civil life were being absorbed into national structures. Nationalisation affected science as well. Academies, universities, scientific societies and even the sciences themselves derived their status from the nation-state to an increasing extent.[6] And what the sciences received they gave back in another form. The science of history, for instance, conferred on the nation-state its own history. Statistics presented a population, a birth rate, a poverty line and in a certain sense ostensibly neutral social phenomena such as crime and unemployment, and as a result became the most 'political' science of all. The data that statisticians produced could be used directly in the day-to-day administration of a country. This did not make the practice of comparative statistics any easier. There was tension between the 'imagined community' of internationally oriented statisticians and the 'imagined community' of the nation.[7] The international statistical congresses soon had to abandon their cosmopolitan character and, to the confusion and annoyance of statisticians themselves, became the battleground for national interests.

This provides the leitmotif of this book: statistics as the field of tension between the scientific claims of neutrality and universality on the one hand and the political and economic reality of the conflicting interests of nation-states on the other. These conflicting interests manifested themselves in a variety of ways. At times the battles constituted genuine tests of strength in international politics, while at others they revolved around laborious comparisons of divergent economies or pragmatic assessments of various methods of registration. These conflicts were most starkly illuminated at the nine international statistical congresses held between 1853 and 1876. As such, they are central to this narrative and give the book its structure. By following the debates from congress to congress we will see a rich tapestry of divergent visions of statistics and the search for ways to facilitate international decision-making.

Statisticians oscillated between universal aspirations and the demands placed on them by the daily practice of statistical research. Whichever topics they discussed, this dilemma resurfaced over and over again in new forms during the congresses. In a sense, this battle with 'reality' continues today. The spirit of Quetelet and his contemporaries lives on in the offices of Eurostat. The nineteenth century was replete with idealism – an idealism so deep-seated that it has outlived its usefulness in some respects. At the congress in The Hague in 1869, Jean Baptist Baron van Hugenpoth tot den Beerenclauw called the gathering 'the tribunal Europe'.[8] Italian politician and statistician Cesare Correnti went so far as to say that the international congress was 'the prophecy of a European parliament'.[9] In hindsight, this may seem to be a portentous statement: a lot of talking but few concrete results. For Correnti, however, the metaphor held the same promise as Italian unification: government on the basis of facts and participation. In the middle of the nineteenth century the step from a unified Italy to a unified Europe did not seem all that great, particularly in the political philosophy of someone like Correnti, a student of the federalist Carlo Cattaneo.

Like idealism, realism was also growing. Fredrik Theodor Berg of Sweden gradually became convinced of the need to allow the statistical Europe to emerge gradually, or incrementally as theorists of European integration would say today. In a letter to the organiser of the sixth international congress, Pietro Maestri, Berg wrote: 'The statistical congresses will, in my opinion, never be truly *international* until they have been held in the capital cities of the most important states and, while moving around, retained a substantial *national* character. I believe their national disposition is a genuine advantage and should not elicit criticism. We must become acquainted with all national circumstances to give attempts at international generalisations a greater chance of success.'[10]

Drawing comparisons followed naturally from counting and was a step towards progress. It is telling that Friedrich Nietzsche called the mid-nineteenth century 'the age of comparison'.[11] An international statistical congress seemed an excellent venue for making systematic comparisons. At the time, this form of communication had not yet crystallised. In 1853 it was not obvious to Quetelet and his contemporaries how the congress should be organised and even less clear how its outcomes should be put into practice. Language was a recurrent issue. French was the lingua franca of science and diplomacy, but in Britain, Austria and Germany no one was willing to consider relinquishing their national language. Each congress drew hundreds of participants, mainly from the host country. This level of interest lent prestige but – in the eyes of the professional statisticians – had the potential to undermine the scientific significance of the congresses, so means were sought to streamline the deliberations and voting. At the third congress in Vienna it was decided that 'pre-congresses' would be convened from then on for the official delegates of the participating countries. At the eighth congress in St Petersburg the delegates considered whether 'post-congresses' should be held as well. The calls for a permanent international statistics committee grew louder. Statisticians not only discussed their field, they also explored forms of scientific and political cooperation. The search for the right form is a thread running through the congresses and is therefore one of the main themes of this book.

A wide-ranging book like this one could never be the result of primary source research alone, although it must be said that the proceedings of the nine congresses were a nearly inexhaustible source of information. The author is indebted to more writers than could be cited without compromising readability. An enlightening example, particularly as regards readability, is Ian Hackings' *The Taming of Chance*, which covers the same period by and large. In his introductory chapter he informs the reader that 'what follows is not history' but rather a philosophical analysis of concepts in their context.[12] Where necessary I have written a history, with particular attention to national diversity, institutions (such as the international statistical congress) and the administrative practices involved in statistical research. My intention was to take different paths than those explored by Theodore Porter, Stephen Stigler and Alain Desrosières in their history of science studies.[13] The growing body of critical research on national statistics is reviewed where appropriate in the respective chapters.

Under the influence of scholars inspired by sociology, such as Michel Foucault and Pierre Bourdieu, I focus less on the institutional, descriptive history of statistics and more on the history of construction and prescription. Rather than providing an objective representation of reality, statistics served as a guide on how to think about reality. The numerous statistical categories that were invented now determine the way we view the world around us. Specific definitions for 'ordinary' words like house, household, family and profession had to be formulated in order to make the categories they represent countable. Along with this controlled perspective came conditioned intervention, for example in the form of an initial, circumspect social politics.

It is not the aim of this book to set out a detached 'archaeology' of statistics in the nineteenth century. Instead, it describes the perceptions, goals and dilemmas of the protagonists and their contact with each other, and in so doing unravels the complex relationships between science, government and society, wherever possible from their point of view. This is not a strictly chronological narrative. As stated above, the book traces the international statistical congresses held in nine European cities between 1853 and 1876. Chapter 8 combines the final congresses in St Petersburg and Budapest, not because what was going on in the field in Russia and Hungary is of less interest – on the contrary – but because the congress movement was clearly on the wane by that time. Each chapter addresses the state of government statistics in the organising country, but the reader who expects to find a systematic comparison of nine national styles of statistics or of the institutionalisation of statistics in nine countries will be disappointed. Such a comparison would make the book nine times as long and a tiresome read.[14]

The various paths of state- and nation-building that European countries traversed in the nineteenth century are recognisable in the objectives of government statistics and are reflected in the topics selected for statistical study and in the categories used in the research. Each congress was clearly dominated by the specific interests – in some cases obsessions – of the country in which the statisticians convened. The aim of this book is to show in each case how the organisation of government statistics and national concerns influenced the international agenda.

The international statistical congresses were the work of a small group of people who saw in Quetelet a pioneer. It is probably no coincidence that there was only one more congress after his death in 1874. The top statisticians in the host countries did just as much to advance the field, and they play a prominent role in the pages of this book. Charles Dupin and Alfred Legoyt of France, Karl von Czoernig of Austria, William Farr of England, Ernst Engel of Germany, Pietro Maestri and Cesare Correnti of Italy, Simon Vissering and Marie Matthieu von Baumhauer of the Netherlands, Petr Petrovich Semenov of Russia and Károly Keleti of Hungary make up the core of an international network of statisticians. This book may also be read as a collective biography of these men. It begins with a journey to Brussels.

Notes

1   According to the Prussian delegate F.G. Schubert, *Rechenschafts-Bericht über die dritte Versammlung des internationalen Congresses für Statistik abgehalten zu Wien vom 31. August bis 5. September 1857* (Vienna 1858), p. 218.

2   G. Rümelin, *Zur Theorie der Statistik* (1863), in G. Rümelin, *Reden und Aufsätze* (Freiburg i. B. 1875) p. 208.

3   Congrès International de Statistique à La Haye, *Compte-rendu des travaux de la septième session. Seconde partie* (The Hague 1870), p. 35.

4   A. Legoyt, 'Du mouvement de la population en France', *Journal de la Société de Statistique de Paris*, 1 (1860), 132.

5   *Ibid.*, 166–167.

6   R. Jessen and J. Vogel, *Wissenschaft und Nation in der europäischen Geschichte* (Frankfurt and New York 2002).

7   B. Anderson, *Imagined Communities: Reflections on the Origins and Spread of Nationalism* (2nd edn, London 1991).

8   Congrès International de Statistique à la Haye, *Compte-rendu des travaux de la septième session. Seconde partie*, p. 444.

9   C. Correnti, 'Congressi di statistica', *Annuario statistico italiano* II (1864), p. xliv.

10 Letter from F.-T. Berg aan P. Maestri, published in *Compte-rendu des travaux de la sixième session du Congrès International de Statistique réunie à Florence les 30 Septembre, 1, 2, 3, 4 et 5 Octobre 1867* (Florence 1868), p. 27.

11 'Zeitalter der Vergleichung' is the title of the 23rd aphorism in F. Nietzsche, *Menschliches, Allzumenschliches* (original edition, Chemnitz 1878).

12 I. Hacking, *The Taming of Chance* (Cambridge 1990, reprinted 1998), p. 7.

13 T.M. Porter, *The Rise of Statistical Thinking: 1820–1900* (Princeton 1986); S.M. Stigler, *The History of Statistics. The Measurement of Uncertainty before 1900* (Cambridge, MA and London 1986); A. Desrosières, *La politique des grands nombres. Histoire de la raison statistique* (Paris 1993).

14 For successful attempts at a comparative history of national statistics, see S.J. Woolf, 'Statistics and the Modern State', *Comparative Studies in Society and History* 31 (1989), 588–604; A. Desrosières, *La politique des grands nombres*; J.-P. Beaud and J.-G. Prévost (eds), *L'ère du chiffre. Systèmes statistiques et traditions nationales* (Québec 2000); L. Schweber, *Disciplining Statistics. Demography and Vital Statistics in France and England, 1830–1885* (Durham and London 2006).

1

The first meeting: Brussels 1853

The genesis of international statistics was inspired by a desire for reform. At the Great Exhibition of 1851 Adolphe Quetelet, born in Ghent in 1796, recognised that Europe was on the cusp of great economic and scientific breakthroughs. Knowledge about the changes taking place was of primary importance if the pace of reform and balance in society were to be maintained. Statistics could provide the information required, but there was no shared body of knowledge about statistics. In Europe, statisticians did not know how others in their field defined statistics or how they were conducting statistical research. So Quetelet invited everyone who was occupied with the subject to Brussels to share their ideas. The scientific congress was a relatively new form of communication that was generating a lot of enthusiasm. It was not difficult to entice the *crème de la crème* of European statistical practice to the Belgian capital.

At midnight on Thursday 15 September 1853, Carl Friedrich Wilhelm Dieterici, director of the Prussian Statistical Office, boarded the night train in Berlin to travel to the congress that would officially begin on 19 September. Taking a train to an international congress on statistics would have been inconceivable just ten years earlier. All the signs indicated that a new Europe was in the making. Dieterici made appreciative use of the new connections and decided to stop in Dortmund, a city on the rise in the western provinces of the Kingdom of Prussia. He arrived at Dortmund station at half past five in the morning. Dieterici was impressed by the growth of the iron and coal industry, and collected material so that he could report on Dortmund to the interior minister when he returned to Berlin. The statistician was determined that the government should have up-to-date factual information in order to monitor the rapid industrialisation of the Ruhrgebiet. This was, after all, one of his office's tasks. After touring the Dortmund area all day, on Friday evening he travelled on to Aachen, where he spent the night before continuing his journey on

Saturday. As he dutifully noted in his report, he arrived at the Prussian mission in the Belgian capital shortly after three o'clock in the afternoon.

Dieterici's next destination was the home of Adolphe Quetelet, the architect and host of the congress. The two men had been corresponding professionally for years but had never met in person. Dieterici was immediately impressed. Quetelet was the consummate scientist, a man who was 'sustained and animated by scientific ideas and views'.[1] The Belgian was also an extremely courteous man who felt at ease in the highest circles. Dieterici believed that Quetelet's excellent standing with the government was the reason statistics was thriving in Belgium. Quetelet told his German colleague Dieterici that it was Humboldt who had urged him to pursue a scientific career and that he had visited Johann Gottfried Hoffmann, Dieterici's predecessor, in Berlin back in the 1820s. Hoffmann gave him a tour of the Royal Statistical Office, which he had founded in 1805. That visit reinforced Quetelet's conviction that statistics was the science of the future, the science that could cultivate prosperity and progress. Though he had been educated as a mathematician and astronomer, he devoted himself to statistics with even greater zeal. Quetelet told Dieterici: 'In the same way that astronomy surveys the celestial bodies and meteorology studies the currents of air, wind and weather, statistics examines the risks that threaten society.'[2] Dieterici was completely won over by Quetelet, and he was not the only one.

That same week some 150 statisticians from every corner of Europe – official government representatives, academics and interested individuals – gathered in Brussels to attend the international statistical congress. They shared a passion for statistics (which was somewhat different from an obsession with numbers), but were it not for the gravitational force of Quetelet's personality, they probably never would have sought each other out. It helped that Quetelet was Belgian. Belgium was a guiding nation for progressive Europe. As a small, neutral, non-threatening country, it could afford to assert a certain degree of independence from the great powers. The revolutions of 1848 did not leave Belgium wholly unscathed, but the political fallout was less dramatic than elsewhere. Radical democrats had had the wind taken out of their sails when the government of Charles Rogier introduced reforms, and a conservative reaction was unthinkable in the young, liberal, unitary state. Belgium had a constitution and a liberal representative system, and could boast of a reasonably stable parliamentary culture. The Belgian constitution of 1831 served as a model for the constitutional law code permitted by King Charles Albert of Sardinia of the House of Savoy in Piedmont in 1848. Belgium's municipal act of 1836 was studied carefully in Turin and The Hague, when the Piedmontese and Dutch governments were devising new local government laws in the late 1840s.

Dieterici, who had briefly been a member of the upper house of the Prussian parliament in 1848, would probably have felt comfortable in the liberal, academic atmosphere of the Belgian capital, though he could not have said so in his official report to the minister. In 1848 he had expressed a positive view of the liberal-nationalist Frankfurt Parliament, but at the same time condemned every radical tendency. Dieterici had classical liberal ideas, believed in the state and in effective legislation, but only if its object was to safeguard the freedom of capital and labour. With this essential restriction he distanced himself from every idea that tended towards socialism. In his view, statistics was a source of knowledge, but his deepest insights were grounded in the conviction that the common good was based on virtuousness, and that government and politics had their roots in moral philosophy and not in class conflict.[3]

Although Dieterici greatly admired Quetelet – in his letters he frequently addressed him as his 'maître' – it is questionable whether they were in complete agreement on the nature and function of statistics. Even if they did agree that statistics was the foundation of good government, they must have realised that applying this idea to the Prussian and Belgian government systems and cultures would most likely lead to very different outcomes. In the nineteenth century, statistics was both a social science and an instrument of government. Nevertheless, every handbook opened with a different definition of statistics and every country had its own way of organising statistical research. The statisticians who gathered in Brussels in 1853 shared a boundless optimism and believed in the scientific neutrality of statistics, but when they tried to put their ideas into practice they encountered many obstacles.

Railway connections to Brussels were excellent. At that time, Belgium had the densest railway network in the world and Brussels was the main hub. International meetings were frequently staged in the city. In the period 1830–1850 Brussels and Paris were the refuges of exiles and political fugitives. In 1841, count David Fredrik Frölich, a lawyer and Member of Parliament from Sweden, had asked the Belgian government to support his initiative to establish an international peace society. The main task of the society, which he wanted to seat in Brussels, would be to collect and publish statistical data that had been 'subjected to philosophical assessment'. The Belgian Central Commission for Statistics, which was ordered to handle this request, decided that it was not possible at that time to integrate science and politics in the way Frölich proposed.[4]

Clearly, though, for many liberals Brussels occupied a central place in their mental map of Europe. In 1852 sanitary reformers, or 'hygienists', held their first congress there. A few weeks before the statistical congress, geographers, meteorologists and naval officers gathered there to discuss the state of the atmosphere and the world's oceans. The aim of that congress was to establish uniformity in meteorological and hydrographical observations made around the world.

Quetelet was in charge of that congress as well, and saw the obvious similarities between the two. Though statisticians were not concerned with air currents and gulf streams, the objective of their congress was no less comprehensive. Quetelet presented it thus at the official opening: 'to study, in another context, the fluctuations, the movements and the obstacles in modern society'.[5]

The first congress

On Sunday 18 September the statisticians held a preparatory meeting. Quetelet addressed the newly arrived participants and proposed to start the sessions with a presentation by the various statistical offices. No one objected, since that is what was stated in the programme. However, the mood was not as harmonious as it seemed. It was clear to everyone that politics had to be kept at bay, but they sensed that domestic and international political relations would make it difficult to maintain scientific neutrality, a feature of statistics that they all held sacred. The sheer diversity in the methods of organising government statistics pointed to governing traditions and principles that could not easily be harmonised. The idea of an international congress was born during the Great Exhibition of 1851 in London, but the coup d'état by Louis Napoleon in France on 2 December 1851 and the international disagreement about Schleswig Holstein in the spring of 1852 delayed preparations for a year. From the start it was clear that it would be difficult to reconcile national interests and the pursuit of international statistics.

In his report Dieterici noted that the congress delegates representing the German state statistical offices were in agreement that the Belgian arrangement – a statistical office under the interior ministry but steered by a scientific central commission – was an imperfect solution. Dieterici and his colleagues put their faith in the primacy of bureaucracy and had doubts about the Belgian practice of 'allowing committees, associations, representatives and delegates, societies, municipalities and interest groups to negotiate everything'.[6] The differences between the respective political and administrative cultures of the two countries were obvious and keenly felt.

Leopold von Ranke, the great German historian who happened to be conducting archival research in Brussels at the time, placed this divarication in an even wider context, calling it a struggle between 'Roman and Germanic ideas'.[7] In the domain of statistics, too, he wrote to his brother Ferdinand, 'the trend of Germanic consciousness has been deeper and more comprehensive than that of Roman consciousness'. The Roman approach, which identified strongly with a linear idea of progress, could not easily accommodate the ideas of the Germans or some Britons for that matter. At the same time, Ranke continued, the Germans were likely to provoke outrage as they adamantly defended their positions, precisely because they were a minority voting bloc and realised that all they had going for them was the impact of their words. Conciliation was out of the question, but there was mutual respect.

Ranke doubted the utility of such confrontations. He saw throughout history an eternal, dialectical interaction of forces and counter-forces, and so he developed a special fascination for times of crisis. This led him to believe that people should express their ideas freely and could learn from each other, but that they should take their time. Development was impossible without exploring every possible relationship between divergent ideas. Ranke abhorred his positivist contemporaries' mechanical faith in progress. With barely concealed pleasure he wrote to his wife Clara that he had managed to undermine the younger congress participants' sense of their own worldly wisdom by positing some well-chosen paradoxes.

Ranke's name was on the official list of participants but he did not attend the sessions. He read about the discussions in the newspaper. At the urging of the Prussian mission, he had stayed in Brussels and, having spent some time scouring the archives and communing with the dead, he was determined to find out what opinions people were professing in the land of the living. He allowed himself the pleasure of attending the banquet King Leopold held in honour of the congress participants. He described to his wife the European luminaries he observed or, in some cases, spoke to. He noted that Lord Ebrington, a member of the British delegation, spoke fluent French, was filled with philanthropic desires and had grilled the aged, bald-headed, earnest, gesticulating Spanish delegate, Ramón de la Sagra. He listened while Jan Ackersdijck, a professor from Utrecht, held forth and finally took refuge in generalities about the welfare of mankind when he could no longer follow his own theories. Ranke was impressed by the cosmopolitanism of Karl von Czoernig, head of statistics in Austria, whose protracted stays in Venice and Dalmatia had helped him understand the complex reality of public administration in his own country. Ranke conversed with Professor Friedrich Von Hermann of Munich University, who was responsible for statistics in Bavaria. Through a colossal effort, the impact of which could still be read in his countenance, Von Hermann had achieved importance in the state and in the literature. According to Ranke, the fact that Von Hermann provoked such opposition in the debates underscored his intellectual prowess. Ranke was struck by the verbosity and remarkable stories of the ageing Louis Villermé, a member of the Académie des Sciences Morales et Politiques. And of course there was the omnipresent Adolphe Quetelet, the host, who Ranke considered to be more a man of the world than a scholar. His fellow countrymen, whom he referred to as the Northern Germans, were convinced that the entire congress would prove futile.[8] We will become better acquainted with all of these men and determine whether the presentiment of Ranke's compatriots proved true.

At the official opening of the congress in the room where Belgium's Royal Academy of Sciences usually met, there was not a hint of uncertainty. The interior minister, Ferdinand Piercot, who was responsible for government statistics, attributed to statistics a key role in social progress and emphasised that it had been a persistent concern for the government since independence. The full-scale census of 1846 was proof of this. Methodological uniformity would further elevate the status of statistics and imbue it with international esteem as a reliable science of public administration. And that was not all. Piercot stressed that 'thus conceived, statistics would strengthen the bonds between nations and the sense of brotherhood and peace, which protect mankind from the resurgence of foolhardy national rivalries, would be deepened everywhere'.[9] Perhaps the minister was referring to the international tensions of recent years, which initially had caused the congress to be postponed.

Preparations

The optimistic words of the Belgian minister echoed the idealism that rang out when the plan for a congress was first presented. Quetelet and Auguste Visschers launched the proposal at the meeting of the Central Commission for Statistics of 11 July 1851. Visschers, born in Maastricht, was a typical liberal reformer striving for a more compassionate world, beginning with better working conditions, fairer criminal law and more humane prisons. Science as the engine of progress: that was Quetelet's and Visschers' motto. The 'European family' would be the better for it: a meeting or even a permanent organisation would be established to carry out the studies that would be initiated on a joint basis. It would 'be to all of Europe what a central commission or a ministerial agency was to a single state'.

Quetelet and Visschers would not go so far as to anticipate 'the day when the states of Europe would have the same laws, the same institutions, the same currency and the same weights and measures', but they were certain that the increase in commercial and scientific contacts would inspire a tendency to copy the recognised improvements conceived in other countries. 'Instead of withdrawing into indolent egoism or clinging to old nationalities, science would organise general schools of thought', which would benefit all of humankind. If the Central Commission found its way clear to approve the proposal, the two initiators would go to the Great Exhibition in London to recruit members of the Statistical Society for the project.[10]

Quetelet knew that they would not encounter any resistance in London. He had been involved in the genesis of the Statistical Society of London, which was founded in 1834 to give the new statistical department of the British Association for the Advancement of Science a broader radius of action. Quetelet had been invited to attend the association's meeting in Cambridge in June of 1833. He was there first and foremost as a representative of the Belgian Royal Academy, in which he played a prominent role until the end of his life (as permanent secretary from 1834 onward). But as an astronomer he could also join in the debate with authority. While in England, he took the opportunity to check data on magnetic forces that he had acquired on the Continent. In the report of his journey he also described various experiments and presentations he attended.[11]

Despite all this activity, his visit in the summer of 1833 would have gone virtually unnoticed had he not discussed his suicide and crime research with Richard Jones, a professor of political economy in London. The latter was intrigued and convened a meeting in his office at Cambridge to which he invited everyone involved in statistics. The seminar could not be part of the main programme because the assembled minds, most of whom were scientists, feared the political implications of the science of statistics. In those days, England was under the spell of a new poor law, which in turn was embedded in a gradual expansion of the state. Numbers may not have played a decisive role in the debates, but the proponents of reform were keenly aware of the power of statistical data.

As the traditional political arguments rooted in philanthropy and paternalism receded into the background, the importance given to numbers grew. The figures from the annual poor relief statistics began to tell a story, 'the story of poor law "abuse", of maladministration, of rate-payers' misery, and of market distortions'.[12] In this climate the scientists were understandably loathe to venture outside their profession and openly join in the political debate.

It was therefore an extraordinary step for Richard Jones to assemble the statisticians, or those who considered themselves such, in his Trinity College office. Along with Quetelet the group included old Thomas Malthus, author of the influential *Essay on the Principle of Population* dating from 1798, Charles Babbage, a mathematician famous for inventing a tabulator, and William Whewell, a Cambridge professor, first of mineralogy and later of moral philosophy. Quetelet had met Babbage in Paris in 1826 and Whewell in Heidelberg in 1829 at a meeting of the Gesellschaft Deutscher Naturförscher und Ärzte.

Despite its curious beginnings, the initiative of Jones, Quetelet and the others was a great success. Within a year, they had established the Statistical Society of London, which is discussed in detail in Chapter 4. This chapter is concerned with Quetelet's key role. He was, of course, the Statistical Society's official correspondent. In Brussels in 1837 he had spent a year teaching the calculus of probability to Prince Albert of Saxe-Coburg-Gotha, who married Queen Victoria of Great Britain in 1840. Since that time, Albert and Quetelet had maintained a fairly regular correspondence.[13] In 1846 Quetelet published a probability study in the form of letters to the prince and his brother Ernst.[14] In 1860, when Albert opened the fourth international statistical congress in London, he lavished praise on his teacher.

When the Belgian initiative to hold a statistical congress in London in 1851 was discussed, it was greeted with joy and optimism, though Quetelet had probably not travelled to London due to illness. That Visschers could speak in his name was enough for the English and foreign visitors to the Great Exhibition. In November 1851 Visschers reported to the Central Commission, informing the members that he had informally consulted a number of foreign experts, such as George Richardson Porter, Joseph Fletcher and William Farr from Britain but also Horace Say and Joseph Garnier from the Société des Economistes, and had received only positive reactions. They proposed to hold the congress in September 1852. The programme would need to be set in advance of the congress. A provisional schedule of sessions was sent to the provincial statistical commissions and to foreign correspondents; in addition, official delegates would be invited through diplomatic channels.

The programme was divided into three sections. The first section would address how statistics was organised in the various countries; in addition this section would focus on the numerical description of the territory and population figures (censuses, registration of births, deaths and marriages, migration – the term 'demography' was not yet in common usage). The second section would concentrate on economic statistics (which the preparation committee considered to include 'workers' budgets'). The third section was intended for the presentation and discussion of statistics on the mental and moral condition of the people (poverty, schools, crime and punishment). This included the causes and effects of emigration.

Evidently, the search for a satisfactory division of tasks (and thus of the topics of statistical research) was still ongoing. In the spring of 1853 the time seemed ripe to start making preparations for the congress. The subcommittee, led by Quetelet and Visschers, had meanwhile revised the programme. The components concerning emigration were incorporated into the first section and the discussion of workers' budgets was moved to the third section. The Central Commission's concise reports do not offer an explanation of this revision.

The relocation of workers' consumption expenditure is particularly telling. What was at first an economic issue became a moral issue with a single stroke of the pen. Workers' budget statistics were highly sensitive. The state's role in alleviating poverty would eventually come up and was sure to spark a fierce political debate. This could explain the caution and uncertainty surrounding the subject, but we will see that other, seemingly neutral topics of statistical research were no less thorny.

Belgians as trailblazers

Belgium's pioneering role in the European statistical movement was informed both by its liberal polity and the special status of statistics within it, and by Quetelet's key position as an intellectual. By the mid-nineteenth century, under Quetelet's leadership a learning process had had an impact on government statistics in Belgium and many practical problems had been resolved. In 1846 a general census of population, industry and agriculture was held in every municipality. Quetelet and his colleagues gained a great deal of experience by conducting the survey and processing the data. In 1853 the Belgians were ready to receive Europe.

The organisation of Belgian statistics was in a way a legacy of the United Kingdom of William I, though it must be said that the heirs received a much higher return on 'capital' than most Northern Netherlanders had thought possible. After years of hesitation, in 1826 William I signed the Royal Decree establishing a statistical office and a statistical commission whose task was to coordinate the work of the office. The period after the fall of Napoleon and withdrawal of the French from the Low Countries had been an uncertain time for the field of statistics. Some ministries accumulated statistical data, but the information was not compiled systematically anywhere. In the provinces, some governors attempted to interest local elites in statistics. Some private individuals published certain statistics. At the universities, statistics was incorporated into the study of law and history, but to professors and students it was no more than a fairly insignificant subsidiary subject.

Those who took the subject of statistics seriously believed that publicity could ensure its future. Development would be impossible unless information about the country, the population and the economy was published. In 1819 the statesman and economist Gijsbert Karel van Hogendorp defined the function of statistics as follows: 'The true foundations of the Economy of the State cannot be generally known and accepted unless statistical pronouncements are made public, as this will concentrate minds, and cause everyone to reason and write about it until, eventually, a public opinion on the subject emerges that is conducive to general prosperity, and could overcome all opposition'.[15] The decision of 1826 was a tentative, overdue response to this implicit plea.

The statistical commission comprised the interior minister Pierre L.J.S. van Gobbelschroy, who hailed from the Southern Netherlands, and several administrative officers from his ministry. The key figure of the commission was the secretary, Édouard Smits, who would emigrate to the new state of Belgium with Quetelet in 1830. Not one to restrict his activity to his official tasks, in 1827 Smits published a commentary on the first series of tables issued by the commission. He embellished his commentary with an explanation of his vision on statistics. His ideas were anything but original. He pursued a synthesis of French political arithmetic and the German cameralistic tradition of the study of *Staatsmerkwürdigkeiten*, but produced no more than an unconvincing hodgepodge. From Joseph Fourier, who had contributed to the then highly esteemed *Recherches statistiques sur la Ville de Paris et le Département de la Seine* (1821–1829), he borrowed a definition of statistics as a science that was limited to facts concerning the power and wealth of the people. Following in the footsteps of the Historical School of Gottfried Achenwall and August Ludwig von Schlözer, he saw statistics as a link between the past, present and future. And as if that were not enough, he believed in the universal and eternal law of nature, which prescribed that the kingdom of the Netherlands was moving towards a state of social perfection, a process that the exertions of statisticians could only accelerate.[16] Statistics was rich in pretention, but still deficient in application.

The commission's most important initiative was the census of 1829 in the United Netherlands. There were large and painful gaps in the existing population statistics. Without a precise population count, the statistics available were unusable. Civil servant and mathematician Rehuel Lobatto, who began publishing an annual containing interesting information about the country and its people in 1826, alerted the statistical commission to the deficiencies in the incomplete population figures, which were calculated on the basis of annual birth and death figures. Lobatto proposed to resolved the problem by holding a census every ten years, an idea that he had borrowed from one of Quetelet's earliest statistical publications, *Recherches sur la population, les naissances, les décès, les depôts de medicité, etc. dans le Royaume des Pays-Bas* (Brussels 1827).

Quetelet in focus

There are several reasons Quetelet's *Recherches* of 1827, a book of less than 70 pages, can be considered the key to nineteenth-century government statistics.

Quetelet was thrust into the limelight as a social statistician, though arguably he could lay little claim to originality. His book addressed the condition of the population in the United Kingdom of the Netherlands. But in addition to the statistical project he discussed all kinds of related phenomena, such as fertility, mortality and birth rates in different months of the year and times of day. For example, the fact that in various parts of the kingdom the death rate bottomed out in July had to be significant, all the more so because Villermé had made similar observations in France. The ratios and averages that Quetelet observed led him to consider possible causes, but also to intuit that there were laws governing the incredible regularity of births and deaths. In his later work, Quetelet would expand this insight into the highly creative, but flawed, theory of the *homme moyen*, the average person. In the *Recherches* he was still very cautious and sought above all more and more reliable numerical data. With great subtlety he also conveyed a political message: population growth would be possible only if agricultural and industrial production were promoted and if the people were given an appropriate degree of freedom that would guarantee public confidence.[17]

The *Recherches* was an eye-opener for King William I and his closest ministers, though they saw in it something different than Quetelet's true intentions. The court regarded Quetelet as the man who, in accordance with the principles of eighteenth-century German cameralism, which was strongly oriented towards the state, could put the Netherlands on the map in the discipline of statistics, and invited him to write a paper comparing the vitality of the Dutch state with that of other states. Quetelet undertook the task, but the finished paper was published in 1829 by a private house and was not issued as a government publication.[18] He could not reconcile the power-politics ambitions of his patrons, who were thinking in terms of the enlightened monarchy, with his belief that statistics should benefit the public or with the high standard of reliability he required of the figures. The *Recherches* of 1827 pointed not to the past but to the future, and in a certain sense to a future that did not materialise until the twentieth century.

Like Lobatto, Quetelet saw the dire necessity of a new census. His education and practical training in mathematics and astronomy led him to a simple and revolutionary solution: it should be possible to count the entire population purely on the basis of the number of births (which was, as a rule, recorded with great precision in the births register), if one only knew which 'multiplier' to use. The multiplier could be calculated as follows. It begins with a careful selection of a small number of municipalities. For each of the municipalities, you determine the total number of births in a number of years and then calculate the variable by which those figures must be multiplied to arrive at the figure for the entire population in the relevant municipality in those years. The outcome is a multiplier that can be used for each region or country to quickly obtain an accurate population figure.

Quetelet derived the probability method underlying this calculation from French mathematician Pierre Simon de Laplace, who himself was indebted to the intellectual milieu of the Académie Royale des Sciences of Paris. Soon after the mid-eighteenth century, political arithmetic received a strong impulse in France.[19] This method was grounded in the development of mathematics; financial considerations undoubtedly also played a role, but the decisive factor was the impossibility in eighteenth-century France of achieving a degree of precision in traditional censuses that would satisfy the scientists of the Académie Royale des Sciences. Despite the incredible efforts of academicians like Condorcet and Laplace to perfect the probability method and its application in public administration, the growing distance between the intellectual aspirations of scientists and the interests of the state after the French Revolution signified the temporary end of political arithmetic. By the time Laplace published his principal works (*Théorie analytique des probabilités*, Paris 1812, and *Essai philosophique sur les probabilités*, Paris 1814), sampling and multipliers were unknown quantities in government statistics.

The fact that Quetelet nevertheless proposed a census in 1827 based on the Laplace method had more to do with his background in mathematics and astronomy than anything else. In 1823 he had received a government grant to go to Paris and learn about astronomy and how to operate an observatory. Quetelet's biographers cannot say for certain whether he was taught by Laplace, but it is indisputable that Laplace had enormous influence in the circles in which Quetelet moved. In 1825, still focused on the idea of establishing an observatory in Brussels, Quetelet launched a scientific journal, the *Correspondance mathématique et physique*, with Frenchman Jean Guillaume Garnier, a professor of mathematics and physical astronomy in Ghent. Though the journal focused on the natural sciences, mathematics, engineering and astronomy, increasingly more space was given to social statistics and related commentary. In the first issue of 1825, Quetelet himself published the average number of births in Brussels over an eighteen-year period categorised by months of the year. The distribution, he noted, could be graphically represented by a sine curve, which we know as the normal distribution.[20] From the various articles that Quetelet wrote on statistics, we can conclude that he presented his data and conclusions to recognised specialists, such as Villermé and Fourier. In addition to population statistics he began to study schools, crime and prisons. His interest in these areas was apparent in the *Recherches*.

The progress that Quetelet made in statistics around 1825 inspired him to propose a new census, based on the Laplace method. He must have had doubts, though, because he appended the commentary of Charles L.G.J. Baron van Keverberg van Kessel to his proposal. Keverberg was somewhat critical of the probability method, which was completely new to him. He did not believe it was possible to select a representative but limited number of municipalities that could do justice to the many aspects of the 'laws' governing birth and death. He cited the differences between urban and rural areas, rich cities and poor municipalities, densely and sparsely populated areas, and pointed to a whole spectrum of geographical circumstances. However, it was typical of the prevailing thought that he nevertheless referred to the 'laws' of birth and death. But the only way to determine how many people lived in the kingdom was to hold a full census, by which he meant lists of all inhabitants, stating their ages and occupations.[21] Only in this way would it be possible to say anything sensible about the laws that governed shifts in the population.

It is no coincidence that Keverberg suggested this. Under French rule, he had been vice prefect of Kleef and under William I governor of Antwerp and later East Flanders. In 1817 in East Flanders he had led the establishment of an association that would coordinate statistics for the province. If there was anyone who was knowledgeable about the practical administrative side of statistics, it was Keverberg.

Quetelet allowed himself to be persuaded by the former governor, although the latter did not omit to stress the difficulties inherent in a large-scale census that would have to be overcome. The state would be dependent on census officials and local governments, which could not all be expected to be equal to the task. Unambiguous questions and thorough checks were therefore absolute conditions. During the French Empire, the state had overloaded the local governments with statistical circulars whose purpose was not always evident. Moreover, the political intricacies of the day were so complex that the interior ministry was unable to devote sufficient attention to the processing of data. Keverberg assured Quetelet that in the current circumstances it was to be expected that a well-structured statistical survey would be more successful. The lower levels of government stood to benefit from the data that they collected. They, too, needed to know what was happening in their territory in order to exercise the constitutional freedoms, however limited, they had acquired in 1815.[22]

Adolphe Quetelet would have thought long and hard about all these observations. When, in his capacity as chairman of the Central Commission for Statistics, he bore responsibility for the first census of Belgium as an independent state, he adhered meticulously to Keverberg's instructions. Apparently, Quetelet was easily dissuaded from his probability plan. He may have felt that he lacked sufficient knowledge of administrative practices and that Keverberg was a reliable authority. Moreover, he had no objection on principle to gathering large quantities of data. But what effect might it have had on government statistics and perhaps even the state if random sampling had been attempted at the beginning of the nineteenth century? The censuses and other large-scale statistical studies that European (and non-European) countries organised throughout the century strengthened the state like no other instrument of government. The masses had little contact with the state, paid no direct taxes and had no voting rights, but the census agents brought the state into their homes.

Quetelet was not intensely involved in the national census that was ultimately held in 1829. He continued to focus his attention on the observatory that he wanted to build in Brussels. In the autumn of 1827 he travelled to England and Scotland. In January 1828 he was made the official astronomer of the observatory, before construction had even begun. In the summer of 1829 he went abroad again, this time to Germany, where he met with many scholars and writers.

The highlight of the trip was undoubtedly his visit with Goethe at his home in Weimar. Goethe was a famous all-rounder, who in old age remained intensely involved in the natural sciences, and morphology in particular. Goethe was envious of Quetelet, who would be attending the forthcoming scientific congress in Heidelberg, because he was anxious about the possibility of his work being subjected to scrutiny there. Like a novice, he insisted that Quetelet inform him about how his ideas were received at the congress. They discussed natural phenomena and the order that was apparent in them. They also talked about Goethe's optical theories. Until Goethe's death in 1832 they exchanged several letters in which Goethe was highly complimentary of Quetelet's wife, who had a hand in managing her husband's social life.[23]

Several decades later, Xavier Heuschling, Quetelet's close colleague at the Central Commission for Statistics, wondered whether Goethe's winged words, which many a statistician cited in his own writings, had been inspired by Quetelet's visit: 'They say that numbers govern the world, but it is certain that numbers show how the world is governed.'[24] Goethe's words did, in fact, date from after their meeting. However, they were prompted by less exceptional circumstances. Biedermann, who published Goethe's conversations, recorded these words as Goethe's reaction to an article in *Le Temps* about the income enjoyed by the English clergy, which was comparable to a good secular income, and as such provoked Goethe's disapproval.

The average man

Following the breakup of the United Kingdom of the Netherlands, the process of renewal that organised statistics had undergone after 1825 was completely undone. The statistical office and the statistical commission faded into obscurity. In Belgium, by contrast, government statistics began to gain momentum. The proclamation of the new state virtually coincided with the founding of a statistical office at the interior ministry. The Belgian constitution dates from 7 February 1831; the decree establishing the statistical office dates from 24 February of the same year. The new state began issuing official statistics publications almost immediately: in 1832 Quetelet and Smits published the *Recherches sur la reproduction et la mortalité de l'homme aux differents âges et sur la population de la Belgique*, a year later the *Statistique des tribunaux de la Belgique*. Other government agencies reported their annual figures, too: on foreign trade, urban excises, justice, land ownership, mining and industry. The young liberal state sought information to affirm its existence and steer its government and the people wanted information that would enable them to exercise their freedom to the fullest extent. It gradually became clear that a degree of uniformity needed to be injected into statistical research for it to remain significant to the state and the public.

To that end, a Central Commission for Statistics was established in 1841. The commission's remit was to homogenise national statistics, in part by detecting lacunas, suppressing superfluous details, creating uniform tables and introducing a clear classification system in published statistics. The chairman of the commission was, of course, Adolphe Quetelet. Most of the other members were representatives of government ministries. In 1843 special commissions were set up in every province. Each of these commissions was chaired by the governor of the province, and was given the task of promoting statistical research at provincial and local level and checking raw data before it was sent to higher authorities.

In the meantime, Quetelet had solidified his reputation as a statistician. The first edition of his *Sur l'homme et le développement de ses facultés, ou Essai de physique sociale* appeared in 1835. It synthesised the whole of his work on social statistics to date. It was the zenith of his search for the laws of society. His goal was to create a new science – social physics – which was concerned with population issues, education, crime, industry and agriculture. It would be a science that made the task of the legislator easier: in today's parlance, it was a policy-relevant science. Quetelet appears to have been unaware of the fact that Auguste Comte had already coined the term 'social physics' to describe the all-encompassing science that he had envisaged. Out of desperation, Comte decided to call his science 'sociology', though he doubted the name would stick.

The great appeal of Quetelet's book lay in the metaphor of the average man. The concept must have captured the imaginations of the denizens of the nineteenth century. It was an idea that soon broke free from its originator's intended meaning. In the same way that Musil's 'Mann ohne Eigenschaften' seemed to capture the essence of twentieth-century man, 'l'homme moyen' represented his nineteenth-century predecessor. Because Quetelet's statistical thinking was grounded in his knowledge of astronomy, he saw in all numerical observations regularity and – above all – an orderly clustering around averages. From his studies in astronomy he understood the notion of the normal distribution, a special kind of frequency distribution that astronomers use to determine the position of celestial bodies. The so-called Gaussian distribution or bell curve is the graphical representation of the normal distribution. In the same way that astronomical observations tend to cluster around the precise position of the stars, sets of physical and moral characteristics of human beings tend to be concentrated in the average person.

'The average man', Quetelet wrote, 'is to a nation what the centre of gravity is to a body; all manifestations of equilibrium and movement can be estimated on that basis.'[25] He gave examples of physical characteristics, such as weight and girth, but the most interesting were of course the moral characteristics of human beings, which if sufficient observations were made would always point to an ideal, average value. In a later work, Quetelet noted: 'For his moral abilities, like his physical abilities, man is subject to minor and major deviations from an average; the variations around this average follow the general law that determines all the fluctuations which a series of phenomena can undergo under the influence of coincidental causes.'[26]

The average man was, in a sense, also a perfect man. Quetelet believed that the progress of civilisation was evident from the closing gap between the highest and lowest values by which human behaviours could be expressed. This was also at the root of Quetelet's anti-revolutionary stance: in situations of equilibrium, revolution was unnecessary and even impossible. In 1830 and even more so in 1848 he tried to steer clear of every form of radicalism. His measured attitude appealed to like-minded individuals who were more closely engaged with political reality.

Vincenzo Gioberti, an Italian nationalist who took inspiration from his Christian faith, wrote to Quetelet from Paris in February 1848, at the height of the riots in the French capital. They knew each other from Gioberti's years of exile in Brussels. Gioberti had just read Quetelet's latest book, *Du système social*, and was deeply affected by the political philosophical wisdom articulated in it. The popular fury and devastation in the city filled the Italian priest with dread. If Louis-Philippe's government had been more mindful of the average man, he wrote, then revolution could have been averted: 'If Louis-Philippe and his wretched ministers had thought about the average man, then they would not have blindly hurled themselves into a system that is precipitating their downfall and may bring great misfortune to France. I have committed myself to rereading and studying your book. I believe that an entire political system can be built upon it.'[27] Quetelet was first and foremost a man of science and distanced himself from explicit political positions. His average man was much more than an engaged citizen.

The perfection that Quetelet saw in the average man was not always easy to explain. After all, it was not just the positive characteristics of people that tended towards a single point, but suicidal and criminal tendencies could also be reduced to average values. Quetelet's article on '*le penchant au crime*' dating from 1831, which he paraphrased in his *Sur l'homme*, stoked some controversy. He was so astonished by the regularity that he saw in crime statistics that he seemed to be saying that every human being was inclined to evil. Every year produced virtually identical totals in the various categories of crime. Obviously a disposition to crime did not conform to the standards of decency of the bourgeoisie, but Quetelet pondered an entirely different explanation of his observations. He was particularly interested in the circumstances that influenced crime, such as climate, seasons, sex, education and, above all, age. If only one could acquire a good understanding of these factors, it would be possible to conceive of ways to suppress the tendency.

Without expressing himself explicitly in political terms, he indicated how the state could employ its resources. Member of Parliament Henri de Brouckère referred to Quetelet in his plea to abolish the death penalty and to take alternative measures during the session of 4 July 1832. Crime statistics were similar from year to year, as was public spending to combat crime and punish convicted offenders. Increasing state expenditure would no doubt have a positive impact on the crime rate. De Brouckère was summarising Quetelet's ideas when he said that crime and punishment were ultimately budgetary matters.[28] While the inclination to commit crime may be a general human trait, it does not necessarily follow that it is immutable. Eliminating certain causes could keep some effects at bay, thus reducing crime, expenditure and inconvenience. In other words, the political counterpart to the notion of the average man was a deep desire to exercise control.

The average man was not a coherent concept in every respect. Quetelet recognised that the measurability of phenomena depended on the 'population'. In the definition from *Sur l'homme* (1835) cited above, he spoke of the nation as the territory of the average man. However, a population was, in theory, even larger. The precision of the average increases as the series of observations expands. According to Quetelet physical characteristics, for example, have not changed throughout the history of humanity, and are therefore most recognisable when the measured group is at its largest. His dream of an international statistics was born of the conviction that everything that could be counted should be counted. On the other hand, he also wrote that the average man is defined by place and time, and that society is not an instrument for men to manipulate at will so that it produces the desired statistical results. In the view of his biographer, Frank H. Hankins, Quetelet did not actually consider this paradox fully.[29]

Others believe that there was no inconsistency and that Quetelet did not seek 'simple', physical laws. According to Stephen M. Stigler, he was fully aware of the complexity of social life and, in fact, wanted only to accumulate as much data as possible and, from that data, distil different categories of causes. If too few causes were identified, mistakes would be made and it would be impossible to discover laws.[30] With Quetelet, it is difficult to separate the ends from the means. Reason took him a long way but did not utterly dominate his thinking. He looked at people the same way he looked at the stars: from a distance. His visions of the concentrated order and of the average man added an extra dimension to his logic: if one could only collect enough data, all diversity would amalgamate into an average, a brilliant focal point. He was blinded by that brilliance. For Quetelet, the truth lay in the middle and nowhere else.

Counting in Belgium

When the Central Commission for Statistics was set up in 1841, no one but Quetelet, by then an internationally renowned statistician, could have been chosen to preside over it as chair. In 1838 his *Sur l'homme* had been translated into German and supplemented by a doctor from Stuttgart, V.A. Riecke. R. Knox, a Scottish doctor, would produce an English translation in 1842. It is no coincidence that both translators were doctors. As we shall see in later chapters, doctors were important actors in the statistical movement. The medical profession was also represented in the Central Commission. Dieudonné Sauveur, inspector-general of the health service and permanent secretary of the Academy of Medicine, was a member for nearly as long as Quetelet himself.

The commission's first major task was to supervise a census of Brussels in 1842. It was obvious to everyone that this was to be a test run for a general census of the entire Belgian population. A national census was the largest statistical lacuna in the young state. In the first part of the *Bulletin de la Commission de Statistique*, Quetelet discussed the Brussels census in detail. The figures and the technical details concerning the implementation were the most important, but Quetelet got carried away with the order he detected in the numbers. First, following Villermé, he studied the city in terms of specific characteristics, such as quality of housing, and then discovered to his surprise that the best districts were the least industrialised, or that income was highest in the parts of the city where the most foreigners lived, 'as if change in the make-up of the population is an element of vitality and prosperity'. It seems that he was really surprised by his own observation that 'the grouping of urban districts by size and quality of dwellings can be seen in a new light if one takes into account that this grouping is inversely proportional to that of the residents in the poverty register?' The conclusion was almost too obvious: 'The results are mutually verifying and provide the ultimate guarantee for the care with which the count was carried out.'[31] Heuschling, the secretary of the commission, went a step further in his interpretation of the data on Brussels. He delved deeper into the relationship between occupational groups and rates of birth out of wedlock, which to his apparent astonishment were highest among domestic workers and day labourers. He also noted that in the case of illegitimate births, the percentage of girls was higher than that of boys (while this was normally the other way around). He concluded from this that 'as previously observed, illegitimate unions appear to be an obstacle to the further development of the male population.'[32] Such categorical conclusions reflect the moralistic undercurrent that pervaded the interests of statisticians, and more generally the anxieties of the moneyed middle classes. That said, statisticians were not overt moralists. It is necessary to read between the lines of their texts and tables and distil their underlying thoughts indirectly from the categories and classifications they employed.

The outcome of the Brussels census was encouraging and reinforced the conviction held by Quetelet and his colleagues that the time was ripe for a national population census. On 28 July 1843 the commission composed a report for the interior minister, which was also published in the *Bulletin*. The report stated that annual population figures were still being based on the count of 1829. The commission suspected that the municipalities were fiddling the numbers to limit the number of militia conscripts. But the liberal state required a precise population count for many of the public bodies that were prescribed by law. For example, the size of the municipal council and some court juries and certain tax rates depended on the number of inhabitants. 'The process of counting and registering the population was an essential component, in fact a *sine qua non*, of liberal government in the Kingdom of Belgium.'[33]

The central state had an ambivalent role: on the one hand, it was the highest manifestation of the concepts of freedom and representativeness, on the other, the state was compelled, not least when conducting statistical research, to intervene vigorously in social life. The commission emphasised the importance of top-down control: 'Government intervention is essential to adequately guarantee the fairness of the count; if we want the count to accurately reflect reality and wish to prevent local authorities from lowering the population figure at will, as they have done in the past, the results must be adequately verified by a higher authority, which in case of doubt as to the precision of the figures obtained will be duty bound to take appropriate measures and, if necessary, order a new count.[34] Clearly, statistics presupposed an active state, though at first glance this appears to contradict the principles of early nineteenth-century liberalism.

Quetelet also emphasised the scientific importance of the census. Regarding the Brussels census of 1842 he wrote: 'It is not enough ... to know a population's quantitative strength. We must also analyse the elements of which it is composed. This analysis will enable us to determine the degree of prosperity, the strength and the needs of that population and form a fairly accurate notion of its future. A population count has more than an absolute value; the population figure is the indispensable element to which we must turn to estimate the mortality rate and find solutions to all manner of problems concerning medical statistics, government and public administration.'[35]

The great census of 1846 shows what effects Quetelet's ideas had in practice. The members of the commission had been working unremittingly on the preparations since 1843. They accumulated the data from the population counts that had been performed within Belgian territory since 1801. They asked the provincial statistical commissions to give their views on how a national census should be held. A myriad of problems presented themselves: whether to count the actual or legal population, distribute census cards per family or per dwelling, monolingual or bilingual cards, how to distinguish the uses of different parts of a house, how to specify the extent to which people depended on poor relief, age and place of birth, degree of sanguinity, language, faith, occupation, etc. The commission also asked the provinces to discuss changing the house numbers, how census agents would perform their task and how information should be extracted from the cards, while it applied itself to the agricultural and industrial censuses that would be conducted simultaneously.

Once the commission had considered every detail, secured a budget from the interior ministry and drafted provisional regulations, another trial count was conducted, this time in Molenbeek-Saint-Jean, covering not only the population but also agriculture and industry. From this test run, the commission concluded that the structure was effective, but consideration would need to be given to popular fears that the primary aim of the exercise was to raise national taxes. On 30 June 1846 the king signed a decree ordering a census of the population, industry and agriculture to be held on 15 October of the same year.

During the period between 30 June and 15 October the commission did not leave the country in peace. On 13 July it had the ministry send out a circular to the governors calling on them to convene meetings of the provincial statistical commissions, district commissioners and mayors. The ministry would send representatives of the central commission to the meetings. The commission's goal was to eliminate every risk of unforeseen problems interfering with the execution and processing of the census. Commission secretary Heuschling put together a programme of excursions to the provinces for the members. At the end of August, the central commission presented the ministry with a report on the results of these information-gathering visits. The remuneration of the census agents and others who were involved in the processing was an important point of discussion. Quetelet and Heuschling pointed out that agents working in the countryside would have to travel long distances and fill in large numbers of census cards themselves because many of the residents could not read or write. The ministry acknowledged the problem and approved a higher fee than had been originally planned. In September, circulars and letters were sent to the governors and various ministries to clear up any remaining questions and issue a few last-minute instructions.

The preparation demonstrates how deeply the operation affected communication between the various levels of government and, in general, between the state and society. The central commission liaised between the ministries involved and the provincial and local governments. The provincial statistical commissions, in which the local elites were strongly represented, provided local support. In the process, the census became an act of national integration.

Contact between the state and the population had never before occurred on such a massive scale. Census cards were delivered to each household a few days before 15 October 1846. Nearly 11,000 cards (plus the forms for agricultural and industrial organisations) were distributed in the city of Bruges alone.[36] The city council appointed ten agents to distribute and retrieve the cards. All of them were municipal employees and this gave them an opportunity to earn a little extra. The governor monitored the procedures very closely and answered the city council's questions in writing. There was a never-ending stream of questions about details. Many people were not considered part of the 'ordinary' population (such as those residing in mental institutions, hospitals, military barracks, prisons, etc.) and the instructions did not cover every eventuality. It took the ten census agents seven half-days to distribute the cards. They were accompanied by police officers.

The municipal executive anticipated that the task of collecting the census cards, for which the royal decree of 30 June prescribed a ten-day period, would pose bigger problems. It was thought that the agents would have to fill in two-thirds of the cards themselves. The agents began their task before the day of the actual census, so that they would only have to check the information on or around 15 October. This was not entirely in keeping with the rules, but the municipal council saw no alternative. In a municipal order issued before the distribution and collection of census cards began, the agents were instructed to start their day at half past eight in the morning; they could break for lunch at half past twelve but had to return to their regular jobs by three o' clock. This schedule turned out to be overly optimistic. Collecting the cards in time demanded an all-out effort. On 4 November the municipal council of Bruges dispatched 10,821 completed and verified cards, in 95 parcels corresponding to the 95 districts in the city, to the governor for further processing. Each parcel contained a list of house numbers, a list of the corresponding census card numbers and a reckoning of the number of people residing in each dwelling.

The other municipalities of Belgium were no less industrious than Bruges. On 10 November, all the census cards were handed over to the provincial authorities. The members of the central commission continued their inspection tours to oversee the processing phase at first hand. On 23 December, Quetelet reported the first authorised results to the minister. Though he could provide only a total population figure for men and women at that time, his tone was irrepressibly elevated. He was deeply convinced of the central commission's mission in the operation. It was as if the words of Luke 2:1 – 'In those days Caesar Augustus issued a decree that a census should be taken of the entire Roman world' – were on his mind. He remarked again on the colossal efforts of the authorities and the population. His words were almost inadequate: 'Persons of every age and both sexes, native born and foreign, who were present on the day of the census were counted at the place where they passed the night.' He examined the methodology and came to the conclusion that the first Belgian census was among the best in the world.[37] Heuschling wrote to Quetelet that the government should make the most of this success, since such comprehensive and rapid administrative results were rarely achieved.[38]

The prospect that from 1 January 1847 local authorities would be required to keep up-to-date population registers only increased the enthusiasm. The census cards would be returned to the Belgian municipalities, which would then be required to set up population registers based on them. This may have been the climax of the census for Quetelet and his colleagues. The households occupying permanent dwellings in the municipalities would be recorded in the registers and special registers would be established for the others. The authorities were most attentive to the advantages of being able to monitor the whereabouts of the 'dangerous classes'. Moreover, 'lawful domicile', a term from the civil code, now had an administrative basis. The statisticians hoped that this would enable them to continually monitor the human universe. To Quetelet, the population register was a microscope on society comparable to the telescope in his observatory that gave him a view of the stars.

The statistical agenda in 1853

Given their value to statisticians, it is no wonder that the implementation and refinement of the census and population registers was an important item on the agenda of the international statistical congress in Brussels. In the congress programme that was dispatched in the spring of 1853, the census was high on the list of discussion topics, second only to the organisation of statistics in general.

In a brief address, the Belgian central commission presented the primary differences between censuses in European countries and in the United States. England and Belgium tallied their actual populations: every person who had spent the night before the census at the dwelling in which they were found was counted. France, Austria, Piedmont and the states of the German Zollverein employed a mixed system in which the actual and legal populations were enumerated. The commission favoured the actual population method, but proposed to leave open the possibility of registering the legal population as well. Rarely did any two countries hold their censuses in the same month or employ the same system of periodisation. The commission proposed setting 31 December 1860 as the next census date, followed by a new census every ten years. December was the month in which German states conducted their surveys and it seemed well chosen, since it was the time of year that people were least itinerant and the 'floating population' was smallest.

The commission had a preference for census cards by household, according to the Belgian system instead of a list by municipality, as in France. In their view, the major advantage of the Belgian method was that people filled in their data themselves, though occasionally under the supervision of government officials. In addition, the household census cards provided varied information, which would be easier to use for other purposes.

The matter of the census agents also required special attention, because the success of counting operations depended strongly on them. In most cases, local governments were responsible for appointing agents. In Württemberg, the local authorities called upon the clergy to assist; in France, they enlisted tax officers; in big cities, the authorities often engaged the help of visitors to the poor or other relief workers. By hook or by crook, the census agents had to make sure the information was filled in properly or complete the forms themselves 'in accordance with the instructions they were given'. Sensibly, the matter of payment was not addressed. The commission concluded with a proposal to formulate a minimum number of fixed questions on matters such as language, religion, occupation, income, illness and disability, and called for every municipality to create a population register to record all movements of the population.

How did the congress respond to this laundry list of preferences, which could have far-reaching effects on statistical practice? The printed report of the discussion is concise. Some of the participants, such as Horace Say of France, were of the opinion that information collected by means of a census should not be too detailed. For example, there were moral and practical reasons not to ask all kinds of questions about illnesses. Say caused some hilarity when he remarked that he found the question on abnormalities of the spinal column, which was inspired by medical debates on the influence of nutrition, climate and physical environment on that part of the body, a rather delicate one. He feared that at least half of humanity would appear in a bad light if questions were asked about physical aberrations of this nature. His countryman Joseph Garnier added that no one would want to interrogate a lady about physical defects.

Disagreement arose in the French camp about the penalty for refusing to furnish requested information. Alfred Legoyt, the head of France's census bureau, the Statistique Générale de France, favoured setting a penalty. Say opposed this idea, opining that people should not be forced to answer questions, as that would only serve to increase their suspicion. Quetelet did not want to attach too much importance to the issue of sanctions and steered the congress to reject Legoyt's motion.[39]

Notably, Dieterici's report of the discussion contradicts the printed proceedings of the congress. The proceedings are probably based on what was said during the plenary sessions and what was recorded in *La Moniteur Belge*, the Belgian Bulletin of Acts, Orders and Decrees; according to Dieterici, the gazette was somewhat selective. He noted in his report that he himself and the other Germans spoke frequently and defended the census method used in the Zollverein: 'Belgium, France and England may reckon as they like, but in my opinion the method employed in the Zollverein is correct and good.'[40] Dieterici wrote to his minister that he had strongly endorsed a three-yearly census because of the rapid pace of population growth in the German states. On this point, Quetelet abandoned the central committee's preference and took the position that the state should hold a census at least once every ten years.

Dieterici found the issue of language somewhat problematic, since he knew that German Poles understood and spoke both their mother tongue and the national language. But Quetelet did not want to dismiss this issue, because it was so important in Belgium. The census of 1846 showed that the majority of the population spoke 'Flemish'. According to Dieterici's summary of Quetelet's remarks on this subject, this finding was significant for the identity of the Flemish people.

With regard to illness and disability, Dieterici's preference was considerably more conservative than the proposal put forward by the central commission. The blind, deaf and mentally disabled could be counted, but dementia needed to be dealt with more carefully, since it was sometimes brought on by ageing and posed no risk or problems outside the household. It was undesirable to count kyphotic or crippled people or amputees. Dieterici was of the opinion that registering these abnormalities was not in the state's interests and, moreover, would demonstrate a lack of humanity. Austrian representative Karl von Czoernig supported his Prussian colleague and remarked drily that counting the number of people on crutches could affect entire villages. The final resolution was more moderate than the proposal: the survey would be restricted to blindness, deafness, mental disability and dementia.

Debates of this nature were frequent during the sessions held between 19 and 22 September 1853. Scientific objectives, state interests and social circumstances provided continuous food for discussion. The participants were well aware of the fact that the resolutions adopted by the congress merely reflected the preferences of the majority of attendees, and that no sanctions could be imposed for non-compliance with those decisions. The discussion concerning the organisation of government statistics made this abundantly clear. How could statisticians compel their governments to establish a central commission for statistics, comprised of expert civil servants and scientists, as proposed by the Belgian organising committee? According to the printed report, the congress skirted the thorny aspects of this issue.

Joseph Garnier, the official rapporteur on this subject, mentioned that consensus proved unattainable in the preparatory discussions held prior to the plenary session. The participants were unwilling to go further than recommending the establishment of a central 'institution' that would promote statistical research and operate independently of government bureaucracy but in contact with local authorities. The congress was disinclined to make an official pronouncement on this matter and restricted itself to adopting a resolution stating that every country should designate a person or body to see to it that foreign and domestic statistical publications were disseminated.

Dieterici's report reveals that there were deep differences of opinion. In his view, the central commission's proposal was predicated on the situation in Belgium and France. Quetelet himself, Dieterici emphasised, was an obvious example of a scientist who had avoided bureaucratic spheres until well into his career. This was also true of Legoyt and of William Farr, coordinator of the English censuses and a doctor by profession. Dieterici observed that these men were prominent scientists but not civil servants in heart and soul. In Prussia, statistics was imbued with the primacy of bureaucracy. Friedrich von Hermann of Bavaria and Czoernig of Austria concurred with him. Dieterici believed that in his fatherland everything could remain as it was. A central commission 'à la Belge' was completely unnecessary because the head of the Prussian statistical office already embodied the union of government and science. Both he and Johann Gottfried Hoffmann were professors of political economy in Berlin. Heuschling, the secretary of the Belgian central commission, supposedly told him in confidence that the commission had been set up primarily to convince parliament that it was safe to earmark funding for statistical objectives.

It is by no means certain that Quetelet would have endorsed this view. He was, after all, a man inclined to compromise. Throughout the congress, he played the role of the mediator, and tried to avoid insurmountable differences of opinion. The central commission's proposal to survey the working class was a sensitive issue. It was an initiative of Auguste Visschers, who explained his proposal to the assembly. In addition to his membership in the central commission, Visschers had a seat on the Mining Council and was well acquainted with the social impact of industrialisation. It was undoubtedly clear from the start that this topic would be a controversial one. There was a serious risk of a politico-ideological debate ensuing about the role of the state in social life. Visschers readily admitted that the plan to map the spending habits of the working class on the basis of questionnaires would usher in a new age of statistical practice. Once the public authorities had officially recognised statistics, 'people would feel the need to go further, to plumb the depths of the social order, with the aim of researching everything of importance to the political community or the circumstances of its members, particularly those who are exposed most to suffering and deprivation'.[41]

Visschers made reference to England where, he claimed, research into workers' circumstances had originated. His proposal was based on a suggestion posed by the recently deceased school inspector Joseph Fletcher. Fletcher had done a great deal of work for the Statistical Society of London, studying the living standards of weavers, the spread of crime and, of course, the moral advantages of common education. Surveys of the working class had indeed been held in England since the 1830s. Visschers learned that government was not always the best-equipped institution to study workers close up, and that it was better to have intermediary agents carry out the task, armed with a list of clear questions. In Belgium, he had commissioned approximately one thousand interviews. Though not all the results had been processed, they gave an impression of the valuable information that could be obtained by this method. Visschers wanted to encourage statisticians from other countries to launch similar studies to gauge the effects of various physical-geographical and economic situations. At the end of his speech, he revealed that some state intervention was desirable to alleviate the direst need. Some schools of economic thought, he said, were too indifferent to the poor; others proposed dangerous systems. Entirely in the style of reformist liberalism, he exhorted his listeners to 'discover the truth' and act accordingly.

The debate on the proposal barely touched on the formulation of the survey questions but, as was to be expected, focused on the underlying ideas. Horace Say objected to being accused of indifference as an adherent of Adam Smith. He simply believed that it was unnecessary for every initiative, including the organisation of statistical research, to come from government. Visschers hastened to add that he had no desire to discredit anyone and was merely searching for solutions to a social problem. The congress decided to approve the questionnaire, but could do no more than recommend that those present adopt the programme put forward by Visscher and his colleagues. The results would then be compared at a subsequent congress. It will come as no surprise that it proved difficult to get this item put on the agenda.

Other topics, such as crime statistics, foreign trade, poverty, education and emigration, were hardly less controversial. There was a relationship between all these and the social tensions fostered by industrialisation, urbanisation and impoverishment. Statisticians believed they could tackle these problems scientifically and impartially. But as it turned out, it wasn't that simple. Most of the issues were politically charged. Charles Babbage, an indefatigable inventor, submitted a paper on lighthouses, which was one of the very few contributions that could be considered neutral. He was designing a system that would make it possible to allocate a unique light sequence to every lighthouse in the world. His paper was more appropriate for the congress of meteorologists and hydrographers that preceded the statistical congress, but it was nevertheless published as an annexe to the *Compte rendu des travaux du congrès général de statistique*. It reflected the statistics community's desire for precision and control, but what was possible for inanimate objects remained a utopia for social statistics. At the time, though, few statisticians realised this.

In September 1853 Brussels was for a short time the centre of statistics. Quetelet's charisma drew all the distinguished statisticians of the day to the Belgian capital. As a small, independent, liberal country, Belgium was the ideal place to host a gathering of scientists. But statisticians had aspirations that reached beyond science. Statistics was traditionally concerned with *Staatsmerkwürdigkeiten*: in the eighteenth century, the primary goal was to reinforce the power of the state and in the nineteenth century, there was a gradual shift in emphasis to improving the lot of the state and its people. The aims of statistical research varied from surveying human and economic potential to increasing the state's understanding and control of the dangers that threatened society. Examples of this will be discussed in later chapters. With such ambitious goals, statistics acquired a political mission that transcended the theoretical.

This burden weighed heavily on the international statistical congress. After Brussels, the statisticians wanted to move on, but the limitations were self-evident. They were unable to agree on the location of the next gathering. Berlin was mentioned, but Dieterici wouldn't commit himself. Legoyt, not wanting to be left behind, pointed out that Paris would be hosting the next World's Fair in 1855. This presented a good opportunity to bring the statisticians together. The choice was ultimately up to the Belgian central commission. After the congress in Brussels, Quetelet asked the *éminence grise* of science, Alexander von Humboldt, for his opinion. According to Humboldt, a long-time resident of cosmopolitan Paris, Berlin was less suitable for international meetings. Perhaps his opinion was decisive for Quetelet. The second congress would be held in Paris.

Most statisticians firmly believed in the possibilities of their branch of science. Unlimited statistical research had many allurements. The illusion of increasing precision was one of them. Quetelet's metaphor of the average man reflected the false certainty harboured by statisticians in the mid-nineteenth century. They all shared a desire for uniformity and a boundless confidence in the future. This optimistic view of statistics was typical of the times. Around 1850, the scientific world experienced a series of revolutions that heralded the birth of modern science. It was the time of Comte, Marx, Darwin, Charles Lyell, Justus von Liebig and many others. One of the main features of the transition was the use of mathematics, which consequently became a universal language.[42] Mathematics was also a highly useful language for statisticians, though government statistics rarely required them to use methods of calculation other than addition, subtraction and averaging.

Faith in numbers or, more precisely, series of numbers had major consequences for bureaucratic practice. For a state to compile its statistics in compliance with the preferences of the international statistical congress, it had to be more 'involved' than was customary. This probably came easiest to the Prussians. It was a simple matter for an authoritarian, bureaucratic state to become a statistical state. In a sense, Belgium had a much more difficult road to travel. There was widespread agreement among political and government elites concerning the importance of statistics to the liberal state. They wanted to conduct statistical research in an environment of openness and public debate. That meant that the state would have to take on the complicated task of creating the institutional and social conditions under which usable statistics could be produced.

In 1853 the belief in scientific progress was stronger than the perception that the realities of politics and bureaucracy could stand in the way of progress. Even Dieterici, who we have come to know as more of a realist than the other participants, decided that despite his low expectations the first international statistical congress promised well: 'The ethical awareness of the progress of the nations, yea of all humanity, through prosperity and moral persuasion, in other words the principle of a noble humanity, dominated the gathering, as divergent as the participants were in their country of origin, religion or personal position in life.'[43] Most of the participants of the first international statistical congress left Brussels with a comparable sense of optimism. They were set to continue their journey of discovery.

Notes

1   Geheimes Staatsarchiv Preußischer Kulturbesitz (hereafter GStA PK), I. Hauptabteilung, Repositur 77, Ministerium des Innern, Abteilung I, Section 13, Nr. 99, Bd. 1 Statistische Generalversammlungen des In- und Auslandes (1853–1859), Report of Dieterici to the Ministry of the Interior, Berlin, 17 October 1853. The description of Dieterici's journey is based on this official report.

2   *Ibid.*

3   (C.)W.(F.) Dieterici, *Über preußische Zustände, über Arbeit und Kapital. Ein politisches Selbstgespräch seinen lieben Mittbürgern gewidmet* (Berlin and Posen 1848), VII.

4   *Bulletin de la Commission de Statistique* 1 (1843), 470, minutes of the session of 22 September 1841.

5   *Compte rendu des travaux du congrès général de statistique réuni à Bruxelles les 19, 20, 21 et 22 septembre 1853* (Brussels 1853), p. 23.

6   GStA PK, Report of Dieterici, 17 October 1853.

7   L. Von Ranke, 'An Ferdinand Ranke (Hannover, 24 September 1853)', in B. Hoeft and H. Herzfeld (eds), *Neue Briefe* (Hamburg 1949), p. 358.

8   L. von Ranke, 'An Clara Ranke (Brussels, 22 September 1853)', in W.P. Fuchs (ed.), *Das Briefwerk* (Hamburg 1949), pp. 373–374.

9   *Compte rendu à Bruxelles 1853*, 19.

10 *Bulletin de la Commission Centrale de Statistique* 5 (1851), 23–25.

11 *Correspondance mathématique et physique* 8 (1835), 1–18.

12 D. Eastwood, 'Rethinking the Debates on the Poor Law in Early Nineteenth-Century England', *Utilitas* 6 (1994), 112.

13 E. Gossart, 'Adolphe Quetelet et le prince Albert de Saxe-Cobourg (1836–1861)', *Bulletins de l'Académie Royale de Belgique, Classe des Lettres et des Sciences Morales e Politiques* (1919), 211–254.

14 A. Quetelet, *Lettres à S.A.R. le duc régnant de Saxe-Coburg et Gotha, sur la théorie des probabilités, appliquée aux sciences morales et politiques* (Brussels 1846; in 1849 the letters were also published in English).

15 G.K. van Hogendorp, *Bijdragen tot de huishouding van staat in het Koninkrijk der Nederlanden*, ed. J.R. Thorbecke (Amsterdam, 2nd edn, n.d.) IV, p. 175.

16 É. Smits, *Nationale statistiek. Ontwikkeling der een-en-dertig tabellen …* (Brussels 1827).

17 A. Quetelet, *Recherches sur la population, les naissances, les décès, les depôts de medicité, etc. dans le Royaume des Pays Bas* (Brussels 1827), p. 68.

18 A. Quetelet, *Recherches statistiques sur le royaume des Pays-Bas* (Brussels 1829).

19 E. Brian, *La mesure de l'État. Administrateurs et géomètres au xviiie siècle* (Paris 1994).

20 *Correspondance mathématique et physique* 1 (1825), 16–18.

21 The mathematical implications of Keverberg's proposal are discussed by S.M. Stigler, *The History of Statistics. The Measurement of Uncertainty before 1900* (Cambridge, MA and London 1986), pp. 163–169.

22 Quetelet, *Recherches sur la population*, 'Notes par M. le baron De Keverberg', pp. 69–77.

23 About Quetelet's visit to Goethe, see V. John, 'Quetelet bei Goethe', in H. Paasche (ed.), *Festgabe für Johannes Conrad. Zur Feier des 25-jährigen Bestehens des staatswissenschaftlichen Seminars zu Halle a. S.* (Jena 1898), pp. 313–334.

24 Archives de l'Académie royale de Belgique (Brussels), Archives Quetelet, letter from Heuschling to Quetelet, 17 November 1865.

25 A. Quetelet, *Sur l'homme et le développement de ses facultés, ou Essai de physique sociale* (Brussels 1836) II, p. 264.

26 A. Quetelet, *Du système social et des lois qui le régissent* (Paris 1848), pp. 91–92.

27 Letter from V. Gioberti to A. Quetelet, Paris, 24 February 1848, in V. Gioberti, *Epistolario*, VII (Florence 1934), p. 279.

28 *Adolphe Quetelet 1796–1874. Exposition documentaire présentée à la Bibliothèque Royale Albert Ier à l'occasion du centenaire de la mort d'Adolphe Quetelet* (Brussels 1974), p. 89.

29 F.H. Hankins, *Adolphe Quetelet as Statistician* (New York 1908), pp. 76–82.

30 S.M. Stigler, 'Adolphe Quetelet: Statistician, Scientist, Builder of Intellectual Institutions', in *Actualité et universalité de la pensée scientifique d'Adophe Quetelet. Actes du colloque organisé à l'occasion du bicentenaire de sa naissance. Palais des Académies 24–25 octobre 1996* (Brussels 1997), pp. 47–61.

31 A. Quetelet, 'Sur le recensement de la population de Bruxelles en 1842', *Bulletin de la Commission de Statistique* 1 (1843), 72.

32 X. Heuschling, 'Des naissances dans la ville de Bruxelles, considérées dans leur rapport avec la population', *Bulletin de la Commission de Statistique* 1 (1843), 172.

33 N. Randeraad, 'Negentiende-eeuwse bevolkingsregisters als statistische bron en middel tot sociale beheersing', *Tijdschrift voor Sociale Geschiedenis* 21 (1995), 328.

34 'Rapport au Ministre de l'intérieur sur la nécessité d'un recensement général de la population du royaume (28 juillet 1843)', *Bulletin de la Commission de Statistique* 1 (1843), 577–578.

35 *Algemene volks-, nijverheids- en handelstelling op 31 december 1947*, I (Brussel 1949), p. 9.

36 The account of the census in Bruges is based on the correspondence deposited with the City Archive in Bruges, Hedendaags Archief, Bevolking en burgerlijke stand, Statistique-recensement de population 1846, no. 1, box VII A 21.

37 A. Quetelet, 'Résultats du recensement de la population. Rapport au Ministre de l'intérieur' (23 December 1846), *Bulletin de la Commission de Statistique* 3 (1847), 152–155.

38 Archives de l'Académie royale de Belgique (Brussels), Archives Quetelet, no. 1298, letter of 25 December 1846.

39 *Compte rendu à Bruxelles 1853*, pp.108–113.

40 GStA PK, Report of Dieterici, 17 October 1853.

41 *Compte rendu à Bruxelles 1853*, p. 87.

42 J. Blum, *In the Beginning. The Advent of the Modern Age. Europe in the 1840s* (New York 1994), p. 119.

43 GStA PK, Report of Dieterici, 17 October 1853.

2

All the world's a stage: Paris 1855

In 1855 Parisians believed that their city was the centre of the world. On 15 May of that year emperor Napoleon III opened the second World's Fair, which would attract over five million visitors. To Napoleon, this exposition was the international affirmation of his reign. Charles Louis Napoleon Bonaparte, the third son of Louis Napoleon Bonaparte, king of Holland, was elected president of the new French Republic in 1848. In 1852, he abandoned his republican ideals and had himself crowned emperor Napoleon III of France. He ordered the construction of the Palais de l'Industrie, a magnificent structure of glass and iron between the Champs-Élysées and the river Seine. The design was reminiscent of the Crystal Palace in London, which had been built for the Great Exhibition of 1851. The colossal Palais provided accommodation for the 21,779 industrial exhibitors. At 250 metres long, 108 metres wide and 35 metres high, it was one of the largest, if not the most elegant, modern structures in Paris according to the *Baedeker* of 1878. The exposition's 2,175 fine art entries were housed in a separate building, the Palais des Beaux-Arts. The construction of the palaces was an integral part of the grandiose urban renewal project that the emperor asked prefect Georges Haussmann to carry out in 1853. The visitors to the World's Fair witnessed the beginning of a demolition and construction craze that would grip the city for years to come.

Napoleon also employed less peaceful means to raise the prestige of his empire. In 1854, France and Britain declared war on Russia. The Crimean War would reach a tragic low point with the siege of Sevastopol, which coincided with the Paris exposition. The siege came to an end when the French breached the Malakoff bastion on 8 September, two days before the opening of the second international statistical congress.

The congress delegates were not especially concerned with the Crimean War. Nevertheless, Carl Friedrich Wilhelm Dieterici, who represented the

Prussian kingdom in 1855 as he had in 1853, observed a bellicose mood among the French.[1] The name of General Pélissier, the hero of the storming of the Malakoff, was on everyone's lips. Dieterici noted that popular dramas and children's theatre showed 'that the French are a bellicose people'. He sensed that the entire French government exuded an aura of command and obedience. It is perhaps astonishing that such descriptions should flow from the pen of a Prussian official, but they reveal the simmering tensions between Prussia and France that slowly but surely were infecting international and personal relations. Dieterici's report of his journey to Paris is permeated with the intense rivalry that was brewing between these two countries. Wherever he discerned economic growth in France, he sought evidence of even greater prosperity in his home country. He admired the French silk industry, but could not resist noting that Prussian silk was of extraordinary quality. He noted, with undisguised pride, that the French held German science in high esteem.

Dieterici was not particularly complimentary about the Paris statistical congress. He thought the programme and the issues presented by the participants were 'too French'. He criticised the lack of scientific principles and the excessive bureaucracy. His criticism is surprising since just two years earlier he had complained about the lack of administrative expertise and the academic mentality of the French and the Belgians. In his letter of 4 May 1855 to Alfred Legoyt, director of the Statistique Générale de France, he had revealed nothing of the scientific aspirations that he emphasised in his report on the congress to the Prussian interior minister. One might wonder what Dieterici's actual objectives were. One of his proposals was to expand transport statistics by including the length of village streets as well as that of major roads, railroads and canals. While this may have been a useful suggestion, it was not an ingenious idea of a great scientist (which he clearly thought he was).[2]

The absence of the peacemaker, Adolphe Quetelet, may be one reason for Dieterici's about-face and less-than-conciliatory attitude towards the French. The great pioneer of European statistics had suffered a stroke in July 1855 and was too ill to travel. Quetelet was a master at engineering compromises and striking the right tone. His absence was nearly as palpable as his presence would have been.

Charles Dupin

The programme for the second international statistical congress was compiled by a commission under the auspices of the French Ministry of Agriculture, Trade and Public Works. Unlike Belgium, France had no permanent central commission for statistics. The ad hoc commission did not meet until April 1855, so there was little time for thorough preparations. Charles Dupin's report on the provisional programme struck a decidedly patriotic tone. That always worked.

Dupin was born in Varzy (near Nevers) in 1784 and educated at the

Polytechnique. During the First Empire, he pursued a career as a naval engineer. His father had been a member of the National Assembly during the revolutionary period and later became a prefect, so it is not surprising that Dupin – like his elder brother André-Marie – had political ambitions. In 1827, he entered Parliament as a liberal. In and outside Parliament, he positioned himself as a naval specialist and a man of extensive knowledge of socio-economic issues. In 1820, he published the six-volume *Force militaire de la Grande-Bretagne*, followed by *Force Commerciale de la Grande-Bretagne* in 1826 and *Forces productives et commerciales de la France* in 1827. These works were steeped in the German tradition of descriptive political science, but also had a numerical foundation. In any case, they gave Dupin national and international prestige.

Forces productives et commerciales contained a shaded map showing the disparities in the state of education in each department. This 'Carte figurative de l'instruction populaire de la France' was the first modern statistical map. It showed the relationship between the entire population of an administrative unit (in this case, the departments) and the number of children in school. The lighter the shading, the more children there were in school relative to the total population of the department; the darker the shading, the fewer children there were in school, or – in the words of Dupin – the more people were needed to send one child to school. In fact, the map gave as much insight into the state of education as the distribution of ignorance.

Dupin made a significant contribution to the dubious practice in statistical geography of dividing France into the virtuous North and the idle, wicked South. By including statistical data about each part of the country at the bottom of the map and in the text of the book, he accentuated the differences between the two regions of France, which were separated by an imaginary line running from Saint Malo to Genève. Southern France was depicted in darker shades because of the smaller percentage of children in school, but also because it had relatively fewer schools, won fewer prizes at industry expositions, had a lower mean household income and much lower tax revenues and, in general, had less 'production capacity'.

Quetelet wrote about Dupin's graphical innovation in his journal, *Correspondance mathématique et physique*, and announced that an education map of the Netherlands was being prepared. Like France's southern departments, the south of the Netherlands was obviously straggling.[3] Édouard Smits, the secretary of the statistical commission for the United Kingdom of the Netherlands, also cited Dupin's work in his discussion of the state of education in the northern and southern Netherlands. 'He has,' Smits wrote of his French inspirator, 'brought about a great leap forward in science; he has used the figures to explain the morality, enlightenment and glory of his countrymen.'[4]

Dupin's moral statistics were part of the liberal, intellectual movement that had defined the statistical environment in France since the 1820s. Ideas about morality were rendered into statistical categories, thereby creating a new reality expressed in 'hard' numbers. This was a reality fraught with threats to bourgeois life, but it showed where state intervention or private initiative was needed to stave off danger. The Brussels edition of *Forces productives et commerciales de la France* contained an homage to the inhabitants of Southern France that the government censor had omitted from the French edition. The south was first defined as a statistical unit and was then given a model 'to be followed prudently'. The model was the north of France: 'a part of the kingdom that has benefited from a long series of events, but especially from its proximity to peoples such as the Britons, the Swiss and the Dutch who are industrially advanced and highly satisfied with their institutions, while your only neighbours are the peoples of Spain and Portugal, of Sardinia and Africa, who were left behind long ago and are underdeveloped due to bad laws and bad governments'.[5]

It was no coincidence that Dupin was so deeply engaged with the working class and the idea that its members could be guided along the right path by a humane state and targeted paternalism. Industrialisation and the rise of the proletariat posed direct threats to the bourgeois order. Dupin made enthusiastic use of numerical data in dealing with this subject. The goal of his investigations into the fortunes and misfortunes of the working class could be inferred from the titles of his writings on this matter: *Sur le sort des ouvriers considéré dans ses rapports avec l'industrie, la liberté et l'ordre public* (1831), *Harmonie des intérêts industriels et des intérêts sociaux* (1833) and *L'avenir de la classe ouvrière* (1833).

By 1855 Dupin had reached the respectable age of 71. His years mattered. He had been appointed to the Senate by Louis Napoleon in 1852, and he was a prominent rapporteur for the imperial commission established to organise the World's Fair of 1855. Dupin opened his report on the programme for the 1855 statistical congress by pointing out how important it was for France – which had an illustrious statistical tradition – to play a leading role at the congress. Nationalism seeped into the debates on statistics and morality virtually unnoticed. Dieterici's criticism of French chauvinism (which was rather like the pot calling the kettle black) was not wholly unfounded. It was obvious to the commission and Dupin that France could claim superiority over other parties when it came to government statistics. Dupin made that perfectly clear. The French government had been ordering intendants in the provinces to gather statistical information since the time of Louis XIV. Under Napoleon I, official statistics received new impulses, and the French Restoration sparked important initiatives, which were imitated by the Belgians and the British. In Dupin's view, the conquest of Algeria was also a victory for statistics: 'Statistics concerning that land, which have been gradually perfected, constitute a periodic commendation, expressed in facts, for the capacity of a great nation to extol the blessings of civilisation in a region that not 25 years ago was in a state of utter barbarism and infancy'.[6] Dupin could not resist mentioning the departmental education maps that had been produced in the past decade, patterned after his example. Initially, his maps drew a great deal of criticism, particularly from the departments that were lagging behind, but the number of schools increased gradually and the map's shadings become lighter and lighter, 'so bright that there was almost no need to publish it'.[7] His recital continued in this vein. The message was clear: a presentation of France's achievements in statistics would have such a salutary effect on other countries that they would be compelled to adopt French statistical practice.

An assessment of French statistics

Dupin's linear progress diktat was well suited to the Napoleonic climate. The statistical traditions of France, however, were much more complex than his argument suggested. Influenced in part by the political regime changes that followed the Revolution, statistics in France underwent a period of turbulent development. Statistics had a long history as an instrument of the state. During the *ancien régime*, the military and financial vicissitudes of the kingdom regularly motivated the king and his ministers to ask the provincial authorities to provide numerical information. However, confidentiality was essential; the royal court was ultimately the only beneficiary of these statistical investigations. In the course of the eighteenth century, various multidisciplinary studies combining political, economic and geographical research were published, many written by members of the Académie des Sciences, which was preparing the way for statistics as a science. Prominent scholars like d'Alembert and Condorcet were developing what was intended to be an explicitly political science. Condorcet called it 'social mathematics'. Around 1760, scholars and public servants began an intensive exchange of ideas. Condorcet, for example, had a close relationship with Turgot, a physiocrat and the financial genius behind Louis XVI. New quantitative methods (e.g. the birth rate multiplier discussed in Chapter 1) were tested but vanished quickly after 1789. At any rate, they were not incorporated into government statistical practice. The theory of probabilities and other complex mathematical methods were being used in the life insurance business and in gambling theory, but statistics would follow another path for the time being.

There is no simple explanation for this. Keverberg's explicit rejection of Quetelet's proposal to conduct a population count based on a kind of sampling (discussed in the previous chapter) echoed the divergence of opinions that marked the last decade of the eighteenth century. Enlightened thinkers, in particular philosophers and mathematicians, were severely shaken by the French Revolution. The rapid succession of political upheavals that began in 1789 undermined their faith in the propensity towards reason, which may have been the preserve of the elite but nevertheless could serve as a moral guide for all. While the eighteenth-century thinker regarded society as a collective of rational individuals and, consequently, an organism governed by order, his nineteenth-century successor saw a society that was guided by order despite the irrational nature of the human beings living in it. Eighteenth-century political probability theory evolved into nineteenth-century statistics, but underwent a radical metamorphosis along the way.[8]

Science was not solely responsible for this transformation. The French

Revolution paved the way to a well-ordered state, which may not have been immediately evident in practice, but the blueprint was there. In 1789–1790 the National Assembly designed a hierarchical, uniform government structure that was meant to facilitate effective centralised control and, at the same time, bring government and the people closer together by means of elections and public education. The government's division of the country into departments was an important step in the process and dissolved the traditional provincial boundaries, forging new territorial loyalties. This turned out to be one of the most enduring reforms of the Revolution. In the nineteenth century, the departments were an essential component in statistical research. The statistical exertions of the revolutionary state were initially limited to research aimed at exploring the new territorial reality. During the Consulate period, at the end of 1799, the government stepped up its statistical research activity, which was coordinated by a statistical bureau operated by the interior ministry. In 1802 the bureau was incorporated into the ministry's Secretariat General and given its own domain, separate from the other ministerial divisions. As such, it became 'the central memory of the state'.[9]

The Napoleonic moment

The statistical bureau rejected probability theory, despite the presence of the mathematician Étienne Duvillard, who had moved in the same circles as Condorcet before the Revolution. In 1806, Duvillard served briefly as director of the bureau, but it was already clear to him that mathematical methods were unwelcome. Jean-Antoine Chaptal, France's interior minister from 1800 to 1804, had firmly rejected Duvillard's proposal to establish a Bureau des Calculs Scientifiques, 'where facts are verified, where essential correlations and laws are sought through mathematical analysis or otherwise deduced if they cannot be identified through direct observation'.[10] In the minister's view, a bureau of this nature and the proposed methods tended too much towards secrecy and held too little promise of producing genuine empirical knowledge.

Due to their vision of good administration, the Consulate regime had a preference for general, descriptive statistics, if necessary numerical but never obtained through deduction. They wanted a precise analysis of where the departments stood and how regional diversity compared to that of the nation. The Statistique Générale de la France, Chaptal's large-scale comparative statistical survey launched in 1801, typified the goals of the Consulate The prefects placed in charge of the departments in early 1800 (a reform with long-lasting effects) were ordered to write descriptive reports in accordance with a fixed plan. They were instructed to address five main topics: topography, population, social circumstances, agriculture and industry; the minister also asked the prefects to compare the pre-1789 situation to the current state of affairs. The circular of the 19th germinal in the revolutionary year IX explaining the project was followed by 25 tabular forms, each accompanied by pages and pages of instructions.[11]

Chaptal's ambitious goal was to produce an highly detailed inventory of France. Precision was the primary requirement: 'saying nothing is a thousand times better than saying something that is incorrect', he wrote to his prefects.[12] The farthest reaches of the country were to be described and Paris would be given access to all the information amassed. The administrative structure and the design of the statistical survey corresponded perfectly. The prefects were well placed to furnish accurate and detailed data; the possibilities were too enticing to be left unexploited. Chaptal rebuked a prefect who thought it would suffice to base his overview of the taxes levied in his department on an average value: 'In this case, using a proportional average will not suffice; that would teach me nothing I do not already know, that would not reveal what I most urgently seek, namely the subtle physical and moral distinctions that distinguish the various parts of France from each other.'[13] Knowledge was power, especially when it was comprised of empirical facts.

In many ways, Napoleonic statistics foreshadowed the form that statistics would take as the nineteenth century progressed. The same bureaucratic hierarchy that was used to carry out statistical investigations could be used to intervene in social life. Statistics legitimised the importance of the state. For a while, there was very little distinction between the science of public administration and statistics. In his authoritative essay on statecraft (three editions between 1808 and 1812), Charles Jean Bonnin wrote: 'Statecraft and statistics, which are mutually enlightening, will contribute to the internal prosperity of states. Like physicists discerning natural laws from the constant facts of nature, so shall governments seek in the knowledge of the facts the remedies specific to the needs of the nations.'[14]

'Governing requires knowledge' was the idea behind the Napoleonic state, and a notion to which the liberal state of the future could subscribe. This seemingly simple aphorism was not as easy to put into practice as one might think, even through the agency of a state as strong as the Napoleonic one. Napoleon had the same problem that liberals encounter when they in power: without the cooperation of the people – and first and foremost the local elites – it would be nigh on impossible to accumulate useful knowledge, let alone undertake specific actions.

The interaction that arose between state and population affected the knowledge that statistical investigations produced. The local elites – notables, landowners and civil servants – who supplied the factual information could not have had a radically different perspective from their principals. They were tied to the classifications and categories they were given to work with. Moreover, it was virtually inevitable that the reports would confirm the divisions between the enlightened statistics compilers and those being described, between the elites and the general population. Descriptions of society indicated the direction of social change. The chasm that existed between government and the governed became increasingly obvious. The elites were self-reverential, were incapable of critical self-reflection and remained largely invisible. The people were the main focus of attention, in part because they were easy to describe, but primarily because they had to be governed and improved. Connections were often drawn between the national character and the physical environment. The observations of the prefect of Ariège (near the Pyrenees) on the local population are typical: 'The inhabitant of Ariège is by nature good and obliging, but also cold, severe and cautious ... He is frugal and patient, and almost impervious to hardship ... Religious fanaticism appears to be at the core of his character.'[15] Generalisations of this kind remained in vogue throughout the nineteenth century (and beyond).

There was another important continuity: Chaptal's statistical topography was not a resounding success. The state was not strong enough and society was not cooperative enough for the project to succeed. Statistics faced constant resistance and aversion. This was no different under Napoleon and, given the frequency of requests for statistical information, the obstinacy of the provinces was completely understandable. The prefects often mentioned the respondents' attempts to dodge the government's constant demand for numbers. And in some cases, they helped to manipulate the figures. In 1805, Chaptal's initiative ultimately resulted in just 47 statistical memorials (out of 111 departments, of which 25 were outside France).[16] This was not an accomplishment that a well-organised state would be proud to claim. The experience that some prefects gained in the process, however, had a long-lasting effect. Gilbert Chabrol de Volvic was responsible for compiling a statistical report on Montenotte in Northern Italy; he made a name for himself later as prefect of the Seine during the Restoration, when he applied his professional skills to produce *Recherches statistiques sur la ville de Paris et le département de la Seine* (four volumes, Paris 1821–1829). As we will soon see, this work was a treasure trove for the 'moral statisticians'.

The end of Chaptal's tenure as interior minister in 1804 marked a transformation in Napoleonic statistics. The practice of producing descriptive departmental statistics made way for targeted, strictly numerical, uniform investigations that directly served the interests of the state.[17] The wars, the continental blockade and the economic crisis strengthened the autocratic elements of the Napoleonic state, and statistics was caught in the current. Interest in broad topographical matters all but disappeared; only meteorological observations were continued because of their importance to agriculture. Surveys were streamlined and covered only a limited list of strictly defined topics, such as the navigability of inland waterways, salt, olives, chestnuts, textiles, agricultural land and livestock.[18]

The guises of statistics after 1815

If the Consulate and Empire periods were the fat years for French statistics, the reign of the Bourbon monarchs (1815–1830) could be regarded as the lean years. Nevertheless, the Restoration was not just a time of statistical decline.

There was no place for a central statistical bureau under the monarchy, but the accumulation of statistics went ahead as usual in the departments. Most mayors continued to produce routine reports on births, marriages, deaths, migration and taxation, and with equal regularity the prefects incorporated the data into their official correspondence. But no national statistical publications of any consequence were produced.

The continuity of statistical research at provincial and local level is most apparent in the *Recherches statistiques sur la ville de Paris et le département de la Seine*, which prefect Chabrol de Volvic helped to compile. Chabrol's tenure as prefect of Paris from 1812 to 1830 is an exceptional example of bureaucratic continuity. In 1817, he ordered an extensive census of the French capital that was reminiscent of Chaptal's statistics project. The survey covered population, climate, geography, institutions and the economy. In 1818, an autonomous bureau for records and statistics was established for the Seine prefecture. Managed by Frédéric Villot, the bureau was involved in implementing the census and processing the data. Villot himself made an important contribution to the *Recherches Statistiques*. In the preface he wrote that statistical investigations were a core element of public administration. And, he continued, 'it often occurs that vital administrative questions arise which could not be probed deeply without resorting to statistical information'.[19] This was clearly reminiscent of Napoleonic practices. At the same time, Chabrol and his colleagues distanced themselves from the politics of the latter years of the Empire by publishing figures and interpretations of the numbers.

In 1818, Chabrol issued a report to the interior minister about the Paris census of the previous year and had it published in the *Recherches Statistiques*. He emphasised that the count was better in many respects than previous ones. The first improvement was that numerical statements noting the number of people in a dwelling were replaced by complete name lists of all inhabitants. In addition to people's names, the new lists included their age, sex, marital status and occupation. Separate sheets were created for each household. Chabrol reported that there were some 200,000 sheets in total. The second improvement was the appointment of special officials to conduct the door-to-door survey. The 150 officials were 'all persons of irreproachable conduct with positions in public service'.[20] The entire operation was completed within ten days to avoid potential counting duplications due to people moving house. Special measures were taken for hospitals, hotels, military barracks and the like. The Dutch and Belgian population censuses of 1829 and 1846 respectively, and the instructions regarding the population registers in those countries, were no doubt based on the Paris operation.

Not only did Chabrol provide a count of the city's inhabitants and a series of sheets containing the most essential information about the population, he also ordered his staff to process the statistical data. For example, they compiled reports summarising data on sex, age and marital status of the inhabitants by street and district. This made it possible to compare different areas of Paris.

Chabrol was also interested in the relationship between the number of births and the total population (a relationship expressed by the 'multiplier', as explained in Chapter 1). Understanding this relationship would make it possible to 'identify the progressive variations in the population and the increase that has taken place since the end of the seventeenth century'.[21] Quetelet was no doubt aware of this passage when he proposed a count using the multiplier in the United Kingdom of the Netherlands. His proposal, however, ignored the fact that a full census had been conducted in Paris first.

Alongside Villot and Chabrol, the mathematician and physicist Joseph Fourier was an authoritative co-author of the *Recherches statistiques*. He wrote several pieces in which he demonstrated that large sets of population data revealed patterns. There can be no doubt that Fourier's contributions provided inspiration for Quetelet's first statistical works on the Kingdom of the Netherlands. The ideas Fourier expressed in the *Recherches statistiques* are also reflected in Quetelet's *Sur l'homme* (1835). But Quetelet was not the only one who drew on the insights and comparative material from the statistics on Paris.

The physician Louis Villermé wrote and published an extensive dissertation on the first volume of the *Recherches statistiques* in 1821. The census data and the related statistical studies were a goldmine for Villermé's project on social medicine. As an army surgeon under Napoleon, he had spent a great deal of time on the battlefield, where he witnessed how quickly epidemics could take hold and how important good hygiene was. After the Napoleonic wars ended, he turned his attention to the role of medicine in peacetime. In an article from 1818, 'On hunger and its impact on health in former theatres of war', Villermé combined his experiences as an army medical officer and as a socially engaged researcher.[22] He was a member of several reformist associations and wrote reports in which he used government statistics to explain aspects of population dynamics. He frequently discussed trends in birth and death rates.

Villermé's articles about difference in the mortality rates of the rich and poor in Paris and in France are typical examples of his approach. It will come as no surprise to us that he discovered pronounced disparities. In the early nineteenth century, such observations invited wild speculation about the future of social relations. At the time, there were fierce debates going on about whether climatological and geographical circumstances affected morbidity and mortality and whether the social environment had an even greater impact. The correlation between progress and health was another topic of discussion. Was it the case that public health improved as society developed, or did progress foster idleness or enflame passions and, if so, did this adversely affect people's health? These were important issues to the emerging bourgeoisie.

In Villermé's opinion, such questions could best be answered by looking at the numbers. He gradually came to believe that poverty was the most malevolent factor and managed to convince his generation of sanitarians that his ideas were right. The cholera epidemic of 1832, which claimed 18,000 victims in Paris alone, was in many ways a test case for the sanitary movement in France. Though Villermé had worked hard to position himself as a social statistician, in 1832 he returned to medicine and joined in the battle against cholera. Unfortunately, medicine was virtually powerless against this devastating disease. He made an important contribution to the report on the epidemic that raged in and around Paris. A special commission compiled the report by order of the state. Villot, as director of the statistical bureau of the prefecture, sat on the commission.[23] Social medicine and statistics were now inextricably linked.

Quetelet was deeply interested in Villermé's work and initiated a public exchange of letters with the Frenchmen in *Correspondance mathématique et physique*. Quetelet adopted Villermé's methods in his own research on monthly fluctuations in birth and death rates, and was receptive to social explanations. Each man strengthened the other's conviction that population dynamics were subject to laws. The contact between Quetelet and Villermé demonstrates the significant role that statistics played in how public health theories developed in the first half of the nineteenth century. The *Annales d'hygiène publique*, first established by Villermé and several other French physicians in 1829, confirmed year after year that quantification was an important instrument for controlling public health. In his principal work, *Sur l'homme*, Quetelet used a great deal of data that he and others had already published in the *Annales d'hygiène publique*.

A movement of 'moral' statisticians gradually took shape after 1830. Moral statisticians were interested in connections between poverty and other social ills on the one hand and disease, death, education and similar issues on the other. They saw unvarying patterns in nearly everything. Rates of suicide, insanity and crime showed the same astonishing regularity, at least in their eyes. In 1833, André Michel Guerry published his popular *Essai sur la statistique morale de la France*, which attracted attention from beyond France's borders. Like Dupin he was partial to graphical representations. And like Dupin in 1829 he published several maps of France showing the relationship between education and crime rates.[24] In his monograph of 1833 he wrote that good education could by no means guarantee a reduction in crime (though he had come to this conclusion in a somewhat arbitrary fashion). Education, he decided, was 'an instrument that can be used for good or for evil'.[25] This notion contradicted the commonly held assumption that the departments where education was poorest had the highest crime rates.

Guerry and other moral statisticians took an extraordinary interest in the topic of suicide. Their unremitting attention for this social phenomenon, this 'moral disease', resulted in a growing body of detailed and precise statistics on the subject. Émile Durkheim's famous book on suicide, published in 1897, was based on over fifty years of intense debate on the issue.

The work produced by Dupin, Villermé, Guerry and others would have been virtually inconceivable without the ever-expanding series of government statistics publications. The Ministry of War had been producing the *Comptes présentés au Roi sur le recrutement de l'armée*, an annual account of matters related to conscription, since 1819 and the Ministry of Justice began publishing criminal statistics regularly in 1827. The *Compte général de l'administration de la justice criminelle*, the longest-running and most homogeneous statistical series on crime, served as a model for many other countries and was a source of raw data for the development of the science of criminology.[26] Guerry based his statistical maps of 1829 on it. Primary education statistics were published from 1831 onwards under the auspices of the Ministry of Education. All of these series had their roots in earlier initiatives, but the regularity with which they were published gave the science of statistics an unprecedented impulse.

The political climate that emerged after the revolution of 1830, which ushered in the July Monarchy, was more favourable for the development of statistics than that of the Restoration. The government strove to adopt legislation that would enable social forces to develop unencumbered. To achieve its goal, the government needed to understand these forces. There was more intellectual freedom, as evidenced by the revitalisation of the Académie Royale des Sciences Morales et Politiques in 1832. One of the Académie's five divisions was devoted to political economy and statistics and its members included illustrious figures like old Abbé Sieyès, who returned from exile in Belgium in 1830, and Charles Maurice de Talleyrand, Auguste Comte, Dupin and Villermé.

The battle against pauperism was an important theme within the Académie des Sciences. In 1834 the minster of education, François Guizot, asked Villermé and the Académie to conduct a statistical investigation of factory workers. The study was published in 1840 under the title *Tableau de l'état physique et moral des ouvriers employés dans les manufactures de coton, de laine et de soie*. Together, Villermé's substantial research report and Edwin Chadwick's *Report on the Sanitary Condition of the Labouring Population of Great Britain* (1842), which is discussed in Chapter 3, constitute a sanitarists' manifest of the first order. Villermé's work was based on numerous visits *in loco*, contained a myriad of tables and typified the role that statistics was playing at the time as a science of social facts. Tables and charts were a widely accepted method of representing data and lent gravitas to opinions. Villermé's *Tableau* was often quoted in debates on the child labour law that parliament ultimately passed in 1841, after it had been watered down.

In 1835 parliament decided to make funds available to set up a statistical collection, demonstrating that statistics was gradually regaining its position within the central state. Two years earlier, Adolphe Thiers, who was minister of trade at the time, had commissioned a translation of the statistical work of Britain's Board of Trade (*Tableau du revenu, de la population, du commerce, etc., du Royaume-Uni et de ses dépendances*, Paris 1833). His aim was to underline the usefulness of a similar publication, namely a new Statistique Générale de la France. Alexandre Moreau de Jonnès was put in charge of the project and would run the bureau of the SGF until 1852.

Moreau had a fairly formalistic view of statistics. 'Statistics is the science of social facts, expressed in numerical terms,' he wrote in an essay in 1847.[27] He believed that statistics did not exist without numbers, and if the numbers bore no relation to social facts, they were not true statistics. He did not think much of the sanitary movement. Though he shared the sanitarians' appetite for

statistics, he preferred absolute numbers and wanted nothing to do with probabilities or any other method of calculation that detracted from the purity of
the number as a direct expression of social reality. He wanted to present only
hard numbers to the minister, not statistical laws or patterns deduced from
the numbers. The sections of the Statistique Générale de la France concerning the territory, the population, the economy and public administration (the
first series was published between 1835 and 1852 in thirteen parts) largely met
Moreau's wishes: a lot of numbers, no debate and no controversial subjects. The
interests of the moral statisticians were ignored.

Nevertheless, the official statistical publications, edited by Moreau, did in
fact express certain ideas about social order. First, the large-scale use of the
machinery of government (the prefects facilitated all the surveys) demonstrated
great confidence in bureaucracy. The relationship between the state and statistics that had evolved during the Napoleonic period was restored. Second, the
Ministry of Agriculture and Trade, which supervised the government statistics,
wanted above all to learn more about France's public resources. In its circulars,
the Ministry of Agriculture and Trade emphasised that the surveys had no fiscal
objectives, but the accumulated information was a welcome source of knowledge for the Ministry of Finance.

The government began collecting statistics on industry in 1839, but stopped
after a year because the public – factory owners in particular – were convinced
that the government was laying the groundwork for a new tax. The industrial
survey was resumed in 1845, not only as a quantitative investigation of the
size and dispersion of factories, but also as a study of the influence of industrial capitalism and the size and composition of the working class. As previous
surveys had revealed, asking the question was (almost) tantamount to answer-
ing it. In 1839, all workshops employing twenty or more labourers were defined
as factories; but during the course of the survey, the threshold was lowered to
ten, drawing a line between industry and trades, 'arts et métiers', which would
be included in a future survey. The prefecture kept copies of the forms that were
filled in for each factory. Knowledge about the dispersion of workers was always
useful.

Unity and diversity at the congress of 1855

Moreau de Jonnès had resigned as director of the bureau of the Statistique
Générale in 1852 and so did not participate in the congress, but did remain
active in the Académie des Sciences. He told Dieterici that the congress was
hostile to science and avoided the real issues that the international statistics
community needed to tackle. 'C'est le pouvoir qui fait la chose' was his devastating judgement. Villermé, who was well over seventy years old, put in an
appearance but did not play a prominent role.

By the time the second international statistical congress began in 1855, statistics had acquired a permanent place in the machinery of government, in the

academies and in public opinion in France. Statistics survived both the revolution of 1848 and France's transition from a republic to the Second Empire, but there was still little consensus about its subject matter and objectives. The emperor was primarily interested in the grandeur of the nation. The executive branch needed a numerical description of society in order to organise and control it. The scientific community wanted to go further, to uncover probabilities and patterns, in short, to organise progress. Numerous statistical essays had been published by then, and each defined the concept of statistics differently.

In the year of the Paris congress, Achille Guillard – teacher, engineer, botanist and statistician – coined a new term, 'demography'. His ambition was to establish a new science. He saw demography, or 'human statistics', as the confluence of the many streams of statistical thought:

> Is it not for the sake of humanity, its progress, its improvement and its well-being that facts concerning agriculture, industry, trade, government, pathology and medicine, and all manner of things are collected? Agricultural, industrial, commercial, financial, administrative, medical and other statistics are merely the branches of the enormous tree of humanity, which covers the whole earth with its green foliage and contributes to the development of everything that it sustains and encompasses. Only human statistics, or demography, has the capacity to depict this in its entirety.[28]

The term demography has withstood the test of time, though Guillard's grand aspirations and the moral undertone of his essay no longer resonate. Tendencies towards specialisation and attempts at synthesis were typical of the turbulent development of statistics in France, and the effects would have been felt at the international congress. The programme was shrouded in mystery until the last moment. The members of the preparatory commission were men of disparate temperament and experience. Bureau directors and members of the Institut de France did not always speak the same language. Guillard, whose work – not by coincidence – was published just days before the congress, could not publicly criticise his countrymen, but did express regret about the lack of focus:

> We shall be permitted to say that unless all sections concern themselves with the necessity of uniformity (without which science will remain uncertain and open to dispute), and unless that necessity is the beacon that enlightens all discussions of a general and a specific nature, there is a danger that the congress will fail in its objective, and that a gathering of scholars whose aim is to discuss their points of view seriously and purge contradictions will turn out to be a futile exhibition of a literary circle.[29]

The pursuit of uniformity united all statisticians, not just the French. However, disagreement ensued whenever an attempt was made to define this endeavour in specific terms. The international setting did not make the task any easier. Differences of opinion between scientists and between countries played a role at the congress of 1855. More cautious than their Belgian predecessors, the French organisers presented the participants with a list of questions and proposals rather than a set of propositions. They decided to hold simultaneous discussion sessions for experts in the morning, followed by an afternoon plenary session at which decisions would be adopted publicly. The meetings were held in the parliament building. Though the official record states that 365 people registered for the congress, only 250 actually attended, the majority of whom (220 according to Dieterici) were residents of France.

The minister of Agriculture and Trade, Eugène Rouher, delivered the opening address in the main hall of the Corps législatif. His grand words were appropriate for the occasion: international statistics would reveal which laws and institutions were most conducive to love of family and country, to mitigating suffering and to elevating the hearts and minds of the people. The modesty of his subsequent observation demonstrated a greater sense of realism: the objective of international statistics could not be realised by one gathering or one country; the Paris congress was therefore only a building block. After Rouher, the directors of the national statistical bureaus took it in turns to address the congress. The participants had their first opportunity for discussion in the special sessions that followed.

Dieterici attended a session on agricultural statistics. He noted that thirty Frenchmen, but only a handful of 'foreigners', took part. In his personal report, he remarked that during the session tasks were assigned to the participants in a 'rather loud and disorderly' manner. There was no substantive discussion on the first day. 'Everything had a rather parliamentary character', he noted disapprovingly, 'and the scientific element was neglected.[30] To him, apparently, the modifier 'parliamentary' stood for boisterous and unprofessional.

Certainly Dieterici's opinion had a strong authoritarian and nationalist tint. Most French participants were proud of their achievements during the congress. Even Guillard, who had been cautiously critical of the representatives of government statistics in his book on demography, joined in the discussion wholeheartedly. He made various attempts to elicit statements about the organisation of statistics from the congress. He also participated in the session on statistics of large cities, a subject that had been disposed of in 1853 with declaration of intent, which stated 'in consideration of the particular phenomena relating to public health, morality, crime et cetera which occur in densely populated agglomerations, special and detailed statistics must be compiled for all large cities.[31] The other themes addressed by the 1855 congress were agriculture statistics, transport statistics, foreign trade, insurance, crime and justice, poverty, disease and mortality.

Some of these subjects had been on the agenda of the Brussels congress, but it was clear from the start that little progress had been made internationally. Furtive attempts to formulate joint guidelines for organising national statistics had produced only meagre results. The establishment of central statistical commissions, another topic addressed in 1853, was on the agenda again. The director of government statistics in Austria, Karl von Czoernig, was the rapporteur for the general debate preparation session. His report provides a good overview of the way statistics was organised in the mid-nineteenth century.

Czoernig observed that the science of statistics was new and the use of statistics for the purposes of public administration was newer still. While the need to acquire data of this kind was obvious, different paths were being taken to achieve the goal. Only a few countries had statistical bureaus, and where they did exist, they were often bound by the domain of the ministry under whose remit they came. In some cases, duplicate information was collected via different channels. Moreover, information sharing between government and science left much to be desired. According to Czoernig, there was only one remedy: national statistics would have to be centralised. He compared the task of the statistician with that of other scientists, such as astronomers or physicians:

> As an astronomer must study the universe to explain the orbit of celestial bodies; as the physician must produce an exact depiction of all the body's organs and every function of the human organism to understand the mechanism of life; to understand and explain the complex mechanism of the life of societies, the statistician must consider the entirety of all possible manifestations of that life.[32]

This objective was attainable only by means of central statistical commissions, based on the Belgian model. Czoernig asserted that France needed a central commission: though more statistical investigations were conducted in France than in any other country, there was no centralisation and the practical value of government statistics was not always obvious. England had a similar problem: there was plenty of statistical material but no uniformity. The German Zollverein had already begun coordinating its surveys and Austria's Direction der administrativen Statistik was, in practice, tantamount to a central commission. Czoernig's Austrian colleague Louis Debrauz supported him and suggested publishing the proposal in the French government gazette, the *Moniteur*, because he anticipated that the national delegates would not have a mandate from their respective governments to approve decisions adopted by the congress.

All the delegates dreamt of uniformity in statistical practice. They wanted to see standardisation in bureaucracy and organisation, terminology and choice of research topics, and this came up for discussion intermittently. Before the Paris congress began, Ernst Engel, who was representing Saxony, made a plea for a multilingual statistics dictionary.[33] During the congress, the Spanish clergyman Bonifacio Sotos Ochando proposed a universal language, a precursor of Esperanto. The participants discussed making French the official language of the congress. Debrauz strongly supported this suggestion, because French was the main language of diplomacy and, in his opinion, science needed a new universal language. However, the assembled statisticians were reluctant to take a decision on the matter and left it up to the organisers of the next congress.

Consensus on the standardisation of currency units, weights and measures – a fervent desire of the French organisers – proved equally difficult to reach. The French delegate Hippolyte Peut, a member of the Paris-based Societé d'Économie Politique, made an impassioned plea in favour of adopting French units of measurement, e.g. the metre, as Piedmont, Switzerland and Belgium had already done. Dieterici noted that the goal of standardisation met with approval all around, but the congress could do no more than urge governments to follow the statisticians' lead. *Voilà tout*. The national authorities had full control over such matters, and Dieterici believed wholeheartedly that this was the way it should be. Moreover, he had doubts about whether the decimal system was the best conceivable system. He had attended a meeting of the Societé d'Économie Politique at which this subject was discussed extensively. In his opinion, the people – the French population included – were not used to counting in units of ten. To him, the discussion was somewhat academic (though, all things considered, he probably appreciated that). What he found most irritating was the self-importance of the French and their assumption that France could influence the domestic agendas of other states.

The French preparatory commission, at the instigation of Alfred Legoyt, considered the issue of population counts, which had also been discussed in depth in 1853, but it turned out that there was no scope for dealing with this matter at the congress. Vexing questions concerning the use of census agents, sanctions for evasion and deception, systemisation of occupation nomenclature, definitions of households and family and enumeration of dwellings remained unanswered. These were the questions that the congress should have tackled to demonstrate that an international statistics framework was a viable pursuit. The fact that the population census would not appear on the agenda again until the London congress in 1860 did not bode well for progress on this front.

The statistics of large cities was an important theme at the Paris congress. This new form of statistical research encompassed every aspect of the nineteenth-century debate on statistics. Growing urbanisation and the attendant misery was the dark side of industrial capitalism, so it is not surprising that statisticians focused their attention on the city as an object of numerical study. The congress in Brussels had pointed the way to urban statistics, but it was up to the French preparatory commission to develop an appropriate programme. The task was in good hands. The French were very proud of Chaptal's pioneering work in Paris in the 1820s. Moreover, the Paris Chamber of Commerce had commissioned an extensive census of Parisian industry in 1847–1848 and published the results in 1851. Though this survey had a limited objective, Legoyt believed that this 'work, worthy of good citizens, was a perpetual and remarkable lesson benefiting the social order.

These were not empty words. The revolution of spring 1848 was accompanied by waves of public protest. The workers took to the streets to protest the rapid growth of unemployment and the closure of national, government-supported workshops. Knowledge concerning the state of business and industry in the capital was not only of economic interest, it was also of value to political leaders. The members of the Chamber of Commerce – the factory and workshop owners who were involved in the industrial statistics – were keen to project an image of a stable economic sector in which workers were simply employees and had no political demands. Both workers and their bosses were classified as *industriels*.

This took the edge off the socialist rhetoric, which emphasised the differences between the two groups. In other ways, too, the *Statistique de l'industrie* was an endorsement of bourgeois morality. Married workers were found to have the highest ethical values. They distanced themselves from worldly lusts and passions and took shelter in the tranquillity of the family. 'Written in the wake of 1848, it [the *Statistique de l'industrie*] was intended to dispute the revolution's most radical economic and political claims and to reassert a vision of economic organisation that had been severely challenged, especially by socialist theorists.'[34]

References to statistics of the Paris Chamber of Commerce such as those of Legoyt were actually allusions to the desire the bourgeoisie had for social and political control. This desire for control stemmed from the uncertainties that were rife in nineteenth-century society, despite the many benefits that the middle class enjoyed. Epidemics, disease, popular uprising, crime and bankruptcy were perpetual threats, particularly in the eyes of the emancipated citizen, who had been liberated from so many chains since the French Revolution. Certainty breeds desire for even greater certainty. This was the reason that insurance statistics were included in the programme. As the origin of both good and evil, the city was the primary focus of attention.

That said, the creation of an international framework for statistics of large cities was more than a conservative project. Urban statistics incorporated virtually all the substantive and ideological aspects of general statistics. Dupin took it upon himself to report on this topic to the congress, and did it with panache. There were innumerable subjects to study: topography, surface area, publicly- and privately-owned buildings, roads, population, public health, consumption, trade and industry, local government, municipal finances, public amusement, poor relief, safety, crime, education and churches. Each of these themes was broken down into subtopics, resulting in a list of questions several pages long. It was no coincidence that *hygiène publique* was the theme that inspired the most questions. There was enormous interest in sewage systems, water mains, bathhouses, medical care, health police, cemeteries and prostitution. A separate questionnaire was drafted to collect data on urban trade and industry and appended to the list. On paper, it was a magnificent project that appealed to the classifying, statistical mind. However, in practice it was almost unworkable in this form.

This did not stop Guillard from remarking, as a congress participant, that some issues pertinent to large cities were missing from Dupin's project. For example, he thought there should be a way to determine whether abandoned children were given shelter inside or outside the city, and whether the number of children born out of wedlock was included in the urban births figure, even if the mothers were from outside the city. Like all statisticians, he had boundless optimism and faith that it was possible to know everything.

There were also smouldering rivalries between cities. The English delegates praised London's statistics and the public sanitation measures the city was implementing. They wanted to include specific questions concerning what they considered to be their areas of expertise, such as water supply.

The urban statistics project foreshadowed future developments. The number of urban statistics bureaus gradually increased. Germany, at the forefront of this development, held a national conference on urban statistics in 1879. By 1900 there were nearly one hundred urban statistic bureaus in Europe. The origins of the Union Internationale des Villes, or International Union of Local Authorities, founded in 1913 could be traced back to the initiatives that were explored in Paris in 1855.

The focus on statistics of large cities was both a low point and a high point in the international statistics movement. *Statistique Internationale des Grandes Villes*, edited by Joseph Körösi, director of the statistics bureau of Budapest, was published in two volumes in 1876 and 1877. Notwithstanding the reports issued by the participants, these were the first official publications of the international statistical congresses that had been held thus far. They fulfilled the promise that Dupin had made in 1855. The subject matter of these volumes (population dynamics and finance) show that only a small portion of the original wish-list was carried out.

The countryside also drew the attention of the statisticians. The congress of 1853 had taken a number of decisions regarding the agricultural census, a subject at least as complex as that of the population census. What was the best month in which to conduct an agricultural census? How often should the census be repeated? Who should be given the task of collecting the data: civil servants, who could easily be suspected of having fiscal motives; ordinary citizens, who would probably lack the right expertise and would demand payment for their efforts; or a special commission, as in France? And what kind of data should be collected and how?

All of these questions and more were raised by the organiser of the agriculture section, Marie Joseph Monny de Monnier, a department head at the Ministry of Trade and Agriculture. The rapporteur for the section, Maurice Block, emphasised the tremendous scope of the problems involved in collecting agricultural statistics. To begin with, there was no government agency that concerned itself directly with agricultural production; it fell to outsiders to classify the questions and data, but first they would have to reach a consensus. Every country had come up with solutions, but on comparison they were found to be very different.

Block referred to ponderous discussions in the closed morning sessions that produced few practical compromises. For example, the participants had a preference for paid, government-appointed census agents, but wanted to maintain commissions, provided that they had the capacity to manage the organisation of the counts and verification of the numbers adeptly. Then there was the matter of how the data should be obtained: by interviewing each agricultural producer or having them fill in questionnaires, or by consulting the land registry to ascertain the surface area that was devoted to each type of land use and then calculate the total production 'based on a certain number of weighings and measurements to be carried out with care and in a variety of circumstances'

– i.e. by means of extrapolation.[35]

Some countries did not maintain a land registry, and many people were sceptical of extrapolation, because they regarded the results of this method as inherently non-representative. The agriculture section endorsed the establishment of land registries, but left it up to each country to decide which methods would produce the best results, given the local situation. With regard to periodicity, too, each country would be free to decide which interval was most appropriate. They did, however, opt for both annual and decennial surveys with varying degrees of precision in the desired data. So, pragmatism prevailed over the quest for uniformity.

These problems were not resolved during the open deliberations, when the assembled participants were given the opportunity to express their opinions on the various proposals. On the contrary, the French could not even agree among themselves. Napoléon Foch, secretary-general of the Hautes-Pyrénées department and father of the famous field marshal, was utterly opposed to the idea of paying census agents. As he saw it, paying agents had not led to improvements anywhere the practice existed. Furthermore, he believed that remuneration was a road to nowhere, because statistics would soon become unaffordable. By contrast, his countryman Hippolyte Peut, a member of the Société d'Économie Politique, believed that paying agents was the only way to guarantee accuracy. This difference of opinion echoed the exchanges that had taken place during the morning sessions.

Dieterici, who witnessed the debate and reported on it to his minister, observed how the French once again commandeered the subject at hand. Block was resolved that only civil servants should be assigned to the task of collecting agricultural data. In Dieterici's opinion, this was a bureaucratic tactic typical of the French. The ministry was primarily interested in defining as many classifications and categories as possible, which was bound to result in chaos. The only thing the ministry and the statistics bureau accomplished, wrote Dieterici, was to make it possible to give a plethora of secondary bodies and persons assignments and instructions, which became the ends rather than the means. He felt confirmed in his views by a French mayor who believed that appointing special civil servants was completely unnecessary because no one was better informed than the local authorities about the situation within their own territory. Moreover, the French assumed that every country maintained a land registry. The Portuguese delegate reported that his country, like half of the states of Europe, had no land registry, and even in France cadastral data was not consistently reliable.

A difference of opinion was also apparent in the discussion about counting livestock, another topic that seemed at first glance unlikely to stoke controversy. However, when it emerged that the French were pushing for an annual inventory in addition to a decennial count – because France had a shortage of livestock and wanted to know whether the West Prussian provinces had surpluses – Dieterici lost his composure. He stated that for fifty years Prussia had conducted triennial counts and that the country had no intention of altering this highly satisfactory practice merely to accommodate the needs of the French.

The debate on agricultural statistics reveals how difficult it was to achieve genuine, workable compromises. People were more willing to introduce a new type of statistics than to change an established practice. The national delegates held fast, in some cases with great obstinacy, to the procedures they were familiar with, and merely took note of the other ideas that were put forward.

In France, there were different 'styles' of statistics, each of which had been more or less institutionalised by the mid-nineteenth century. Government bodies favoured descriptive statistics, a style that was based on combining 'hard' numbers and qualitative descriptions and assumed that reality could be interpreted directly from numbers. During the revolutionary period and under Napoleon I, the foundations had been laid for identifying statistics as an element of good government. Statistics had served so well as the language of bureaucracy that it had become an inextricable part of national government, even though some political regimes (and France experienced quite a few regime changes in the nineteenth century) were less favourably disposed towards it than others. Scientific statistics, in which trends and probabilities dominated the style of discourse, was firmly anchored in the public sphere. The sanitarians, under the leadership of Villermé, were particularly adept at propagating and using statistics as a weapon in their struggle. Members of institutions like the Académie des Sciences Morales et Politiques and the Société d'Économie Politique saw statistics as a means of shaping society in accordance with liberal values. Villermé, who remained active until his death in 1863, supported the establishment of the Société de statistique de Paris in 1860. The Société tried to serve as a bridge between 'official' statistics and the various groups of users, of which the moral statisticians were the most active. The international congress's aspiration of centralisation was finally achieved in 1885, when the government set up the Conseil supérieur de la statistique.

Though the spheres in which statistics was practiced in France overlapped, the convictions and aspirations of statisticians were often irreconcilable. This was the reality in France, and the same paradox was even more clearly evident at the international forum convened in Paris in 1855. National incongruities stood in the way of the consensus to which the statisticians aspired. Uniformity was their common goal, but they were driven apart by the consequences of pursuing that endeavour. Proposals to standardise practices in urban and agricultural statistics provoked considerable discussion, but competition and envy made compromise difficult.

Notes

1   GStA PK, I. Hauptabteilung, Repositur 77, Ministerium des Innern, Abteilung I, Section 13, No. 99, Bd. 1 Statistische Generalversammlungen des In- und Auslandes (1853–1859), report by Dieterici to the Minister of the Interior, Berlin, 18 October 1855.

2   *Compte rendu de la deuxième session du congrès international de statistique réuni à Paris les 10, 12, 13, 14 et 15 septembre 1855* (Paris 1856), XXVII.

3   *Correspondance mathématique et physique* 3 (1827), 253–255. The map showing the state of popular education in the Netherlands, designed by Somerhausen, can be found in Part II of C. Dupin, *Forces productives et commerciales de la France* (Paris 1827, copy Universiteitsbibliotheek Universiteit van Amsterdam).

4   É. Smits, *Nationale statistiek. Ontwikkeling der een-en-dertig tabellen ...* (Brussels 1827), p. 65.

5   C. Dupin, *Forces productives et commerciales de la France*, I (Brussels 1828), XV–XVI.

6   *Compte rendu de la deuxième session du congrès international de statistique*, p. 14.

7   *Ibid.*, p. 15.

8   L. Daston, 'Rational Individuals versus Laws of Society: From Probability to Statistics', in L. Krüger, L.J. Daston, M. Heidelberger (eds.), *The Probabilistic Revolution*, I, *Ideas in History* (Cambridge, MA and London 1987), p. 300.

9   M.-N. Bourguet, *Déchiffrer la France. La statistique départementale à l'époque napoléonienne* (Paris 1988), p. 101.

10 Cited in *ibid.*, p. 105.

11 *Ibid.*, pp. 64–82.

12 Cited in M. Armatte, 'Une discipline dans tous ses états: la statistique à travers ses traités (1800–1914)', *Revue de synthèse* 112 (1991), p. 171.

13 Cited in Bourguet, *Déchiffrer la France*, pp. 80–81.

14 Cited in F. Sofia, *Una scienza per l'amministrazione. Statistica e pubblici apparati tra età rivoluzionaria e restaurazione*, (Rome 1988), p. 104.

15 M.-N. Bourguet, 'Décrire, Compter, Calculer: The Debate over Statistics during the Napoleonic Period', in Krüger, Daston, Heidelberger (eds), *The Probabilistic Revolution*, I, p. 311.

16 S.J. Woolf, *Napoleone e la conquista dell'Europa* (Rome/Bari 1990), p. 108.

17 Bourguet, *Déchiffrer la France*, pp. 301–313.

18 S.J. Woolf, 'Towards the History of the Origins of Statistics: France 1789–1815', in J.-C. Perrot and S.J. Woolf, *State and Statistics in France 1789–1815* (London 1984), pp. 132–155.

19 *Recherches statistiques sur la ville de Paris et le département de la Seine, Année 1821* (Paris 1823) I, III; see also B.-P. Lécuyer, 'The Statistician's Role in Society: the Institutional Establishment of Statistics in France', *Minerva. Review of Science, Learning and Policy* 25 (1987), 41.

20 'Extrait d'un rapport fait à son excellence le ministre de l'Intérieur par monsieur le comte de Chabrol, conseiller d'État, préfet du département de la Seine (3 juillet 1818)', in *Recherches statistiques*, LXXXI.

21 *Ibidem*, LXXXVIII.

22 J.-P. Chaline, 'Louis-René Villermé: l'homme et l'œuvre', in L.-R. Villermé, *Tableau de l'état physique et moral des ouvriers employés dans les manufactures de coton, de laine et de soie* (Paris 1989; 1st edn 1840), p. 15.

23 A.F. La Berge, *Mission and Method. The Early Nineteenth-Century French Public Health Movement* (Cambridge 1992), pp. 59–75.

24 A.M. Guerry and A. Balbi, *Statistique comparée de l'état de l'instruction et du nombre des crimes dans les divers arrondissements des académies et des cours royales de France* (n.p. 1829).

25 A.M. Guerry, *Essai sur la statistique morale de la France* (Paris 1833), p. 51.

26 M. Perrot, 'Premières mesures des faits sociaux: les débuts de la statistique criminelle en France (1780–1830)', in *Pour une histoire de la statistique*, I (Paris 1977), 127.

27 A. Moreau de Jonnès, *Éléments de statistique comprenant les principes généraux de cette science et un aperçu historique de ses progrès* (Paris 1847), p. 1.

28 A. Guillard, *Éléments de statistique humaine ou démographie comparée* (Paris 1855), XXV–XXVI.

29 *Ibid.*, XXXII.

30 GStA PK, I. Hauptabteilung, Repositur 77, Ministerium des Innern, Abteilung I, Section 13, Nr. 99, Bd. 1 Statistische Generalversammlungen des In- und Auslandes (1853–1859), letter from Dieterici to the minister of the Interior, Berlin, 25 March 1857, p. 282f.

31 *Compte rendu des travaux du congrès général de statistique* (Brussel 1853), p. 165.

32 *Compte rendu de la deuxième session du congrès international de statistique*, pp. 367–368.
33 *Ibid.*, XXXII.
34 J.W. Scott, 'Statistical Representations of Work: The Politics of the Chamber of Commerce's *Statistique de l'Industrie à Paris, 1847–48*', in S.L. Kaplan and C.J. Koepp (eds), *Work in France. Representations, Meaning, Organization, and Practice* (Ithaca and London 1986), p. 363.
35 *Compte rendu de la deuxième session du congrès international de statistique*, p. 389.

3

The expansion of Europe: Vienna 1857

The year 1857 was the last carefree year of the Austrian Empire, geographically the second largest state in Europe after Russia. Its territory stretched from Bregenz and Milan in the west to Braşov and Lviv in the east, from Prague in the north to Dalmatia on the Adriatic Sea. The colossal multi-ethnic empire had many enemies, inside and outside its borders. Rising nationalism was a threat to domestic stability, and neighbouring powers were waiting for an opportunity to profit from the internal tensions. In 1858, emperor Napoleon III and Piedmontese statesman Camillo Benso di Cavour met in Plombières, where they agreed that France would support Piedmont (or rather the kingdom of Sardinia) in its goal of liberating the Italian peninsula from Austrian domination. The agreement strengthened Piedmont's self-confidence and led to a war in the spring of 1859 between Austria and the northern Italian kingdom. The Austrian army suffered crushing defeats at Magenta and Solferino. At the Conference of Villafranca, emperor Franz Joseph I was forced to cede Lombardy to the kingdom of Sardinia, an act which set off the formation of the Italian state. Austria's defeat cost it dearly. In 1866, it was compelled to surrender Venice to Italy, too. The proud Habsburg monarchy thus began a long descent that would end in the total collapse of the empire in 1918.

But the end of the empire was unthinkable in 1857. The Austrian ruling class lived in another world: not in Stefan Zweig's 'world of yesterday' but in an even older world. Admittedly, the revolution of 1848 had undermined the power of the Habsburgs, but the accession of Franz Joseph in the same year and the cautious politics of Prime Minister Felix zu Schwarzenberg and his successors re-established the empire among Europe's great powers. Austria was an obvious choice to host the third international statistical congress. The government was eager to enhance its international standing by demonstrating its ability to facilitate cooperation between the state and science.

Under the inspired leadership of Karl von Czoernig, statistics quickly became a valued service in the administrative apparatus of the monarchy. The rapid rise of statistics was linked to the political course Austria took in the years after 1850. The emperor and the government intended to halt democratic reforms and saw statistics as a source of reliable, neutral knowledge that transcended the promises of the political and nationalist opposition movements. In practice, statistics was also an effective instrument of government which offered a partial solution to the language problem. Like German, statistics was an efficient means of communication between administrative levels within the empire, a transnational language that did not appear to favour any one ethnic group. It was in the interests of the central government in Vienna to perfect this language.

Some of the statisticians at the Paris congress of 1855 called for the next gathering to be held in the German-speaking region of Europe, though Britain had explicitly volunteered to host the next event. As a Prussian, Dieterici kept a low profile during the decision making (the French preparatory commission had the final say), but he agreed that the organisation should move to a German city. In Germany, he reasoned in his usual anti-French manner, more attention would be given to the scientific basis of statistics as a matter of course, without administrative and legislative issues coming into play. By the time Vienna was chosen, though, Dieterici had lost all interest in the matter, which left Prussia in the remarkable position of having no official delegate to the congress in 1857. The good news was that the great and ancient powers of Russia and Turkey would be sending representatives for the first time. Expectations were running high.

Karl von Czoernig and his mission

Karl von Czoernig, the director of government statistics in Austria, had made a big impression at the congresses in Brussels and Paris, not least on Leopold von Ranke, who characterised him as someone who 'lives entirely in the present, strong and resolute, with a broad world view'.[1] Czoernig was a man of many talents. Besides being a statistician, he was also a creative artist. In 1856 he painted *Ansicht des Dachsteins*, a work that ended up in the collection of the Louvain town hall in 1879 through the agency of Xavier Heuschling, Quetelet's right hand.[2] Czoernig, born in Tschernhausen (Černousy) in 1804, near Liberec (then Reichenberg) in North Bohemia, studied law in Prague and Vienna and developed a passion for political science and statistics early in life. His first individual publication was a historical statistical study in the eighteenth-century German tradition of 'state description', *Topografisch-historisch-statistische Beschreibung von Reichenberg* (Vienna 1829). In 1828 he joined the civil service. He was first stationed in Trieste, and from 1831 in Milan, where he served as secretary ('Präsidialsekretär') to the governor of Lombardy from 1834. His statistical work continued to attract attention while he was in Italy. In 1841 he was appointed director of 'administrative statistics' and transferred to Vienna.

In 1848 Czoernig was elected to the liberal Frankfurt Parliament by the inhabitants of his native district, without his cooperation (or so it says in his obituary of 1889).[3] This so-called 'parliament of professors' counted other statisticians among its members, such as Friedrich Wilhelm Freiherr von Reden, co-founder of the *Zeitschrift des Vereins für deutsche Statistik*, and Johannes Fallati, author of *Einleitung in die Wissenschaft der Statistik* (Tübingen 1843). Czoernig was a member of the right-leaning liberal majority, which supported a constitutional monarchy and a federal political structure. He was unable – and unwilling – to accomplish much in Frankfurt. After the success of the Kleindeutschland movement, the failure of the Vienna Revolution and the adoption of the 'chartered' constitution of March 1849, he returned to Vienna for good. Czoernig was appointed to a high office in the Ministry of Trade, where he had oversight of official statistics and carried out a series of special projects. He was dispatched to Trieste to reorganise the central shipping agency and, for a while, he managed the state railway service. In 1852 he set up a commission for the study and preservation of Austrian monuments, which he chaired for over ten years. In 1854 he was sent on a mission to the major banking houses in the capitals of Europe, including Amsterdam, to negotiate large loans for the Austrian state, which was perennially short of cash.

Czoernig was above all a technocrat and felt comfortable with the bureaucracy of the neo-absolutist monarchy of Franz Joseph. After the liberal revolution in Austria failed, the emperor rejected parliamentary experimentation. He relied on strong military bureaucratic power and staked everything on economic modernisation, investing heavily in the railways. In 1857, the year of the statistical congress, Czoernig published the second volume of his major work *Ethnographie der österreichischen Monarchie* (Vienna 1855, 1857), which dealt with Austria's government reforms from 1848. A year later Cotta in Stuttgart published the volume with a new foreword under the title *Oesterreich's Neugestaltung 1848–1858*. It was a eulogy to the state and bureaucracy. He dutifully wrote that the emperor was the source of unity in the Habsburg Empire. He underlined the role of the Reichsrat, an advisory council to the emperor, which the constitution of March 1849 had introduced as a counterweight to parliament and the council of ministers. With the 'Sylvesterpatent' and retraction of the constitution on 31 December 1851 the Reichsrat was the only remaining political check on the emperor's power, but in fact it was virtually ineffective as such. The centralised bureaucracy – in combination with the army – was the instrument by which the emperor governed; but the bureaucracy also steered and influenced imperial power more than any other political body. Czoernig saw that and could live with it. Moreover, he had little interest in political reform, as long as the mechanism of the state was able to operate effectively and efficiently. Austrian 'Neugestaltung', or reorganisation, was in his view primarily a matter of 'good administration'.

Statistics offered Czoernig many excellent opportunities to put his ideas concerning public administration into practice. In 1841, when he was made director of government statistics, the agency was in need of a complete overhaul.

Since 1829 there had been a statistical bureau at the General-Rechnungs-Direktorium, a kind of court of audit responsible for examining government expenditure. Before 1829 statistics in Austria consisted of incidental population censuses and private monographs in the tradition of eighteenth-century political science. In 1827 professor Joseph Rohrer of Lemberg (Lviv) published a *Statistik des österreichischen Kaiserthums*, claiming he had gathered the material for his work during his travels around the empire, which he had paid for himself. In other countries, Austrian statistics were considered to be unreliable and cloaked in secrecy. Wilhelm Ludwig Volz, a high official in the Grand Duchy of Baden and expert on German statistics, did not mince words when, after touring the region, he wrote that of all the German states Austria produced the worst statistics; even the population censuses were extremely inaccurate. He claimed that Vienna knew nothing about Hungary, Galicia or Transylvania.[4] This was probably an exaggeration, but it was true that in comparison to French and Belgian statistics, Austria's did not amount to much until Czoernig appeared on the scene. The state had neither assumed responsibility for organising systematic statistical research, nor permitted statistics to play a role of any significance in the public domain.

The civil servants who manned the statistical bureau founded in 1829 were primarily accountants. Emperor Francis I had consented to its establishment under the limiting condition that 'no new personnel or increases would be derived from it; no controversial surveys would be commissioned; and finally completed statistics would not be disclosed to authorities or persons who were not entitled to be informed of them by virtue of their position'.[5] Czoernig was disappointed. The idea behind the development of a new imperial department of statistics (k.k. Direktion der administrativen Statistik) in 1840 was to give government statistics a more authoritative role, and Czoernig was just the man to do it. The new agency would inject uniformity and comprehensiveness into the process of obtaining and processing statistical information about the empire. In addition, the information would be made universally accessible.

Czoernig applied himself to the completion and publication of the *Tafeln zur Statistik der österreichischen Monarchie*, which had been produced in small print runs for internal government use since 1829. Initially, these statistical tables were secret and only the highest-ranking officials in Vienna and the provincial governors had access to them. One hundred copies were printed of the first edition, six of which were intended for the Court. The Court's copies were more lavish than the others, which emphasised the exclusive nature of the series. They featured a copper-engraved title page, a reproduction of a watercolour by Thomas Ender depicting Vienna as seen from the countryside surrounding the city, and a series of financial tables which were apparently intended for use by only the highest-ranking individuals. When Czoernig took charge of government statistics, the tables were made more widely available for general official use; only the financial and military data remained classified. In 1848, the year of revolution, the combined volumes of the 1845 and 1846 *Tafeln*, including the previously classified parts, were published in full. This act of decensorship did not benefit the public directly, however. The tables were published in folio and were expensive, but at least they could be viewed at libraries and exchanged for foreign statistical publications.

After his statistics department moved to the Ministry of Trade in 1848, Czoernig began publishing the *Mittheilungen über Handel, Gewerbe und Verkehrsmittel sowie aus dem Gebiete der Statistik* (issued monthly from 1850, quarterly from 1852 and under the abridged title *Mittheilungen aus dem Gebiete der Statistik*). The aim of the report was in essence the same as that of the daily newspaper *Austria* published under the auspices of Czoernig's department in 1849: to present current economic numbers and infrastructural data.

In his opening address at the statistical congress of 1857, Czoernig justified his publications and his efforts to reform the statistics agency:

> But the improvements in the work of the administrative statistics department would have been of little use if, as in accordance with custom, only the smallest circle of officials had been permitted to make use of it; because if a scientific achievement is not exposed to the light of day, there is a danger that it may fossilise or fade; and it is not just statesmen who feel the urge and the need to stay abreast of national statistics. The entire educated public is interested in public affairs and a very large number of businessmen participate directly in economic life.[6]

Czoernig wanted producers to provide him with data on industry and agriculture directly and knew that he would have to give them something in return. Publication was meant to encourage precision.

Czoernig's statistics project was first and foremost a practical undertaking intended to streamline administrative processes. Public disclosure of the data was a sincere aim in itself, but it ultimately served the interests of the state. Citizens, especially educated ones, were entitled to have access to information about the power of the state and, as a result, gain a true sense of their citizenship. Entrepreneurs needed access to key economic data. Political rights, however, were of minor importance. When Czoernig was ennobled in 1852 and given the title Freiherr von Czernhausen, he had his coat of arms engraved with Bacon's words 'Wissen ist Macht'. This was Czoernig's scientific and political creed.

Czoernig firmly believed in the Austrian Gesamtstaat. His Bohemian origins and bureaucratic career in Northern Italy sowed the seeds of his conviction that many peoples could live together under a single emperor, even without political concessions. The constitution of 1849 had granted equal status to all nationalities living within the borders of the empire, but the Sylvesterpatent of 1851, which cut political liberalism off at the pass, left few of these rights intact. Domestic policy was aimed at fully depoliticising nationalist aspirations. Czoernig made an interesting contribution to this endeavour. His *Ethnographie der österreichischen Monarchie* and the accompanying ethnographic map were an unprecedentedly accurate, empirical description of the 'Vielvölkerstaat'. It was based on the population census of 1851, but presented little numerical data. The work was steeped in the German tradition of descriptive statistics, but also attempted to breathe new life into that tradition.

'Staatenkunde' (political science), the predecessor of descriptive statistics, had incorporated geographical and topographical descriptions since the eighteenth century. Professor August Ludwig von Schlözer of Göttingen, a renowned champion of government statistics, was already using the terms 'Völkerkunde' (ethnology) and 'Ethnographie' (ethnography) in 1771, and developing methods of drawing comparisons between peoples and societies. Josef Mader, a professor of history and political science in Prague, mentioned ethnology explicitly in his *Materialien zur alten und neuen Statistik von Böhmen* (Prague 1787). Czoernig was sufficiently knowledgeable about topographical statistics from his earlier work and education, but his descriptive account of the monarchy was more than an ethnographic study. In the same way that the Frenchman Guillard introduced 'demography' as the core concept of statistics, and scrutinised demographic developments in France in order to truly understand them, Czoernig proposed that ethnography be employed as an auxiliary science to statistics in order to give the nationality issue in the Austrian empire a scientific dimension and to offer solutions based on science rather than political rights. His aspiration did not go unnoticed. Emperor Franz Joseph took a personal interest in Czoernig's ethnography and kept a copy in his private library.

Czoernig's objective was to find a historical justification for an 'empire' that did not want to be, and could not be, a 'nation'. His ethnographic description was so detailed that it defied every large-scale ethno-nationalist claim: the Austrian monarchy comprised nearly 150 geo-administrative units, 22 language communities and four large ethnic groups (Germans, Slavs, Romans and 'Asian tribes'). Amid such diversity, neither autonomy nor popular sovereignty was an option. One glance at the map and it was obvious that the empire was a historically constituted multi-ethnic state whose right to exist lay in the hereditary monarchy and in the anti-nationalist 'ethnographic element', in which neither language nor population size was of overriding importance. Hungarian nationalism, Italian nationalism and every other nationalism that existed within the borders of the empire were, in Czoernig's view, merely fads without any true cultural-historical basis.

In *Oesterreich's Neugestaltung* Czoernig used the Italian example to illustrate his point. He believed that the peninsula was geographically unsuitable for establishing a unitary state. Moreover, there was enormous 'racial diversity' in Italy, which could be traced back to pre-Roman times and was still recognisable. The Italian language, he continued, was not spoken by the people. With all these differences, the Italians would be better off abandoning nationalism, because 'still today, once the thin veneer of polished urban civilization is removed, in customs and traditions, in physique and facial expression the powerful son of the graceful Celtic tribe could never be mistaken for the gentle, southern Trinacrian, so fond of the Oriental emotional life, nor could the mild, well-spoken Venetian, whose Greek origins are still phonetically audible, be confused with the roughly-aspirating, jovial Tuscan or with the Roman, considered the prototype of manly beauty'.[7] The Italian nationalists of Czoernig's time entertained, in his view, only subversive plans; their invocation of a national identity masked political self-interest. Whatever benefits they associated with unity, it was clear to Czoernig that Italy had rendered its greatest cultural achievements in a time of geopolitical fragmentation.

Implicit in this was a justification of the Habsburg Empire, which was trying to preserve itself in a time of rising nationalism. The paradox of Czoernig's ethnographic statistical study is that it strengthened the ethnic identity of the peoples he described, which in turn stirred their desire for autonomy. Like statistics, ethnography was open to interpretation, and could serve highly divergent interests. For example, a Hungarian ethnography published in 1876, the year the international statistical congress was held in Budapest, attempted to define the Hungarian people on the basis of a common linguistic history and, in doing so, provide a scientific justification for the Ausgleich of 1867.[8]

Ethnography

It was no coincidence that Czoernig completed his *Ethnographie* in 1857 and published part of it separately. His aim was to position himself internationally as an authoritative statistician with a mission. Czoernig was the first to introduce ethnographic statistics in the international arena. Dieterici, still in charge of the Prussian bureau in 1857, was unable to muster any enthusiasm for a third attempt to get international statistics off the ground. He would turn 67 shortly before the Vienna congress and was no longer interested in adventure. In his report on the Paris congress he had complained about the lack of scientific interest among the participants. He did not believe that ethnic diversity in the Austrian monarchy would bring any progress to the development of international statistics as he had envisaged it. Furthermore, there was no evidence in his public demeanour or private correspondence to suggest that his scientific aspirations went beyond Prussian interests. In a letter to his minister, he wrote that Czoernig was primarily concerned with practical matters, such as the railways, and like Freiherr von Reden, he had not penetrated the essence of statistics as a science. Dieterici added 'that Vienna, the capital of an empire comprised of multiple nationalities (Germans, Slavs, Hungarians, Italians), would have difficulty unifying the scientific community on statistical matters'.[9] But the Austrian attempted to transform this apparent weakness into a strength by including ethnographic statistics on the congress agenda.

Czoernig defined ethnography as the science 'that studies individual ethnic groups on the basis of their rise and disappearance, their development and decline, their influence on political, social and religious life in the present and in the past, and the characteristics of their language, life, customs and development, examining each one in isolation and in interaction with the other groups with which it comes into contact'.[10] His positioning of ethnography between history and statistics echoes Schlözer's definitions of history as perpetual statistics and statistics as stationary, present-day history. As an auxiliary science to the former, ethnography examines the historical development of peoples; as an auxiliary science to the latter, it is concerned with the present-day territorial distribution of peoples.

The congress was not the appropriate place to consider the historical element, but it would no doubt provide fertile ground for ethnographic statistics. Czoernig proposed to design a survey that would address the following 'ethnographic-statistical moments': territorial distribution of the 'races' (the term used in the French translation) within the boundaries of the state, the population of the individual races and size of their territory, and an outline of the primary physical, linguistic and cultural characteristics of each one. Naturally, Czoernig presented his illustrated Austrian ethnography to the congress, pointing out that his experience had taught him that 'the organic characteristics of the ethnographic moment in the society of the peoples of a state frequently emerge if the state unites in itself diverse ethnographic elements and if these elements assume political significance or even decisively affect the structure of public life, the activities of the government and the position of the state in the larger community of states within the civilised world'.[11] The Austrian Empire was proof of this claim. There can be no doubt that Czoernig was specifically addressing Russia and Turkey, which were similar, ethnically divided states. In this sense, the third international statistical congress was broader than the previous two had been in terms of subject matter and participating countries. It served the interests of the organising state, but tried to avoid stirring up nationalist sentiments.

Czoernig's proposal was discussed along with two other matters: the relationship between statistics and the natural sciences, and the use of graphic representation. Apparently Czoernig did not dare to couple ethnography with population censuses on the agenda, a theme that had featured in congress programmes from the very start and had much in common with ethnographic statistics.[12] For most European states ethnicity was unimportant, but in Austria, Turkey and Russia it was a highly sensitive issue. To the casual observer it might seem that nature and cartography had little to do with ethnographic statistics, but the organising committee felt that the three topics were closely connected. The relationship between statistics and the 'natural sciences' – geography, meteorology, botany, zoology and the like – raised questions concerning the domain of statistics and where its boundaries lay, questions that would remain unanswered in the second half of the century. But what really mattered were the 'physical' subjects considered relevant to public administration. The discussion turned to matters like variations in land elevation, water levels and vegetation, features that could be illustrated on maps in one way or another.

Czoernig strongly advocated using maps in statistical publications and said so in his opening speech. He pointed out that coloured maps, with or without symbols, enabled the reader to see the spatial dimension of the numerical data at a glance. He undoubtedly had his own ethnographic map in mind. Moreover, messages could often be conveyed faster and more clearly using symbols. Reaching international agreement on the symbols used was at least as important as international standardisation in numerical statistics. These ideas may seem obvious to us now, but graphic representations and maps were scarce in the statistical works of the day. Dupin's 'education map', discussed in Chapter 2, was imitated in France, but there was absolutely no international standardisation. In his *Commercial and Political Atlas* of 1786 and in later works, William Playfair had shown examples of 'linear arithmetic', including the coloured diagrams illustrating trade between Britain and North America, but there was no break-through in this area during the first half of the nineteenth century.[13] Given the situation, the discussion at the congress of 1857 might have been an important step, but as it turned out the results were meagre at best. By the time the topic was put on the agenda of The Hague congress in 1869, little progress had been made. The only examples of the graphic method in the congress report of 1857 were two road and river maps and a complicated table on literary production in the crown-lands of the Habsburg state.

Franz Ritter von Hauslab, a field marshal and corresponding member of the Austrian Academy of Sciences, had prepared an impressive report on statisti-cal cartography. His military background betrays the origin of his interest. The cartography department was an important military service, richly endowed with knowledge of graphics methods. The director of the institute of military geography in Vienna, August von Fligély, was a member of the preparatory commission. And it is reasonable to assume that the representatives of the Austrian army (ten were present according to the printed attendance lists) followed this part of the congress with special interest.

Hauslab argued that statistics had three resources at its disposal: numbers, words and symbols. Which of the three was most appropriate depended on the nature of the subject matter. If graphic representation was your instrument of choice, you would need to consider what it was you wanted to represent. Hauslab believed there were nine forms in which statistical data could be depicted: 1) maps showing the specific location of factories, animals, plants and miner-als; 2) maps showing regional population densities; 3) graphic representations showing the absolute population number in various regions; 4) incremental graphic representations of water levels and temperature; 5) ethnographic maps; 6) comparative graphic representations of the surface area of different countries; 7) maps showing the relationship between the location of goods production and the places where the goods were sold, consumed or exported; 8) graphic representations of temperature and barometric pressure at different times and in different places; 9) flood maps. Hauslab concluded his list with the apodictic words: 'every graphic representation used for statistical purposes can be clas-sified under one of these nine categories'.[14] It was no more than logical that he considered the statistics of agriculture, industry and transport roads eminently well-suited for conversion into the language of symbols.

The apparent inconsistency of this list demonstrates how little systematic thought went into the graphics methods used in statistics in 1857, in our eyes at least. For many people, series of numbers were difficult enough to under-stand; graphs and charts posed an even greater challenge. When this issue was discussed during the congress, it became clear that when people thought in images they were more likely to envisage maps than graphs or diagrams, preferably in full colour. It was easier to depict the increase and decrease of certain phenomena on a map using colour. Valentin Streffleur, a director at the Ministry of Finance and member of the preparatory commission, came up with a series of three basic colours plus white, and their twelve combinations (e.g. yellow shading on a white background or blue cross-hatching on a red background). Gradations of light and dark could be used to illustrate rankings or changes, such as an increase in industrial output, crops or population.

The statistical maps that were published in the first half of the nineteenth century were primarily geographical maps showing the distribution of a particular phenomenon (e.g. cholera) – in some cases relative to a population figure. People worked mainly with absolute numbers, quantities that were directly related to reality. Proportions and other quantitative relationships were more complicated, especially when they were lifted out of the geographical context.

Ernst Engel, who still represented government statistics in Saxony in 1857 (he would transfer to the Prussian bureau in 1859), expressed doubts about graphic representation. While he acknowledged that there were some benefits to processing absolute numbers in statistical topographical maps, he believed there was absolutely no scientific advantage in comparing quantities, since the relative numbers that resulted from such exercises usually referred to a single relationship, at best depicted by a few steps. Like many of his colleagues, Engel was wary of simplifications. Moreover, colours or other symbols used to designate spatial distribution could easily cause confusion. In his eyes, a wide range of spatial, chronological and practical information could be presented in tables without creating a disorderly impression or oversimplifying matters.[15] In this light, it is not surprising that the congress was loathe to take any decisions about standards for colours or symbols; the best they could do was to defer the issue to the next congress.

Neither the official *Rechenschafts-Bericht* of the congress nor the detailed report drawn up by Adolf Ficker, a staff member at the Direktion der administrativen Statistik, mentioned a lively discussion about ethnographic statistics. Someone remarked that studying the characteristics of peoples in the manner Czoernig proposed would not necessarily yield numerical data and therefore this method could not be considered statistical by Quetelet's definition. It would be more useful to study only those characteristics that lent themselves to statistical research, because ethnography would otherwise consist of 'blosse Schilderungen' (mere descriptions) and it would be impossible to calculate the influence of the 'nationality' factor – alongside a range of other factors – on human development.[16] Nevertheless, Czoernig's proposal was adopted virtually verbatim. Only Austrians had been engaged in this subject and their interest was merely descriptive; the others had no real affinity with it or abstained from expressing an opinion.

The fact that Austrians were overrepresented in the discussion was not solely due to the topic at hand. At any given congress, nationals of the host country made up a large majority of the participants. In fact, attendance at every international statistical congress held between 1853 and 1876 was dominated by inhabitants of the organising country. In this respect, the Vienna congress of 1857 was a low point: only 14 per cent of participants came from outside the Habsburg Empire.[17] For the first time, German was the official language of the congress. In Brussels and Paris it had not occurred to anyone to deviate from the French, the most widely used diplomatic language in Europe. The Austrian preparatory commission decided that the conclusions of the sessions held prior to the plenaries would be presented in both French and German. Participants would be allowed to use either language during the discussion, and if anyone wished to address the congress in a third language (not inconceivable considering the location), that would be possible, provided he was able to submit a written translation of his remarks in one of the main languages. In addition, Czoernig – a polyglot – made sure that in informal situations he addressed people in their own language whenever possible. After the congress, Samuel Brown, who represented the Statistical Society of London, wrote 'nor can the foreign members of the Congress easily forget the courtesy and attentions which they individually received from him during its whole continuance'.[18]

Counting money

Financial statistics was another subject that captured the particular attention of the Austrian government. At the Paris congress there had been calls for more international attention to this matter, and it was not surprising that the Austrians took an interest in expanding on it. It was widely known that the Austrian state had a large budget deficit and was interested in any means – including the statistical – of making matters appear rosier than they probably were.

Besides this concern, which was not openly discussed of course, there were others underlying the extensive nomenclature that the preparatory commission presented for discussion. In the tradition of state descriptions, government revenue and expenditure was a primary theme, though the *ancien régime* was a stickler for secrecy when it came to this issue. The Austrian government was unaccustomed to justifying its budgets and accounts to the public. It was under no constitutional obligation to do so and, besides, no one was interested in exposing the colossal deficits that kept the treasury under almost constant pressure. During the Restoration and the Vormärz, the Austrian economy had a strong, early modern, decentralised character, which was difficult to control. It was vital to avoid repeating the national bankruptcy of 1811 and even more important to dispel the impression that the imperial court and the government bureaucracy were the main culprits.

Czoernig was one of the few who realised that there were potential advantages to greater transparency. In the first place, disclosure would require the state to have a full understanding of the revenue and spending of all its bodies.

This was no mean task, given the complexities of the Austrian state apparatus. The reward for the state's efforts in this respect would be the improvement of its ability to conduct audits and obtain credit.

The revolution of 1848 and its outcome were advantageous to Czoernig. Parliamentary control was still out the question, but the state was in favour of economic and bureaucratic modernisation. A financially sophisticated economy was in keeping with this goal. An adequate budget and account would enable the government to better harmonise revenues, investments, tax policy and economic reforms. Not a word was said about a role for parliament. Later Czoernig wrote: 'today there is no better means of assessing a state, its administration and its agencies than by subjecting the budget to a thorough audit'.[19] Again, his interest in financial statistics betrays his technocratic tendencies and his focus on bureaucratic and statistical innovation, rather than on political reform.

Like the Austrian bureaucrats, representatives of the smaller German states were also interested in financial statistics. These states had been part of the Zollverein since 1834 (since 1853 Austria had had an affiliation with the union in the form of a trade agreement with Prussia) and stood to benefit from shared knowledge and uniformity in financial matters. Karl Ritter von Hock, a department head at the finance ministry, introduced the discussion at the congress. He came to the disheartening conclusion that even if it were possible to categorise all sums of money from every financial account there would still be no solution to the problem of the different origins of the sums. It was virtually impossible to determine for each country what part the state, the local authorities and other institutions had in monetary flows. And even if this problem could somehow be solved, there was the matter of the state's capital and reserves. Data on a state's assets were extremely hard to come by, either for technical reasons (how should the value of a piece of infrastructure be calculated?) or due to rules of secrecy. But Hock was implacable: even if all this information could be obtained, he would also want to know how 'expansible' national incomes were, i.e. what was their growth potential? This seemed a mammoth task for statistics bureaus of the age. For the time being, it would remain impossible to come up with methodological criteria to make a clear distinction between statistics and economics.

Be that as it may, the preparatory commission submitted a detailed financial nomenclature, aimed at generating some progress. This topic was largely debated during the morning sessions of experts and was highly technical and formalistic. The majority of participants were statisticians from the German-speaking countries, but occasionally an outsider would speak up. The Dutch liberal economist Simon Vissering, for example, drew the participants' attention to the major significance of colonies for a number of countries and opined that statistics should take this factor into account. No one took the trouble to revisit the proposal in its adapted form during the plenary session. A representative from Baden said he thought Hock's contribution should be published in its entirety in the *Wiener Zeitung*, so that everyone could study it in their spare time. How many might have answered that call?

Austria did not reap the benefits that Czoernig had hoped for. In his comparative financial statistics of 1862, written after Austria had finally begun publishing its annual accounts in 1860, he admitted that the recommendations of the 1857 congress had yielded little. His Direktion der administrativen Statistik was 'unable to adhere strictly to the regime for financial statistics laid down at the Vienna congress, because the science was insufficiently developed and the public administration bodies were not in a position to furnish the necessary material'.[20] Statistics gained little from the attempts of the congress to acquire a modicum of international insight and the Austrian treasury was unable to profit from the appealing but impractical European statistics programme. Austria's financial situation remained extremely precarious. In 1866 the government seriously considered offering the former Dutch finance minister, Pieter Philip van Bosse, the same portfolio in Austria.[21]

The art of combining

In addition to finance and ethnography, the main topics of the third international statistical congress were education, industry, mortality, hospitals and nursing homes, criminal and civil law, the allocation of land ownership and rates. The overarching challenge statisticians faced with respect to all these issues was to find a way to learn about and enumerate the profusion of social phenomena without losing sight of the requirements of and limitations inherent in the science of statistics. The thirst for knowledge overwhelmed them time and again, and the illusion persisted that the world could be fully described by statistical means. Paradoxically, this universalist aspiration accentuated the diversity that existed among nations – and the particularities within nations. The Vienna congress produced seemingly endless lists of questions on all these subjects. However, the requisite statistical research was probably not feasible, and even if the raw data could be collected everywhere they would probably be ill-suited to international comparison.

Of course, this is easily said in hindsight. Czoernig told the congress that the merging of statistics and the state would automatically resolve the scientific sticking points: 'From the perspective of statistics, today we require not just a numerical description of various elements of the state as they are at present or were in the recent past, but also evidence – in a usable form – of the causal link between all significant phenomena in political and economic life.'[22] To Czoernig it was clear as day that government was the only institution that could furnish the data and cohesion.

Czoernig's state was not neutral, however. The rhetoric of efficiency and comprehensiveness shrouded the interests of the conservative Austrian elite: bureaucratic reform and economic modernisation, but no new political freedoms. Yet it was not just established state interests that determined statistical themes and methodologies. The nomenclature of causes of death, for example, was first and foremost a medical matter, but medical science was far from being able to furnish a universal list of causes of death that was acceptable to everyone. Medical training differed from country to country, and so did the definitions of diseases and causes of death. The cholera epidemic and other waves of disease induced governments to seek harmonisation of medical nomenclature. Mortality development was of crucial importance to life insurance companies, too. They required reliable mortality tables but also needed to be able to assess risk by population group and life circumstances.

Sanitarians like Villermé in France and reformers like Chadwick in Britain cranked up the public debate on causes of death. Like so many of their contemporaries, they were painfully aware of the fact that average life expectancy was approximately 35 years. They also knew that there were wide variations between countries and enormous disparities between industrial cities and the countryside. They were deeply committed to a state role – however limited – in regulating social life. Government was the institution that was best able to alleviate the poverty and suffering that contributed to the high mortality rate among some population groups. This position transformed the debate on causes of death into a political issue that the international statistical congress was ill-equipped to handle. The statisticians were not opposed to collecting data on death and disease, but many were averse to every form of government intervention ensuing from statistical research.

They preferred to restrict their discussion of mortality to the nomenclature of the causes of death, a difficult enough subject in its own right. Three lists were in circulation: one compiled by the British sanitarian William Farr, head of the statistical department of the General Register Office, one by Marc d'Espine, a physician from Geneva, and a compromise list that had been put forward at the Paris congress. The Vienna preparatory commission produced a fourth list, in which no distinction was made between acute and chronic diseases leading to death (as d'Espine had proposed) nor between infectious, constitutional and local diseases (as in Farr's list). Other important issues included the determination of death as such (the fear of being buried while still alive was widespread) and an official death certificate, preferably drawn up by the attending doctor. The death certificate was to state whether the fatal illness had been acute or chronic, and epidemic or sporadic. It was acknowledged, though, that there would not always be a doctor in attendance to determine death and establish the cause of death.

The preparatory sessions attended by the medical statistics specialists were lively gatherings, and confirmed that the statistics of death were dealt with very differently from country to country. The experts ultimately agreed on a nomenclature that distinguished the following causes of death: stillbirth, congenital defects (causing death in the first week), old age (after age 60), violence, disease and unknown causes. They also spoke at length about making post-mortem examination a common practice everywhere, and the possibility of having physicians conduct them as a matter of course. The post-mortem had been widely introduced to prevent live burials. The statisticians saw this practice as an opportunity to learn more about the causes of death in general, but clearly there were too few doctors for the post-mortem examination to be a statistical instrument. Once again, their desire to quantify and create order overrode their sense of reality.

The plenary discussion focused on establishing medical statistics bureaux to process the information on the death certificate. The Frenchman Legoyt was concerned about high costs and preferred to see physicians assigned to existing statistical bureaus. He thought most of the work could be done by non-practitioners. Farr disputed this on the grounds of his experience in Britain, but confirmed that a single physician could process the death certificates of an entire country. The proposal that was adopted in the end did not specify how statistics pertaining to cause of death should be processed. This compromise was hardly conducive to standardisation.

Industrial statistics had been a regular item on the congress agenda since 1853, but thus far no agreement had been reached on a joint approach. In every country attempts had been made to conduct industrial counts but it was not unusual for one count to deviate significantly from another. Industrial development was moving full steam ahead. The nomenclature of French industrial statistics changed considerably between the periods of 1839–1847 and 1860–1865. The matter was rendered more complicated by the preference some economists had for incorporating labour statistics into industrial statistics. If they had their way, questions about female and child labour, wages, working conditions and living standards would have to be included. This posed an obvious problem, as it would allow social issues to be surreptitiously slipped into the statistics.

When Czoernig tabled industrial statistics again in 1857, he tried to marginalise the labour factor. He concentrated almost exclusively on production statistics. That is how he had dealt with Austria's industrial statistics in the *Tafeln* since 1845, how he had built up a degree of trust among entrepreneurs and how he intended to win over the international community. He told the congress that the greatest challenge of industrial statistics was the classification of products and industrial activity, a theme on which no agreement had been reached at the world's fairs in London and Paris. By proposing an extremely precise classification system for industrial goods (34 classes and 185 subcategories), he diverted attention from the workers and their circumstances, and expunged a thorny political issue.

Czoernig may not have been consciously motivated by strategic, political considerations, but rather by the complexity of this research area. In statistical terms, the numbers of workers, the ratio of men to women and children and working hours were not controversial. Whether the minimum working age was 14 or 16 years was seen as a relatively simple matter of measurement, not a social issue. Much more difficult – and therefore much more appealing and relevant – was the matter of classifying industrial products and distinguishing between raw materials, semi-manufactures and end products.

There were plenty of obstacles for the true statistician. The industrial statistics rapporteurs were Ernst Engel, director of the Saxony statistical bureau, and Auguste Visschers, member of the Belgian Central Commission for Statistics. Visschers, who had stepped into the breach for workers' budgets in 1853, was consumed by classification and information collection methods. He posed no major objections, but emphasised the importance of accurate bureaucratic control. Czoernig found in Engel a kindred spirit, who was in no small way obsessed with the direct transmission of reality in numbers. It was not merely by chance that Ernst Engel, whose later activities as director of Prussian statistics are described in detail further on in this book, gave serious consideration to the definition of industry (Gewerbe): 'Who would be able to keep a tally of the industrial labours of all people and discover every room where spinning, knitting, sewing, carving, washing or ironing takes place?'[23] And how should manufacturing be distinguished from craftwork? Inevitably, arbitrary choices would have to be made, a task to which the statistician was well suited.

Of even greater interest to statisticians in 1857 was the exchange of ideas regarding data collection methods. A classic problem was the reluctance of industrial producers to furnish reliable numbers. To make matters worse, it was virtually impossible to acquire and process information about every single business in every part of the country. Czoernig had introduced the 'combination' method to deal with this problem. It was a mathematical trick for calculating large unknown quantities similar to probability calculation:

> For the statistician who studies situations that change every day, there is no absolute truth; he must seek the truth in approximation. If the approximation is based on precisely defined elements applied in the right combination, and thus succeeds, it will render the relationship under investigation in such a way that statistical conclusions may be drawn from it and produce the only possible expression, within a given period, of continually mutating facts.[24]

Engel delved more deeply into the 'combination' method, which he defined as follows: 'inferring small quantities that resist observation and measurement from a larger number of measured and observed quantities'. He emphasised that this was not 'conjectural statistics', probability or even what would now be called extrapolation. In the world of administrative statistics such methods were out of the question. The larger quantity had to be measured first, and statisticians could play only with the resulting hard numbers. Still, this did not prevent the value of 'combined' numbers being called into question. Some believed that if civil servants began applying 'subjective' criteria their credibility would be undermined. Others were of the opinion 'that the combination method of completion through inference of the small from the much larger was not subjective, but rather the result of calculation, and was therefore justified in claiming credibility, especially if a detailed explanation of the calculation process was given in each case, as had been proposed'.[25]

This compromise was particularly popular among government representatives. In the 1850s government statistics was still influenced by the Napoleonic tradition of 'good administration', grounded in reliable, comprehensive statistics.

Only full knowledge based on hard numbers would suffice. The power of the number was absolute. Or as Engel remarked during the debate: 'as the culture of material interests moves to the foreground in our time, governments and the governed will have an ever increasing need to express the significance of this culture in numbers'.[26]

As it turned out, the statisticians had difficulty seeing the implications of 'expressing culture in numbers'. Causes of death, industry and the other themes on the agenda all brought the same dilemmas to light. Efforts towards completeness were impeded at every turn. And when practical barriers were lifted, they were replaced by ideological or political obstacles, particularly if agreement had to be reached internationally.

The Austrian trade minister, Georg Ritter von Toggenburg, had called upon the German-speaking statisticians to enter into a closer cooperative relationship. Karl Joseph Kreutzberg, chairman of the Prague trade association, filed a motion proposing the establishment of a German Centralverein für Statistik and a journal. He wanted to discuss his proposal in detail in one of the sessions, and explained that statistics, in his view, should be more than just an instrument of the state, but also 'a public good of the nation'. What Kreutzberg had in mind was a grossdeutsch nation: 'There is a great power that stretches from the Baltic coast to the Adriatic Sea: it is the power of the German spirit.' He continued: 'There is a heavenly body that we gaze upon in Germany, in the high mountains and in the Taunus range, on the banks of the Danube and the mouth of the Elbe, and it is German research.' And to press home the point: 'There is a cathedral being built by the same method everywhere, in Göttingen and in Graz, in Königsberg and in Freiburg, and it is German science.'[27]

Louis Wolowski, a member of the Institut de France, gave a predictable response. An international congress was no place for a debate on a grossdeutsch unification. Czoernig, too, would have preferred to call the proposal out of order. But Kreutzberg wanted to bring his motion to a vote come what may, and the chairman could not refuse. Most participants with a vote were against the motion, so further discussion of the proposal was ruled out. Engel tried to salvage the situation by remarking that 'in accordance with German parliamentary procedure' a minority of at least twelve proponents was sufficient to pass a motion. Czoernig pointed out that the congress rules did not permit this procedure.

The representatives of the statistical bureaux of the German states, including Professor Friedrich Wilhelm Schubert of Prussia, decided to stay two days longer and meet separately on 7 September – after the official closing of the congress – to discuss whether a statistics association and a statistics journal were feasible for Grossdeutschland. Back in 1846 Freiherr von Reden had set up a general German statistics periodical, but his initiative died a premature death when publication was suspended during the revolutionary strife of 1848. The intellectual objectives of the German statistical partnership were largely the same as those of the international statistical congress, but given the common language and existing agreements (particularly the toll treaties) between the German states it seemed simpler to establish a concrete voluntary agreement than to impose uniformisation. They discussed setting up an official association of statistical bureaux, using common forms, instituting a regular exchange of documents, publishing a German statistics annual and maintaining a statistical bibliography.

As logical as this course of action seemed, the German statisticians were unable to reach concrete agreements. They parted promising to inform their respective governments of the initiative. This had become common practice at the international congresses, and it proved equally unsuccessful for the German statisticians. Grossdeutsch statistics would not become a reality until Kaiser Wilhelm I and Otto von Bismarck deployed the Prussian armies and brought about German unity. By then, Austria's role was over.

The preparatory commission arranged two post-congress river cruises, one on the Semmering and one on the Danube to Pressburg in Bratislava. Apparently, during these outings the gentlemen discussed topics that they had not dared to broach even in the corridors of the Austrian House of Representatives. They talked about women and mathematics, and about Julia, Duchess of Giovane, probably the first woman statistician. In 1796 she published her *Plan pour faire servir les voyages à la culture des jeunes gens qui se vouent au service de l'Etat dans la carrière politique, accompagné d'une table pour faciliter les observations statistiques et politiques et de l'esquisse d'une carte statistique*. Remarkably, this seems to sum up nineteenth-century statistics.

The third international statistical congress in Vienna continued along the course set by the Paris congress. As before, the preparatory commission put several topics on the agenda which received special attention from the assembled statisticians. The advantage of this procedure was that it precluded the need to address the entire international statistics project. On the other hand, it gave Austria the power to set the agenda, which it did. The dominance of the Austrian contribution was also evident from the list of participants, most of whom hailed from the Habsburg monarchy. As a result, the Austrian style of practicing statistics was very apparent and statistics was identified much more closely with the state than it had been at the Belgian and French congresses.

Czoernig, the undisputed leader of Austrian government statistics, was the ideal advocate of neo-absolutist statistics. He could circumvent politically sensitive subjects with ease or obfuscate them with technocratic deliberations. To him, professionalism was a matter of administrative perfection; politics seemed to be secondary. But he was also conciliatory, and a man of imagination who spoke several languages. These were talents that served him well in the international milieu. He remained at the helm of Austrian statistics until 1865. In 1863 he was appointed the first chairman of the Statistische Zentralkommission and in 1864 he launched a statistics seminar for civil servants, after the Prussian example. The international congress saw at least one of its wishes fulfilled when the central commission was established.

Notes

1   L. von Ranke, 'An Clara Ranke (Brussels, 22 September 1853)', in W.P. Fuchs (ed.), *Das Briefwerk* (Hamburg 1949), p. 373.

2   In 1898 the painting was still part of the municipal collection. During the First World War it disappeared. It may have been stolen by the German occupying forces, who used the Louvain city hall as their headquarters (information by Veronique Vandekerchove, curator of the Museum Vander Kelen-Mertens in Louvain).

3   'Carl Freiherr von Czörnig', *Statistische Monatsschrift* 15 (1889), 546.

4   Generallandesarchiv Karlsruhe, Abt. 237, Finanz Ministerium, no. 7119, report by Volz, 31 December 1835.

5   Letter from Emperor Francis I to Anton Freiherr von Baldacci, 6 April 1829, cited in *Denkschrift der k.k. statistischen Zentralkommission zur ihrer fünfzigjährigen Bestandes* (Vienna 1913), p. 12.

6   Karl Freiherr von Czoernig, 'Bericht über den Entwurf eines Programmes für die dritte Versammlung des internationalen statistischen Congresses', in *Rechenschafts-Bericht über die dritte Versammlung des internationalen Congresses für Statistik abgehalten zu Wien vom 31. August bis 5. September 1857* (Vienna 1858), p. 12.

7   C. von Czoernig, *Oesterreich's Neugestaltung 1848–1858* (Stuttgart and Augsburg 1858), pp. 17–18.

8   Pál Hunfalvy, *Magyarország ethnographiája* (Budapest 1876), also published in German in 1877, see Z. Tóth, 'Liberale Auffassung der Ethnizität in der "Ethnographie von Ungarn" von Pál Hunfalvy', in C. Kiss, E. Kiss and J. Stagl (eds), *Nation und Nationalismus in wissenschaftlichen Standardwerken Österreich-Ungarns, ca. 1867–1918* (Vienna 1997), pp. 57–64.

9   GStA PK, I. Hauptabteilung, Repositur 77, Ministerium des Innern, Abteilung I, Section 13, Nr. 99, Bd. 1 Statistische Generalversammlungen des In- und Auslandes (1853–1859), letter from Dieterici to the Ministry of the Interior, Berlin, 25 March 1857.

10 C. von Czoernig, 'Statistik der ethnographischen Verschiedenheiten eines Staates. Bericht', in *Rechenschafts-Bericht über die dritte Versammlung des internationalen Congresses für Statistik*, p. 207.

11 *Ibid.*, p. 208.

12 M. Labbé, 'Le projet d'une statistique des nationalités discuté dans les sessions du Congrès International de Statistique (1853–1876)', in H. le Bras, F. Ronsin, E. Zucker-Rouvillois, *Démographie et Politique* (Dijon 1997), pp. 127–142.

13 G. Palsky, *Des chiffres et des cartes. Naissance et développement de la cartographie quantitative française au XIXᵉ siècle* (Paris 1996), pp. 53–56.

14 F. Ritter von Hauslab, 'Anwendung der Kartographie und der Graphik überhaupt auf die Zwecke der Statistik', in *Rechenschafts-Bericht über die dritte Versammlung des internationalen Congresses für Statistik*, p. 202.

15 *Rechenschafts-Bericht über die dritte Versammlung des internationalen Congresses für Statistik*, p. 428; also observed in the report of A. Ficker, 'Die dritte Versammlung des internationalen Congresses für Statistik zu Wien om september 1857', *Mittheilungen aus dem Gebiete der Statistik* 6:3 (1857), 134.

16 *Rechenschafts-Berichtüber über die dritte Versammlung des internationalen Congresses für Statistik*, p. 548.

17 E. Brian, 'Observations sur les origines et sur les activités du congrès international de statistique (1853–1876)', *Bulletin de l'Institut International de Statistique. Actes de la 47ème session*, Tome LIII, Livraison I (Paris 1989), 127.

18 Cited from the *Quarterly Journal* in A. Ficker, 'Die dritte Versammlung', p. 48.

19 C. Freiherr von Czoernig, *Systematische Darstellung der Budgets von Grossbritannien (1862)*,

Frankreich (1862) und Preussen (1861), nebst einer Uebersicht der Budgets von Baiern, Belgien, den Niederlanden, Portugal, Spanien und Russland (Vienna 1862), p. 4.

20 *Ibidem*, vii–viii.

21 F. van der Woude, *Minister Mr. P.P. van Bosse en de fiscale wetgeving rond het midden van de 19e eeuw* (Ph.D. dissertation, Rijksuniversiteit Groningen 1997), p. 85. I should like to thank Christianne Smit for this piece of information.

22 *Rechenschafts-Bericht über die dritte Versammlung des internationalen Congresses für Statistik*, pp. 15–16.

23 *Ibid.*, p. 288.

24 *Ibid.*, p. 149.

25 *Ibid.*, pp. 290–291.

26 *Ibid.*, p. 283.

27 *Ibid.*, p. 270.

4

On waves of passion: London 1860

London was the fountainhead of international statistics. Adolphe Quetelet enjoyed visiting the British capital. Early in his career he had discovered that many British thinkers shared his vision of statistics. He had a hand in the establishment of the Statistical Section (Section F) of the British Association for the Advancement of Science and the Statistical Society of London. In 1851 he chose the Great Exhibition of London as the stage for launching the European statistical congress. He expected the British to be very supportive and the Crystal Palace seemed the ideal place to introduce the international plans being developed by statisticians. The immense exhibition building defied the imagination and exuded confidence in the future. No cast-iron structure had ever been built on this scale. Joseph Paxton, a former gardener, had designed a modern, covered Garden of Eden. It was surrounded by pavilions displaying the most amazing and ingenious inventions of the day and in the centre there were fountains, boscages and towering elms. Birds flew around overhead. It was as if you could touch the sky, which is precisely what statisticians wanted to do.

Statisticians found an attentive listener in Prince Albert, Queen Victoria's German husband and the initiator of the Great Exhibition. As a former student of Adolphe Quetelet, he was well-versed in statistics. He became the patron and honorary chairman of the Statistical Society of London shortly after his marriage and relocation to Britain in 1840. There is no doubt that he was an active proponent of his former teacher's plans in 1851 and, wherever possible, mobilised scientists to support the initiative. When the fourth international statistical congress was held in London in 1860, there was no one better suited to opening the proceedings than Prince Albert. Quetelet and the Prince corresponded regularly. In 1859, on behalf of the statistics community Quetelet invited the Prince to attend the forthcoming congress.[1] The organisers had apparently intended to convene the congress in the summer of 1859, but the war between Austria and Piedmont made it necessary to postpone.

Albert carried the boundless scientific optimism of the Great Exhibition with him until his premature death in 1861. He corresponded with prominent scientists and scholars and regularly attended scientific gatherings. In 1859, at the annual meeting of the British Association for the Advancement of Science, he made an impassioned plea for the unification of science and public administration. He asked William Farr, the most authoritative English statistician of the day, to help him prepare his opening address at the statistical congress on 16 July 1860. The prince purportedly said: 'Now, Dr Farr, I wish to suck your brains'. But he did not restrict himself to picking Farr's brains. Dr Farr later acknowledged that the prince had digested much more than the one report he had sent him. Albert's speech was his own work.[2]

That speech may have marked the highpoint of nineteenth-century statistics. Never before had any member of a royal court or government spoken with such authority about statistics. Albert began by focusing on the congress's public and national character, which was entirely consistent with the high intensity of political life in Britain where every important issue was debated in the public arena.[3] In Albert's view, statistics was everyone's business: everyone in the country should be able to access statistical information, and everyone should contribute to it. A tradition of openness and participation typified the role of statistics in Britain. Like so many others, Albert saw Britain as the birthplace of statistics: the eleventh-century *Domesday Book* was 'one of the oldest and most complete monuments' of that field of inquiry. And, of course, he was able to report that the idea of an international statistical congress germinated when visitors from all over the world gathered together 'at the Great Exhibition of 1851 to exhibit their science, skill and industry in noble rivalry'.

It was then that Albert's speech took a serious turn. He shifted away from dutiful expressions of pride to tackle some of the big issues in statistics. First, he spoke of the alleged dullness of figures and tables. Statistics held little appeal for the general public, a fact that was as understandable as it was regrettable. 'The public generally … connect in their minds statistics, if not with unwelcome taxation (for which they naturally form an important basis), certainly with political controversies, in which they are in the habit of seeing public men making use of the most opposite statistical results, with equal assurance in support of the most opposite arguments'. There was no justification for manipulating numbers and calculations but, in Albert's opinion, the fact that men of science and politics were relying on statistical data more and more meant they were attributing growing importance to statistics. Whatever the prejudices, statistics was there to stay.

The prince went on to say that while statistics appeared to be an imperfect science – more an auxiliary discipline than an autonomous field of inquiry – this was not actually the case. Statistics abstained from the discovery and presentation of universal laws, which was the province of politics and the natural sciences, but did so out of 'self-imposed abnegation'. 'Those general laws, therefore, in the knowledge of which we recognise one of the highest treasures of man on earth, are often left unexpressed, though rendered self-apparent, as they may be read in the uncompromising, rigid figures placed before them'.

The crux of his argument lay in his next point: the belief that statistics was an attack on the Christian faith. The year 1860 was a turbulent time for faith and religion in Britain. A fierce public debate about Charles Darwin's *The Origin of Species* (1859) had erupted and had converged around the dichotomy between creation and evolution, between faith and science. And if that were not enough, in 1860 colleagues of Benjamin Jowett, a professor of Greek, compiled a controversial book entitled *Essays and Reviews* in which they defended the proposition that the Bible should be interpreted like any other book and the Scriptures could be analysed like the great classics of Antiquity. There was a considerable risk that statistics would be tarred with the same brush as godless science. Albert understood this and tried to knock the bottom out of the argument. First, he summarised the fears of the opponents: statistics robbed the Almighty of His power, transformed His world into a machine and led to fatalism because it reduced human beings to mere cogs in the machine with no will of their own. The prince's rejoinder to this criticism is a paragon of rhetoric:

> Is the power of God destroyed or diminished by the discovery of the fact that the earth requires 365 revolutions upon its own axis to every revolution round the sun, giving us so many days to our year, and that the moon changes 13 times during that period, that the tide changes every six hours, that water boils at a temperature of 212 degrees Fahrenheit, that the nightingale sings only in April and May, that all birds lay eggs, that 105 boys are born to every 100 girls? Or is a man a less free agent because it has been ascertained that a generation lasts about forty years; that there are annually put in the post-offices the same number of letters on which the writers had forgotten to place any address; that the number of crimes committed under the same local, national, and social conditions is constant; that the full-grown man ceases to find amusement in the sports of the child?

Albert went on to explain that the field of statistics did not claim that this was how things should be, only that this was how things had always been, and as long as the same causes persisted, it was highly likely that the same effects would be produced. In nature there are no certainties, only likelihoods. Albert marvelled at how statistical data could be used to determine human life expectancy so precisely that life insurance companies could create a specially adapted policy for any individual. Without, he emphasised, disrespectfully attempting to determine the person's date of death.

Albert's best defence against religiously inspired opposition was his proposition that the general laws and patterns revealed by statistics were not applicable to each individual case, and therefore did not restrict human freedom. The only real connection between statistics and the Almighty was that the former showed that He had created a world governed by unchanging laws, but where every human being was a free agent, with full and free command of his faculties. This was met with thunderous applause.

Having cracked the hardest nut, Albert ended his speech in style. He stressed the importance of international congresses: which 'pave the way to an agreement among different Governments and nations'. He reiterated the basics of statistics that Quetelet, his teacher, had formulated seven years before at the opening of the first congress: to study many facts, varied facts, comparable facts and facts collected at different times and places. The previous congresses had issued many recommendations to answer this call. Albert had to admit that some states had failed to comply fully. Since he could not possibly blame his guests, he acknowledged that Britain had not toed the line on population and law enforcement statistics. On the other hand, he hoped that other countries would follow Britain's good example in the areas of agricultural and trade statistics. Albert predicted that the figures would show how interdependent nations had become. In this interdependent world, competition and rivalry were beneficial, as long as peace and goodwill were preserved.

Goodwill was indeed essential but difficult to orchestrate. A curious incident occurred immediately after the opening session on 16 July. Old Lord Brougham, as radical at 82 as he was in his youth and not one to mince his words, stood up and addressed the American ambassador, George Mifflin Dallas. The political climate in the United States was highly charged (the Civil War would begin a few months later) and the world had taken notice. Dallas had been ambassador under President Lincoln's predecessor, James Buchanan, and as such had been involved in several diplomatic conflicts between Britain and the United States concerning the slave trade. Brougham maliciously asked whether Dallas had noticed that there was a black man in the room. Dallas remained uncomfortably silent, but Martin R. Delany, the black man in question, took it upon himself to reassure Prince Albert and Lord Brougham, stating simply 'I am a man'. According to his biographer, this was his shortest but most effective speech.[4] Delany had been invited to the congress because of his struggle for a homeland in Africa for black Americans, an endeavour that had found some support in Britain. The Times wrote the next day that Lord Brougham's impertinent question 'elicited a round of cheering very extraordinary for an assemblage of sedate statisticians'. It took a great deal of effort to prevent a disruption of diplomatic relations between Britain and the United States. It was clear that the congress was not immured from political issues, however much the statisticians or Prince Albert, for that matter, wished it was.

The Times was rather critical of the state of statistics in Britain. In an article published on 17 July the paper saw the fact that the Prince had opened the congress as evidence that the true value of statistics was not appreciated in government circles. A minister would have little to say if asked about the application of statistics in legislation. According to The Times, politics was about interests, conflicts and sentiments, but 'dry statistics are very seldom mentioned, except to be disposed of'. The science of statistics was not part of 'hard politics' in Britain, although it had proven that certain occupations, bad drains, crowded buildings, bad water and leaky gaspipes were life-threatening (as was the polluted Thames). Boisterous speakers, the paper continued, were ready to flatly deny that there was any danger at all to be concerned about or perhaps claim, but only under duress, that a slight shortening of the lifespan was insignificant. 'Nothing but the small still voice of a statistical demonstration will beat these loud talkers off the field'.

Albert's speech set the tone for the congress, but not the language. Once again there was a debate about what the official language should be. As he had in Paris before, Debrauz proposed to accept French as the lingua franca, cleverly appealing to the 'British freedom' of which Prince Albert had spoken so highly. But Debrauz was fighting a losing battle; Farr, the organiser of the London congress, had already announced that both English and French could be spoken. The session chairman, William Francis Cowper, soothed a potential conflict by deciding that the congress would follow the same procedure as the last one, namely that the language of the host country and French would be accepted.

All the afternoon plenary sessions were held in the Large Hall of King's College in Somerset House, a colossal complex between the Strand and what is now Victoria Embankment. Somerset House accommodated several administrative services, including the Inland Revenue Office, the Audit Office, the Wills Office and the General Register Office, and a few learned societies, such as the Geological Society and the Royal Society of Antiquaries. King's College occupied the east wing. It was the ideal place to hold a congress. Numerous rooms with a scholarly ambiance were available for the morning sessions. And hotels were abundant in the neighbourhood.

Many of the official delegates travelled to London a few days before the congress began. After three congresses, a kind of fellowship had arisen among the regular participants and they had agreed to meet up in London in advance of the official proceedings. Jan Ackersdijck, one of the Dutch delegates, arrived on 11 July and took a room near the British Museum. He participated in various preparatory meetings and went on a tourist excursion with Berg, Engel, Hopf, Quetelet, Czoernig, Asher, Sierakowski, Von Bouschen, Von Baumhauer, Brown and Hendricks, the crème de la crème of international statistics. On 13 July he joined the company of statisticians who in those days met regularly at the home of Florence Nightingale, who incidentally did not participate in the discussions.[5] She wrote to her father that he should send her all of his flowers, fruit, vegetables and whatever else he could spare. This was a major event that would 'cement the peace of Europe'.[6] Expectations were high, and not just Nightingale's. Farr and all the regular congress participants were determined to create as much harmony among themselves as possible before the official activities commenced. Only then was there a chance that their governments would accept the resolutions adopted by the congress. After three congresses, it was high time they did.

Political arithmetic and other roots of statistics

Britain had much to offer the international statistical community. Notwithstanding *The Times*'s bitter commentary on the disparagement of statistics in government circles, the country had a rich statistical tradition. The manuals that didn't hark back to the *Domesday Book* proudly referred to the seventeenth-century numerical exercises of William Petty and John Graunt, which were generally considered to be precursors of statistics. Petty coined the term 'political arithmetic' to express his predilection for numbers. 'The method I take ... is not very usual; for instead of using only comparative and superlative Words, and intellectual Arguments, I have taken the course ... to express myself in Terms of *Number, Weight*, or *Measure*.'[7] Petty's zeal for numbers pertaining to population, housing, capital, trade and other economic indicators sprang from the desire to set numerical criteria for state power. His contemporary, Graunt, was particularly interested in mortality rates, which he attempted to couple with birth and immigration rates. He observed many trends that tempted him to make pronouncements about population dynamics in London and elsewhere in Britain. The belief in order and constant ratios would turn out to be trap that only a few statisticians would manage to avoid in the centuries that followed.

The concept of statistics entered the English language at the end of the eighteenth century. John Sinclair's *Statistical Account of Scotland*, which was published in volumes between 1791 and 1799, made it a permanent fixture. Sinclair was responsible for the frequently cited distinction between the German notion of statistics (i.e. investigation of national political power and thus limited to state affairs) and the Anglo-Saxon interpretation, which was based on the idea that the well-being of the country's population was the object of statistical research. It is an appealing contrast, but ultimately this two-dimensional portrayal of the relationship between the state, society and statistics in the nineteenth century falls flat.

Britain itself is a case in point. In the first half of the century, the development of British statistics was more varied than Sinclair's dichotomy would suggest. There was great political freedom, which meant it was possible to experiment with statistics in many different areas. Since 1801 Britain had been conducting a census every ten years. Initially the counts were crude but they foreshadowed a more extensive government statistics; Malthus's frightening proposition that population growth could only be restrained by famine, disease and crime sparked an interest in accurate population figures; and among political economists the clamour for reliable statistics was growing louder. There was no single statistics movement, as has been suggested. At most, there was an emerging 'tendency' – as Quetelet would have put it – to substantiate arguments with statistical data. For example, in the introduction to the first edition of *Das Kapital* (1867) Karl Marx cast back to a tradition of social statistics, which manifested itself in an endless series of reports by factory inspectors, physicians and commissioners charged with studying women's labour and child labour, living conditions and nutrition.[8]

The tradition to which Marx referred was more recent than he may have thought. It was not until the years after 1830 – the same period when statistical activity began to diversify – that people started conducting social surveys in the large cities. It was not by accident that the rise of statistics in those years coincided with a strengthening of the central state, which – until then – bore little resemblance to states like France, Prussia and Austria. Very much depended on the cooperation and motivation of local government. The centralisation of knowledge coincided with, and in some ways even laid the foundation for, the revolution in public administration that Britain underwent in the mid-nineteenth century. A feature of the revolution was that access to expertise gradually came to replace dependence on local government. A new class of civil servants was needed to collect and process statistical information, and would end up shaping the modern state.[9]

The rapid development of statistics applications was propelled from many directions. As in many countries on the European continent, the cholera epidemic of the early 1830s terrified the British population. There was no cure for the disease, but sanitary reformers like Thomas Southwood Smith and Edwin Chadwick (Villermé's intellectual confederates) called for improvements to living conditions in the slums of industrial cities. Using inductive logic and basing their analyses on as much factual information as possible, they attempted to refute what they considered to be unsubstantiated claims of contemporary medical theory by giving more credence to measurements than a priori assumptions. So, statistics was an important instrument. The severe fever epidemic that swept through the slums of London in the winter of 1837–1838 precipitated a socio-medical study that paved the way for Chadwick's startling *Report on the Sanitary Condition of the Labouring Population of Great Britain* in 1842. The sanitarians sought explanations for disease and death in the physical, social, hereditary and psychological environments. Their approach distanced itself from traditional medicine and encompassed all of society, which did not facilitate their endeavours. Reforming medical science went hand in hand with a call for political and administrative reform.

William Farr, too, was an early convert to the objectives of the sanitarian movement. After medical school, he made a study trip to Paris in 1829–1830. His interest was piqued by results that French sanitary reformers had achieved under Villermé's leadership. He noticed that population statistics, and disease and mortality statistics in particular, were an important part of their programme, and lamented that the central state in his home country took little interest in such matters.

Back in Britain, Farr tried his hand at medical journalism. In 1837 he launched the *British Annals of Medicine, Pharmacy, Vital Statistics, and General Science*, probably modelled on the *Annales d'hygiène publique*. This undertaking was short-lived but demonstrated Farr's special interest in statistics. In the same year, he reached a larger audience with his contribution on population statistics to the authoritative statistical review of the British Empire compiled by political economist John Ramsay McCulloch.[10] Like Quetelet, Farr believed there were laws governing the dynamics of birth and death rates, though he did admit – in the same vein as his Belgian confrère – that 'even if the knowledge of those laws gave men no more power over the course of human existence than the meteorologist wields over the storms of the atmosphere, or the astronomer over the revolutions of the heavens'.[11] While he was writing the article for McCulloch, Parliament adopted the Births and Deaths Registration and Marriage Acts (1836). In a footnote he speculated on the transformation that population statistics would undergo. He probably hoped to have a hand in it himself and was angling for an appointment to the new population registry, the General Register Office (GRO), which would also be given oversight of the decennial census.

Farr's oblique job application was successful. In 1839 he was given a permanent appointment to the GRO, where he would stay until he retired in 1880. Farr was able to play a pivotal role in British government statistics for decades. Nevertheless, sanitary reform ideas did not dominate the agenda at the GRO. Tracing the administrative and parliamentary preamble that led to the creation of the agency reveals that determining rights of ownership and establishing causes of death for the benefit of life insurance companies were equally important considerations.[12] This also underlines the vast diversity of statistical sources in Britain.

The key innovation of the 1830s was that the central state began to play a more prominent role in the processing of statistical data. For example, a statistical department was set up at the Board of Trade in 1833 to steer economic statistics in the right direction.[13] The Poor Law Amendment Act of 1834 provided for new territorial administrative units which, a few years later, would form the basis for the registration of births, marriages and deaths. In addition, the Act established a central Poor Law Commission, which would conduct systematic research into conditions in the parishes. Chadwick was secretary to Commission. The findings of the Commission prompted further socio-medical research, which in turn ultimately led to the aforementioned report on sanitary conditions in Britain.

Statistics flourished outside the machinery of government, too. In 1833, during a visit by Quetelet, a small group of experts seized the opportunity to set up a separate statistical section (Section F) at the British Association for the Advancement of Science. The same group (Malthus, Babbage, Jones and Whewell, supported from a distance by Quetelet) founded the Statistical Society of London in 1834. They envisaged a learned society that would support and lend continuity and weight to their deliberations and hoped to establish a new social science in that way. In comparison with Section F, the Statistical Society had a much more diverse membership, with politicians and civil servants occupying prominent places. This had a constraining effect on the Society. Politically charged subjects had to be avoided or approached with great caution. After all, the Society's badge, in the shape of a wheat sheaf, originally bore the Latin tag *Aliis Exterendum* ('to be threshed out by others'), which was nevertheless dropped in 1858. The prospectus of 1834 emphasised that 'opinions' would be excluded from all activities and publications.

The foreword of the first issue of the *Journal of the Statistical Society of London* stated that the province of the science of statistics was to collect, process and compare data. In contrast to political economy, statistics would not be concerned with cause and effect. In its early years the Society concentrated on general research into the 'Condition of Britain', while eschewing explanation and speculation. This principle was at odds with the leading scientific pretentions of the day. The Society's initiators were soon disenchanted with their creation. Malthus died in 1834, Quetelet lived far away, Babbage had countless other interests and Jones resigned from the board in 1838. The optimism that had pervaded the founding session faded with time. Attendance at the meetings dropped and at times there was not even a quorum.

Yet, the activities of the Statistical Society's early years say a great deal about the issues that were associated with statistics in Britain in the second quarter of the nineteenth century. Most of the papers presented at the meetings concerned population and medical statistics; education and crime garnered special attention, too. Though the Statistical Society claimed to avoid them, opinion and speculation could be found lurking in its research reports. For example, Woronzow Greig's 'impressionistic' report on the character and circumstances of the Irish worker was 'full of opinions but practically devoid of statistics'.[14] Other contributions from the early years (on statistical reports originating from Odessa and Venice, on the accounts of the Devon and Exeter Savings Bank) gave little hope that the Society would likely acquire a prominent position in the British public domain. Moreover, the sub-departments for economic, political, medical and moral statistics were performing poorly. Nevertheless, the early fervour was re-ignited when Rawson W. Rawson, George Richardson Porter, head of the statistical department at the Board of Trade, and William Farr became the new faces of the Society at the end of the 1830s.

London was not the only city to have founded a statistical society. Manchester had done so a few months before the capital, and industrial centres such as Glasgow, Birmingham, Bristol, Leeds, Liverpool, Newcastle and Belfast soon followed. In Britain, there was a special connection between cities and statistics. This resulted in a long series of door-to-door surveys – frequently restricted to poor districts – that typified British social statistics, which would reach a pinnacle in the excessively detailed reports compiled by Charles Booth in the 1880s and 1890s.

These statistical societies were mainly interested in studying the adverse effects of urbanisation: poverty, disease and crime. The risks associated with these problems could not be expressed in numbers alone, though numbers were considered essential for a sound understanding of reality. In an article on crime statistics in England and Wales for the Statistical Society of London, Rawson wrote in 1839 that 'the collection of large masses of the population in crowded cities conduces more than anything else to the creation of those causes, whatever they be, which stimulate the commission of crime'.[15] In the 1840s, Joseph Fletcher, following Dupin and Guerry, wrote extensively about the relationship between the state of education and criminal tendencies. Chadwick's *Sanitary Report* was full of accounts of the abominable living conditions of the poor. It was his unwavering opinion that an unhealthy living environment fostered low moral standards.

In a lecture for the Statistical Society on causes of death, based on the findings of his controversial report and a number of foreign cases, Chadwick described the filthy conditions in which the proletariat lived and worked, and concluded that 'the moral atmosphere under which a population is so situated is as offensive and depressing and pestilential as the physical atmosphere under which it suffers; and it is grievous to experience, and melancholy to contemplate'.[16] And to think that Chadwick began his presentation by announcing that would be explaining the best way to set up a register of deaths. On further reflection, the British statisticians were preoccupied with the moral decay that they associated with impoverishment. As much as they professed to be objective and impartial, nearly every statistical study engendered a call for moral reform.

Statistics was more closely associated with morality in Britain than anywhere else. For the most part, social statistics was based on an implicit polarity. For example, there was a clear dividing line between honourable citizens and the dangerous classes, which were inclined to crime, prostitution and licentiousness. There was a less obvious but equally telling division between government and the governed. The statistical laws that Farr and other demographers *avant la lettre* believed they could infer from the data they accumulated were primarily applicable to the world of workers, the unemployed and their families. This brought morality within the scope of science and government. The 'laws' governing disease, death and crime worked only in certain circumstances – which explains their interest in the physical environment – but when circumstances changed, the 'laws' changed too. Farr and his colleagues also thought that circumstances could be altered through government intervention. And therein lies the essence of the modern interventionist state: 'We obtain data about a governed class whose deportment is offensive, and then attempt to alter what we guess are relevant conditions of that class in order to change the laws of statistics that the class obeys'.[17]

Many members of the Statistical Society of London concurred. Joseph Fletcher considered education to be a complete package of potentially positive influences on the individual, which also had the potential to avert the risk of social revolution. In 1849 in the presence of Prince Albert he delivered a detailed speech on the role of education in combating crime. Briefly stated, Fletcher's position was that even the bare minimum of education had a positive impact on the crime rate. He agreed with Quetelet who had written that 'we can modify, the causes which rule our social system, and thereby modify also the deplorable results which are annually read in the annals of crime and suicide'.[18]

The close relationship between statistical laws and morality was a thorny issue. Statisticians insisted that the laws they formulated were mutable, but in the arena of public opinion there were concerns about what the laws said about free will and the possibility of moral reform. Public anxiety was fuelled by Henry Buckle's much-read *History of Civilization in England* (1857). Buckle advocated a remarkable kind of statistical determinism, which he had drawn from the work of Quetelet, only he was much more rigorous, much more direct and undaunted by criticism. His interpretation of crime and suicide statistics caused a commotion. He declared in no uncertain terms that in every society a given number of people would take their own lives and no amount of charity or fear of the afterlife could influence that general law. In combination with Darwin's theory of evolution – or rather a simplified version of it – Buckle's view deeply affected the moral and religious perceptions of the British public.

Roots of globalisation

The fourth international statistical congress began on 16 July 1860 and coincided with the fierce debate about God, evolution and free will that erupted following publication of Buckle's and Darwin's works. In his opening speech Prince Albert deliberately took the time to address these issues and the criticisms being heaped on statistics. Among themselves, though, the statisticians were tackling other problems. To them, the usefulness of statistics was obvious. They wanted to concentrate on the programme that William Farr had presented to them. In the morning the participants attended simultaneous sessions in which they debated topics agreed in advance. In the afternoon, everyone reconvened in plenary session to listen to the presentations by the official delegates and debate the resolutions that had been prepared in the morning sessions.

The United Kingdom national presentation consisted of several parts, which demonstrated the breadth of British statistics. Richard Valpy discussed the publications issued by the statistical department of the Board of Trade. William Newmarch introduced the Statistical Society of London. He explained that some of the topics that the Society had reckoned among its own at first, such as population and poverty statistics, had been absorbed by government statistics in the meantime. Recently, said Newmarch, the Statistical Society had been concentrating on economic and financial statistics. He also applauded the congress for discussing methodology as a separate issue. It had become obvious within the Society, too, that this was necessary.

Samuel Brown talked about the statistical activities of the Institute of Actuaries, which had been set up in 1849 to handle 'all monetary questions involving a consideration of the separate or combined effects of interest and probability'.[19] The life insurance business, endowment societies, friendly societies and sick funds were growing enormously. These institutions were heavily dependent on reliable, comprehensive vital statistics and a thorough understanding of probability theory. The members of the Institute of Actuaries were specialists in these areas, and maintained close ties with the Statistical Society. This gave statistics a commercial application.

Farr ran through the steps that the British government had taken to implement the decisions adopted by the Vienna congress. The British had not been extraordinarily successful in this respect, but Farr cleverly diverted attention away from this fact by turning to the statistics of the British colonies, which were well-represented at the congress. Farr said, 'Our colonial administrators are anxious to avail themselves of all European discoveries; and the delegates will diffuse the principles which you establish over all parts of the globe'.[20] Most of the colonial delegates proudly presented the enormous statistical efforts they had made in their 'country'.

The colonial presentations were a conspicuous novelty at the congress. Lord Brougham and Martin Delany had unwittingly furnished an appropriate introduction on opening day. Never before had the international statistical congress taken such pains to look beyond Europe's borders. It is no wonder that the London congress was the one to bring about this change. The subtext was that in statistical terms the British Empire was a global leader. There were presentations about India, British Guyana, Cape of Good Hope, Ceylon, Jamaica, Barbados, Mauritius and the Ionian Islands (in British possession until 1864). The reiterative message was that the state of statistics in these regions was also a measure of their civilisation, which indirectly derived from the mother country. There were also representatives of more or less independent states outside Europe. The Brazilian report drew a parallel between the development of statistics and the formation of the new state. Despite the tensions between the United Kingdom and the United States, which had been aired at the start of the congress, Edward Jarvis, the president of the American Statistical Society, was given ample opportunity to present America's achievements in statistics. Edward Hamilton of Australia had also submitted an interesting and detailed report, which included his thoughts on the impact of gold discoveries on statistical inquiry.

The global perspective reinforced a latent anthropometric tendency in statistics. Hermann and Robert Schlagintweit, Munich-born explorers, submitted a proposal on racial anthropometry to the fifth section of the congress. The Schlagintweit brothers wrote that while statisticians in civilised countries could refer to the social, moral and physical condition of the population, travellers in uncivilised parts of the world could only collect statistical data about the physical condition of the people. With the support of the Prussian king, the British East India Company and Alexander von Humboldt, they had made a grand tour through India and the Himalayas, which had cost their third brother, Adolf, his life. Before starting off on their trip around the world, they had sought information from Quetelet, who apparently answered their queries. They compiled a list of over thirty measurements of the head, body and limbs which they intended to discuss with the congress participants. However, the proceedings of the congress contain only the text of the proposal.[21] There is no mention of any discussion on this topic.

With some effort it is possible to find tangential links to anthropometrics, eugenics and racism in discussion among statisticians around the middle of the century. Quetelet had already shown in his earliest work that, in his opinion, there were statistical laws governing the physical traits of a population group.

In 1870 he published his *Anthropométrie ou mesure des différentes facultés de l'homme*, which summarised his observations on this matter without offering many novelties. Somewhat later, Cesare Lombroso and Alphonse Bertillon also travelled down this sinister road, but in new directions. William Farr had come to the conclusion, based on the British census of 1851, that the quality of the race could be improved significantly and 'without cruelty' by restricting the marriage rights of 'the incurably criminal, idle, insane, idiotic, or unhappily organized parts of the population.'[22] There can be no doubt that such ideas prompted the eugenics work of Francis Galton and Karl Pearson.

Nevertheless, statisticians like Quetelet and Farr were not specifically concerned about improving the race. Their positivism was aimed at generalisation, not specialisation. They were more interested in the largest common denominator than ostensible outliers and extremes. Cowper, the chairman of the organising committee, summed up the general feeling: 'We are convinced that the human mind is substantially the same in all countries; that though there may be varieties, yet that man is substantially the same being, under whatever tribe or under whatever coloured skin he may be. And in order to study human nature, we cannot confine ourselves to the limits of any single kingdom, but we must endeavour, as far as we can, to extend our observations over the whole human race.'[23]

This could have come straight from Quetelet's playbook. He was the first to address the congress after all the national and colonial reports had been presented in the plenary sessions. He wanted to return to the central idea on which the congress had originally been founded. As chairman of the session on statistical methods and signs, he submitted a paper on comparative statistics. He called for a general list of each country's 'most essential numbers' to be compiled by a special committee of the most prominent statisticians in every country. Quetelet 'appointments' included Farr for Britain, Czoernig for Austria, Legoyt for France, Von Baumhauer and Ackersdijck for the Netherlands, Engel for Prussia and Heuschling and himself for Belgium. The initiative was probably intended to partition off a domain for official statistics, which was completely reliant on government support. National public authorities were not inclined to support a congress that gave a voice to everyone who thought they could use statistics to solve a political or social problem. From the start, Quetelet's plan was implicit in the objective of the international congresses; at the same time, by attempting to demarcate a separate field for official statistics, it heralded their end. So far the congresses had existed only because statisticians of different stripes – from the research community, from public administration and from the private sector – agreed to meet with each other and exchange ideas. But in London, Quetelet opened the door to a different future. As we shall see, his plan eventually led to the establishment of a permanent international commission which would ultimately serve as a link between the international congresses and the International Statistical Institute, founded in 1885.

Health statistics: a kaleidoscope of society

In addition to Quetelet's sixth section on the nature and methods of statistics, there were five other sections on special subjects: the first section on civil and criminal statistics, the second on health, the third on agriculture, mining, textiles and railways, the fourth on economic statistics (prices and wages, banks) and the fifth on the census and related population statistics. Health received the most attention by far, which was not surprising considering Britain's traditional interest in the subject. Yet, Britain's predominance was an obstacle to international discussion, which was the aim of the congress. The host country set the agenda and monopolised the debate.

The topics addressed in the health section demonstrated that statistics and social reform were two sides of the same coin. A paper concerning the statistics of wet-nursing submitted by Mrs M.A. Baines of Brighton (who, incidentally, was not in attendance) was an attempt to explain the high mortality rate among infants fed by wet nurses. This was a social and financial problem in Britain: many such infants were registered with 'burial clubs', which offered a kind of cooperative funeral insurance, and the high mortality rate drove up the costs. Moreover, Baines suggested, there was cause for concern about the protection provided by parents and wet nurses when the infants in their care were registered with one or more 'burial clubs'. Mortality statistics in Britain did not lend themselves to a methodical analysis of causes of death among newborns, and some observers pointed to abuse of the insurance system.

Edwin Chadwick added a macabre detail. According to a physician friend of his, the drop in the number of women who breast-fed their babies was due to the rough treatment girls received at boarding school. As if that weren't enough, the seventh Earl of Shaftesbury opined that female industrial labour was also a problem. Factory mothers were forced to leave their children at home at a very tender age; the children were given sedatives like opium, 'black drops' and Godfrey's Cordial to keep them quiet. There was enough material to inspire a library full of Charles Dickens novels. But while the British presented a litany of social evils as statistical problems, the only foreigner to engage in the debate took a less sensationalist view. Physician and statistician Georg Varrentrapp of Frankfurt said that the German experience with wet-nursing was extremely positive and the circumstances described by the British were alien to him. The section decided to pass on Baines's report to physicians and registrars in Britain, and the problem remained a domestic issue.

The British wanted to convince the world of its expertise in health statistics. Chadwick and Farr, who had a reputation in this area, were active participants in the debate. Yet, their achievements paled in comparison to a woman whose fame was unequalled in Britain and abroad. Since the newspapers began singing the praises of Florence Nightingale and her good work during the Crimean War, she had become a major public figure despite her failing health. As was so often the case, she was conspicuous by her absence from the congress. Being a close acquaintance of Farr's, she had received the most prominent statisticians at her home prior to the congress. Nightingale submitted an article on hospital statistics for the second section and surprised the congress with an open letter, in which she urged those present to make progress in the fight against disease and high mortality rates in their own home countries, and present the results of their efforts at the next congress.

William Farr met Florence Nightingale in 1856, after her triumphant return from the Crimean War. Their agendas and characters complemented each other. Nightingale was passionate, restless and engaged; Farr was no less involved, but measured in his behaviour and accustomed to the slow grind of bureaucracy. They shared an intense interest in public health and sanitation issues. Above all, they had a deep, almost reverent, faith in statistics. Like Prince Albert, Nightingale believed that statistics could help people understand God's plan, and thus bring it closer to fruition. Farr and Nightingale worked together in various health commissions and wrote to each other frequently.

Nightingale was fascinated by Quetelet's work. Early on, she showed an interest in mathematics and had taken lessons in the subject against her father's will. After finding a job in health care, she also studied bookkeeping and accounting. She became an advocate of hospital statistics even before she discovered their practical wartime uses. She was delighted to meet Quetelet in 1860; afterwards, they would maintain regular contact. She encouraged Quetelet to publish a new edition of *Sur l'homme*. When he sent it to her, she read through the book enthusiastically and made copious notes in the margins. She was convinced that his ideas had great practical value for politics, economics and charity. Moreover, she recognised in Quetelet the conviction that there was consistency between statistical laws and God's plan. She was conscious of the issue of free will that some connected to this, but in her opinion the discovery of statistical laws actually conferred free will: the laws enabled people to govern well. All her marginal notes in Quetelet's book speak to this view. One note read: 'God governs by his laws – but so do we – when we have discovered them.'[24] In an unpublished 'In memoriam' on Quetelet, Nightingale wrote: 'When we have discovered & acted upon the "Laws" which register the connection of Physical Condition with Moral Actions: *not*, as in (a), that we must expect from year to year to see the same crimes, suicides, the same pauperism recurring: but – under such & such Social conditions, there will be only so many crimes: under such other, so many more: under still worse Social conditions, so many more.'[25]

The congress participants were in awe of the 'The Lady with the Lamp'. Nightingale's blueprint for hospital statistics was the first item of business at the plenary meeting on the second section proposals. The delegates decided to present her plan to their respective national governments. This international success increased Nightingale's clout in London, and with that, Farr had fulfilled his duty towards her. However, he had much more on his agenda, particularly in the health statistics section. John Sutherland, a physician in Nightingale's and Farr's circle of acquaintances, presented a proposal for general health statistics to the second section. It was a project of cyclopean proportions. The idea was to collect statistical data on mortality in different population groups, climate variations, soil types, urban surface areas, street lengths, dwellings and their layouts, water supply, food supply, occupations etc. There was a long debate about classification, first in the section and later during the plenary session. In short, this was a project in keeping with the usual combination of utopian beliefs and regulatory ambitions among the conferees.

Discussions of this kind reveal a lot about the conferees' conceptions of society, conceptions that usually remained hidden behind an apparent desire for more factual knowledge. Chadwick, for example, wanted mortality rates for specific 'classes' as well as separate occupation groups. En passant he provided insights into class relationships as he perceived them: at the top were the gentry, the clergy, the medical professions, lawyers, 'rentiers', the principal merchants and manufacturers and 'others living in first-class houses'. The second class comprised tradesmen, shopkeepers 'and others living in towns in second-class houses … including clerks'. Next came the wage class (which could be broken down in to subclasses). The fourth class encompassed the paupers, who lived in workhouses, and finally the 'undescribed' class: people who are not described in the registers.[26] Not only did Chadwick's system emphasise the importance to the British of class divisions, but it also showed how difficult it was to formulate statistics such that they could be compared internationally, while taking into account the researchers' perceptions and the economic realities of the country or region.

William Farr also submitted a paper to the public health section of the congress. He proposed to analyse the state of health of every country – district by district – by establishing the number of deaths per thousand inhabitants over several years. He also called for mortality tables and lists of fatal diseases to be produced at both national and local level. He displayed a map showing mortality rates by district in England and wanted France, Germany, Sweden and even Russia to do the same, 'and in that rough way we should like to see the present sanitary state of the whole of Europe, and gradually invade Asia'. He continued: 'I do not know whether we should not enter even China, with the intention of propagating our sanitary principles there.'[27] Statistical zeal was sometimes laced with imperialistic tendencies.

In the same proposal, Farr suggested that the health of a people could be determined by studying physique, weight, strength and intelligence. He wanted to commission a study of these indicators by age group. Intelligence was, of course, a stumbling block, not because there was any doubt about the close connection between 'mens sana' and 'corpus sanum', but because no one knew how intelligence could best be measured. Farr could do no more than express his hope that statistics would uncover new instruments of analysis and new means of gauging the intelligence of a people.[28] As a branch of anthropometrics, this bold idea would take dubious forms a half century later, with devastating consequences.

Whatever the topic of discussion, the participants of this section always assumed that the physical environment had a strong influence on mental and physical health. Obviously, they talked about cholera epidemics, which were the scourge of the whole world; and no one knew precisely what caused them. The proposal for an international epidemic register should be seen in this light. Like so many times before, the discussion tended to revolve around whether cholera was transmitted by human contact or in some other way, by air or through contaminated water. Another proposal submitted to the health section dealt with improving worker housing. Every congress since Brussels had attempted to tackle the subject of workers' living conditions, but there was always a risk of the discussion getting bogged down in political debate. The British organisers probably reckoned that this risk was even greater if the topic was broached within the context of public health. The statistical questionnaire appended to the proposal was so exhaustive that there were sure to be all kinds of practical impediments to using it. Sir David Brewster, a Scottish physicist and the inventor of the kaleidoscope, launched another far-fetched plan in the same section. Brewster believed it would be possible to illuminate the narrow streets of industrial cities, where hundreds of people lived in darkness, using an ingenious system of mirrors. As we have seen before, the conferees' habit of suggesting unworkable plans was one of the biggest problems the congress faced. Their hunger for facts, however, was often greater than their sense of reality.

The continuing census debate

Every congress put population statistics and the census in the programme. For the London edition, the organisers decided to analyse the extent to which the participating countries had managed to implement previous resolutions on this topic. There was an inherent risk to this plan since statisticians, though virtually powerless to execute congress decisions, were the ones held to account. General census guidelines had been issued at the Brussels congress. James T. Hammack, who was affiliated with the General Register Office and a close colleague of Farr's, had taken on the thankless task of gathering information about the state of affairs in various countries. His findings were so discouraging that there was no further discussion of the matter in the section or the plenary session. Some countries had not responded at all, while others had proposed all kinds of changes. As a consequence, Hammack's office drafted two lists of additional instructions: one on questions that should be compulsory in every census, and the other containing optional questions. The questions sparked extensive debate, not just among the British delegates but also among the most prominent national representatives. These talks fulfilled part of the mission of the congress, namely to facilitate the international exchange of knowledge. At the same time, though, they revealed countless seemingly irreconcilable differences. This must have brought many conferees to the brink of desperation.

Alfred Legoyt, the director of French government statistics, was highly vocal in this section. He went back to a matter that he thought had been unjustifiably abandoned in 1853, namely the penalisation of people who gave incorrect information or no information at all. At the time, a majority was convinced that the scientific objectives of the census should not be sullied by association with the criminal code. They would just have to wait until the general public came to understand the liberal ideas behind statistical surveys. But Legoyt felt that perceptions had changed in the meantime. First, public authorities clearly needed accurate statistics to carry out their administrative duties properly; second, he feared that the public might never see the light; third, his experience in France had taught him that sometimes even the highest social class refused to cooperate; and finally, he believed that a specific sanction should punish only those who systematically obstructed the state (and he had no sympathy for such individuals). Legoyt was very persuasive and his proposal on penalisation was incorporated into the final resolution.

Age was another interesting point. 'How old are you?' was certainly not the most difficult census question to answer. In early censuses, it was customary to ask a person's age, but statisticians doubted the reliability of the answers. The section chair, Earl Stanhope, pointed out that many people, particularly those belonging to 'the fairer sex', were more willing to give their year of birth than their age.[29] The Dutch statistician Marie Matthieu von Baumhauer and the Swedish delegate Fredrik Theodor Berg reported that in their respective countries the births register was so accurate that the question on date of birth posed no problems whatsoever.

Legoyt had another compelling argument to hand. He noted that establishing the exact age distribution was very important for the mortality tables. There was but one method of achieving precision and that method would 'require, it's true, state intervention'.[30] As the French emperor's representative, Legoyt had no problem with that. His proposal cast a long shadow, probably longer than he himself could have imagined. Legoyt wanted every inhabitant to request a copy of his birth certificate six months before the census. This document could be used for every census during the person's life and after his death his surviving relatives could hand it over to the local registrar. Proof of identification was born.

Farr was less pessimistic about women's inclination towards honesty. And as for birth certificates, he said that most dates of birth could be found in the family Bible. Farr believed that each government should decide for itself what method of determining age would guarantee the most certainty.

Another topic that revealed the dramatic differences in how people lived was that of residency. The British preparatory commission had decided to place the residency question in the non-compulsory part of the census. Ackersdijck disagreed. Russian delegate Ivan Vernadski wondered whether his Dutch colleague realised that such questions could be highly problematic in a country as vast as Russia. What was to be done about seasonal workers? And what about 'floating' population groups, which incidentally included Jews? Ernst Engel of Prussia agreed with Vernadski. He also saw insurmountable problems and the majority of the section concurred.

Ackersdijck tried to win over the section again during the discussion on registers of births, deaths and marriages. The congress of 1853 had decided that every country should establish population registers, but nothing came of it. Legoyt explained why. In his opinion, only small countries could maintain registers. Engel added that Berlin had had a register but it was unreliable because there was no way of keeping track of people's movements in and out of the city on a daily basis. The participants agreed on a draft resolution stating that the congress recommended registers but only if there were no prohibitive objections. This remarkable condition weakened the resolution considerably.

Statistics as method

The multiplicity of units of weight, measure and currency in use in Europe and America formed a serious impediment to uniformity, a priority issue since the first congress in 1853. The Paris conferees had entreated countries not using the decimal system to add a conversion column to their government statistics reports. In London, they wanted to set the bar even higher, but it was in Britain that opposition was strongest to introducing a uniform unit of measurement different from its own. The former governor of Hong Kong Sir John Bowring, though a proponent of using the decimal standard for the English pound, was conscious of the colossal burden the congress was imposing on his country: 'if there be a country in the world where influence is great, and where the difficulties presented by routine and long habit appear insuperable, this is the country'.[31] It is interesting to note that the introduction of a common currency was already on the agenda in 1860. However, the very idea of having to accept the franc or florin was abhorrent to the British. For that matter, continental states would have been no more amenable to using pounds sterling. William Miller of the Bank of England said, 'the question of an international coin is one hardly ripe for discussion unless somebody proposed an international system of coinage'.[32] Miller had a dream, but could not have known that it would one day become a reality. Some utopian ideas survive their progenitors.

The idea of a decimal standard was in itself highly problematic. Due to Britain's dominance in large parts of the world, there were practical barriers to changing its units of measure, however illogical they were. The congress decided to adopt a resolution stating that statistics intended for an international audience should contain a decimal conversion. In addition, the official representatives were instructed to try to persuade their respective governments of the benefits of the decimal system. Finally, an international commission would draft a report for the next congress and provide recommendations for implementing a uniform system.

The aim of statistical uniformity quickly led to unrealistic ambitions. It seemed that introducing an international standard for weights, measures and coinage was a prerequisite for realising Quetelet's master plan, but it was also a Trojan horse. Changing weights and measures was a bridge too far, but the sixth section had many such items on the agenda, some more realistic than others. For example, they discussed an international library classification system, a subject that would occupy statisticians and public administrators for years until Melvin Dewey's system was made the standard at the beginning of the twentieth century. The library classification system was a good idea, but the proposal to divide up the year into cold and warm periods seemed odd by comparison. It was, however, in keeping with the tenor of the London congress, and revealed something about the unspoken assumptions held by many statisticians.

William A. Guy, an esteemed guest at the Statistical Society of London, suggesting replacing the four seasons with four cold, four warm and four temperate periods. He believed that this division would make it easier to see how diseases and causes of death were related to weather conditions. The matter was discussed very seriously. Some thought that the periods should be shorter, others pointed out that weather defied consistent classification across Europe. The members of the section dissented when Guy explained that he was seeking affirmation that the human mind was more excitable in warm weather than in cold conditions. It was not that they disagreed with his proposition, but they thought that the periods should be reconfigured. Nevertheless, Guy felt misunderstood and withdrew his draft resolution.

This was only one of Guy's noteworthy suggestions. He also submitted a proposal on the importance of signs and symbols in statistical work, or more precisely among 'statists', as he called the practitioners of statistical investigations. His proposal inspired a lively debate about the 'language of signs' which even took a philosophical turn ('when should the symbol resemble the thing or idea it represents?'). More interesting – in view of the prevailing conceptions of statistics – was the brief exchange about Guy's deliberate use of the word 'statist' instead of 'statistician'. He explained the term in the section and again during the plenary session. In keeping with the eighteenth-century German tradition, he understood the science of statistics to be a science of states but distinct from every political implication. 'Old' writers like William Shakespeare, Francis Beaumont and John Fletcher (three names not often mentioned in the same sentence) would have used the word 'statist' to describe someone who displayed statesmanship, or more specifically someone who took a 'scientific' approach to statesmanship. Authoritative scientists like Babbage and Farr concurred.[33] It was clear that statistics was still regarded by a majority as a classical science; statistics of the more mathematical and economic kind would not gain a foothold in Britain for a while.

In the decades prior to 1860, statistics had manifested itself in a variety of ways in Britain's public domain. Debates about poor relief, public health and urbanisation would have been unthinkable without statistical input. Statistics was the language of reformers. In the 1830s statistics became institutionalised, in public administration, science and economic life. Various government services began to systematically gather and process statistical data. The British Association for the Advancement of Science set up a statistical department. Statistical societies were established in several large cities, bringing together local experts, public administrators and business owners who shared a passion for facts and for the theories based on them. But statistics still lacked a nucleus, a centre, and that would remain so. There was no chance that Britain would establish a central statistical committee, though it was the profound wish of the international congress.

There was also opposition to the increasing use of statistics in the public domain. Charles Dickens was an avowed opponent of statisticians. In 1837 he wrote a satirical piece called the 'Full Report of the First Meeting of the Mudfog Association for the Advancement of Everything', in which he mercilessly ridiculed the statistical research community.[34] In 1860, as we have seen, *The Times* was justifiably pessimistic about the limited practical value of statistics in the legislative process. The government and Parliament were still making laws without taking guidance from numerical research. The strongest opposition to statistics came from conservative religious circles, which identified the science with fatalism and determinism. As such, statistics was a risk to man's free will and divine providence. The defenders of statistics – Prince Albert, Florence Nightingale, William Farr and others – faced an awesome challenge.

The international statistical congress of 1860 was a superb opportunity to make their case. They found the conferees amenable to their message. There was harmony of purpose among the statisticians, despite their periodic inability to defend their positions against public opinion and their weakness vis-à-vis political leaders. Moved by passion, the congress extended its reach beyond Europe's borders. Representatives of independent states in North and South America and British colonies shed light on the state of statistical practice in their territories. At the same time, European statisticians were able to effectively propagate European ideas about statistics and the social phenomena that were the objects of statistical inquiry.

The deliberations on public health attracted the most attention. This is not surprising, given that British statisticians had positioned themselves prominently in that field since the 1830s. Most were convinced that living conditions had a profound impact on health. It was the task of the statistics community to map the environmental factors – sometimes literally – and offer carefully considered solutions based on their findings. The congress drafted a number of lofty resolutions, but they were practically unachievable. In this respect, the London congress was no different from its predecessors. Not surprisingly, a commentator in *The Economist* railed against the congress's circuitous procedures and recommended that 'the purposeless speeches and the offensive frequency of mutual compliments which disfigure the general miscellaneous meetings should be abated with a vigorous hand, as blemishes discreditable in themselves and full of danger'.[35] Would the organisers of the fifth congress in Berlin succeed where London had fallen short?

Notes

1   Letter from Quetelet to Prince Albert, 12 January 1859, published in E. Gossart, 'Adolphe

Quetelet et le prince Albert de Saxe-Cobourg (1836–1861)', Académie Royale de Belgique, *Bulletins de l'Académie Royale de Belgique, Classe des Lettres et des Sciences Morales et Politiques* (1919), 244–245.

2   S. Weintraub, *Albert. Uncrowned King* (London 1997), p. 387.

3   All quotes from Prince Albert's speech are from the *Report of the Proceedings of the Fourth Session of the International Statistical Congress Held in London July 16th, 1860, and the Five following Days* (London 1861), pp. 2–7.

4   D. Sterling, *The Making of an Afro-American. Martin Robison Delany 1812–1885* (New York 1971), p. 214.

5   Universiteitsbibliotheek Utrecht, Collectie Ackersdijck, Hs 21 A 12.

6   M. Vicinus and B. Niergaard (eds), *Ever Yours, Florence Nightingale. Selected Letters* (London 1989), p. 208.

7   Cited in D.R. Headrick, *When Information Came of Age. Technologies of Knowledge in the Age of Reason and Revolution, 1700–1850* (Oxford 2000), p. 62.

8   K. Marx, *Das Kapital. Kritik der politischen Ökonomie*, I (Berlin 1981), p. 15.

9   D. Eastwood, '"Amplifying the Province of the Legislature": the Flow of Information and the English State in the Early Nineteenth Century', *Historical Research* 62 (1989), 276–294, specifically 291–294.

10 W. Farr, 'Vital Statistics; or the Statistics of Health, Sickness, Diseases, and Death', in J.R. McCulloch (ed.), *A Statistical Account of the British Empire: Exhibiting Its Extent, Physical Capacities, Population, Industry, and Civil and Religious Institutions* (London 1837) II, pp. 567–601.

11 Cited by J.M. Eyler, *Victorian Social Medicine. The Ideas and Methods of William Farr* (Baltimore, MD and London 1979), p. 33.

12 E. Higgs, 'A cuckoo in the nest? The origins of civil registration and state medical statistics in England and Wales', *Continuity and Change* 11 (1996), 115–134.

13 L. Brown, *The Board of Trade and the Free-Trade Movement 1830–1842* (Oxford 1958), pp. 76–93.

14 M.J. Cullen, *The Statistical Movement in Early Victorian Britain. The Foundations of Empirical Social Research* (New York 1975), p. 88.

15 R.W. Rawson, 'An Inquiry into the Statistics of Crime in England and Wales', *Journal of the Statistical Society of London* 2 (1839), 344.

16 E. Chadwick, 'On the best Modes of representing accurately, by Statistical Returns, the Duration of Life, and the Pressure and Progress of the Causes of Mortality amongst different Classes of the Community, and amongst the Populations of different Districts and Countries', *Journal of the Statistical Society of London* 7 (1844), 31–32.

17 I. Hacking, *The Taming of Chance* (Cambridge 1990), p. 119.

18 J. Fletcher, 'Moral and Educational Statistics of England and Wales', *Journal of the Statistical Society of London* 12 (1849), 231.

19 *Report of the Proceedings of the Fourth Session*, p. 117.

20 *Ibid.*, p. 113.

21 *Ibid.*, p. 500.

22 Cited in V.L. Hilts, *Statist and Statistician: Three Studies in the History of Nineteenth Century English Statistical Thought* (Ph.D. thesis, Harvard University, Cambridge, MA 1967), p. 235.

23 *Report of the Proceedings of the Fourth Session*, p. 206.

24 M. Diamond and M. Stone, 'Nightingale on Quetelet', *Journal of the Royal Statistical Society* 144 A (1981), part 2, 187.

25 *Ibid.*, part 3, 346.

26 *Report of the Proceedings of the Fourth Session*, p. 264.

27 *Ibid.*, p. 277.

28 *Ibid.*, pp. 277–278.

29 *Ibid.*, p. 348.

30 *Ibid.*

31 *Ibid.*, p. 385.
32 *Ibid.*, p. 391.
33 *Ibid.*, p. 148; p. 380.
34 Cited in M. Poovey, 'Figures of Arithmetic, Figures of Speech: The Discourse of Statistics in the 1830s', in J. Chandler, A.I. Davidson en H. Harootunian (eds), *Questions of Evidence. Proof, Practice, and Persuasion across the Disciplines* (Chicago and London 1994), pp. 414–415.
35 Also published in the *Journal of the Statistical Society of London* 23 (1860), 368.

5

The German phoenix: Berlin 1863

Berlin underwent a period of prodigious growth in the mid-nineteenth century. Between 1850 and 1870 its population doubled from approximately 400,000 to 800,000, making it the largest city in German-speaking Europe, larger even than Vienna. In just a few decades the city had shed its provincial image and was able to compete with metropolises like London and Paris on the strength of its economic, cultural and scientific credentials. In 1871 Berlin would become the proud capital city of the new German Empire.

Berlin's growth mirrored the general expansion of Prussia. The political development of the German states had accelerated since the Italian wars of 1859–1860. Central Europe would not accept the borders of 1815 for much longer. The formation of a unified German state was inevitable, but what kind of Germany would it be? A Grossdeutschland solution, integrating Austria and Prussia in a single large state, seemed increasingly less likely, while the Kleindeutschland solution had begun to resemble a 'Greater Prussia' arrangement. Prussia appeared to be fully capable of orchestrating such an arrangement flawlessly under Bismarck's leadership.

German statisticians went about their business amid the political turbulence. Statistics was not a significant topic in the debate on Germany's national future. Within the Zollverein (the German Customs Union), statisticians from the German states met regularly (as they had after the close of the Vienna congress in 1857), but they had no influence of any significance on diplomatic relations. The Zentralbureau des Zollvereins, located in Berlin since 1833, barely had a public function. Yet in many respects statistical practice was bound up with the German question, which had a national component ('Deutschland, aber wo liegt es?'), a political component (who should be involved in the conversation and decision making?) and a social component (how could the effects of economic growth be managed?) The corresponding questions for the German statisticians were: how do we organise a national statistics, who should be involved, and in what form can statistics contribute to the management of major social change? Though the fifth statistical congress had a strong international orientation, these German issues were an implicit part of the programme.

At first, tensions in German and international relations threatened to jeopardise the continuity of the international statistical congresses. A row over a Franco-German trade agreement was used as a pretext for postponing the congress, which had originally been planned for 1862. More serious than the trade conflicts, though, was the domestic political crisis of the spring and summer of 1862, which brought Bismarck to power. The crisis arose when the Prussian House of Representatives refused to approve a military spending increase. King Wilhelm I of Prussia and his ministers sought to provoke a confrontation with parliament. The appointment of Bismarck as prime minister may have had the appearance of a compromise at first, but it soon became clear that the 'white revolutionary' was not much enamoured of parliament. He saw the crisis not as a conflict between liberals, conservatives and other political movements, but rather a battle between the monarchical and parliamentary forms of government. The latter had to be vanquished, whatever the cost.[1] Wilhelm agreed with Bismarck's reasoning entirely, and both remained loyal to the principle of the strong state throughout their lives.

A strong state was certainly not detrimental to statistics, as Chapters 2 and 3 on France and Austria show. However, it would be wrong to view German government statistics as merely a lifeless appendage of an authoritarian state power. Statistics was a refuge for a more liberal Germany, even in Prussian Berlin. There were few conservative aristocrats among the active statisticians, and it was no coincidence that prominent statisticians like Friedrich Wilhelm Schubert, Johannes Fallati and Friedrich Wilhelm von Reden had been members of the Frankfurt Parliament of 1848–1849. The demise of that liberal episode in German history seemed to spell the end of their role, but the ideas of social progress and prudent steering of state intervention based on the results of statistical inquiry lived on in the universities and statistical bureaux of the German states. For a long time there was no visible political scope for implementing these ideas, which overlapped with the ambitions of the Kathedersocialists, but there is no question that Bismarck's social legislation in the period 1883–1891 was rooted in the body of thought promulgated by most German statisticians around the middle of the century.

Once the first Bismarck government was firmly in charge, the objections to planning the congress evaporated. The Prussian foreign minister, count Friedrich A. zu Eulenburg, was well disposed to the cause (believing as he did that he could completely depoliticise statistics) and delegated the organisation of the congress to his officials. As Alexander von Humboldt's home base, Berlin exerted an undeniable attraction on scientists and scholars. Though the congress had been planned for September, the official preparatory commission did not officially convene until June. Yet, if there had ever been a moment in the history of the international statistical congress when it could be elevated to a higher plane, then it was 1863, in Berlin. Ernst Engel, the director of the Prussian statistical bureau, was intent on making the Berlin congress a resounding success. The key to it all was the alpha and omega of Engel's thinking: organisation.

Ernst Engel

Engel personified nineteenth-century statistics, perhaps more than any other statistician discussed in this book. If he could have organised and registered his own birth, he would have. Statistics, he once wrote, 'accompanies a person throughout their entire earthly existence … and leaves him only after death – once the precise age of the deceased and the cause of death have been established'.[2] Ernst Engel was born in Dresden in the Kingdom of Saxony in 1821. He studied mining engineering and visited factories in France, Britain and Belgium in 1847. During his trip, he met Adolphe Quetelet, who made an indelible impression on him. Engel would refer to the Belgian statistician frequently in his writings. In 1883 – after his retirement – Engel published a paper on one of his favourite topics, the economic value of the individual, in which he again lavished praise on Quetelet as the founding father of the inductive method.[3] In a publication dating from 1895, more than two decades after Quetelet's death, Engel introduced a new unit of measure, which he intended to be used as a basis for the statistics of consumptive spending. He called it the 'Quet', hoping that the name of his intellectual father would live on in common parlance, like Watt and Ampère. However, while Engel's name lives on in the law named for him (the proportion of income spent on basic necessities decreases as income increases), it is not associated with the quet, a concept which has completely evaporated.

In 1848 Engel was appointed to an official commission set up to issue recommendations on industrial labour relations. His performance inspired such confidence that he was appointed secretary of the new statistical bureau of Saxony's interior ministry in 1850. The Saxon government intended to take over the organisation and control of statistics from the Statistische Vereinigung für das Königreich Sachsen, which operated partly outside of the government bureaucracy. However, the new statistical bureau had few resources. Apart from Engel there was no permanent staff, no discretionary funds, and it had only limited authority to conduct its own correspondence. It is a testament to Engel's commitment and diligence as an organiser and publicist that the bureau was soon coordinating a host of activities. Engel also edited several statistical periodicals, which were notable for their substantiated and accurate presentation of figures. Everything he undertook demonstrated that he was a specialist who was firmly committed to his work.

Engel remained with the Saxon bureau for eight years, during which time he planted the seeds of his future reputation as the director of the Prussian statistical bureau. What he introduced in Prussia after 1860, he had already tried repeatedly in Saxony. In 1855 he launched a journal entitled *Zeitschrift des Statistischen Bureaus des Königlich Sächsischen Ministeriums des Innern,* producing a large part of the copy himself. He had done most of the writing for the *Mittheilungen des Statistischen Bureaus* since 1851 and in 1853 he filled an entire statistics annual on Saxony. Engel used the journal to disseminate his views on the function of statistics as well as his statistical data. Public disclosure, Engel wrote in the introduction to the first issue, is the foundation of statistics. It was also the rationale behind his drive to publish. Citizens had a right to information about their country, just as the state had a right to receive accurate data from its citizens. Unfortunately, both parties failed dismally to fulfil their obligations to one another. Farmers, for example, were reluctant to give an accurate count of their livestock for fear of incurring tax increases. And the state made hardly any effort at all to prove that there was no direct relationship between statistics and taxation.

This situation distressed Engel. Statistics, in his view, was the foundation of state knowledge and government, and a bridge between the interests of the state and those of its citizens. Statistical data revealed the laws that govern the 'mechanism' of social life. With this imagery he broke with the laissez-faire ideology of his time and evoked the eighteenth-century idea of the state as machine. The essence of the comparison was the increasing complexity of society. The older the machine, the more its cogs interlocked and altered each other's speed and direction. Those 'at the controls' needed not only knowledge of the parts, but also insight into the laws governing their movement. That 'insight', applied to the state, was statistics. And, according to Engel, that was something fundamentally different than collecting data without system or context.[4] Data on a country and its people accumulated and presented systematically was the instrument that enabled the government to manage society. With this interpretation, Engel began to transcend the ways of thinking of his eighteenth-century predecessors.

In the journal's first year of publication, Engel alluded to every topic that occupied the attention of the international community of statisticians. He was clearly well versed in the debates. Like so many European statisticians, he feared the decline of morality, and that was undoubtedly the driving force behind his endeavours. Engel thought a great deal about the statistics of crime and punishment, for example. He believed that prison statistics should be structured so as to answer questions about what the best punishments were for reducing recidivism. His interests went beyond contemplating the numbers and how they were presented. He also called for the prison system to be reorganised and patterned after the mining industry: in the same way that ores are processed by different methods depending on their composition and texture, prisoners should be dealt with – individually or in small groups – on the basis of their moral, intellectual and physical characteristics.[5] Engel was both a statistician and a moralist, and – whenever possible – a reformer, an amalgam not uncommon among his colleagues.

The most important component of statistics – in Saxony as elsewhere – was the census. A new census and livestock count were due to be held at the end of

1855, the ninth since the introduction of the triennial count in Saxony in 1832. Engel used his journal as a platform to explain the benefits of such surveys. He based his case in part on the work of Achille Guillard, the man who coined the term 'demography', whom he had met at the Paris congress in September 1855. As he had done before, he explained that the statistician was in search of the laws that govern human society, like the astronomer investigates the laws that determine the movements of celestial bodies (he knew his Quetelet!) He also gave an example of what he called a 'natural law': the more densely populated a country is, the richer it is and the better the conditions are for further increasing its wealth.[6] Apparently, the notion of 'natural law' was elastic.

The objective of the census was 'to paint as complete and faithful a portrait as possible of the cultural condition of the state of Saxony and the Saxon people'.[7] The 'portrait' was to contain the following elements: numbers, physical characteristics (sex, age, physical defects), mental condition (i.e. psychological defects), religious denomination (Engel noted that Jews, like the Slavs, were to be registered as a separate race), social circumstances (marital status, occupation, social class, place of residence). These data could be combined in endless ways, for the benefit of the state as well as private initiatives (e.g. life insurance companies). The economy, according to Engel, is driven by the human compulsion to satisfy one's needs: 'while the reader of these pages drinks a cup of coffee, he has the power, whether he realises it or not, to move people of every country, every tribe and every generation to action'.[8]

Engel also addressed the different ways that a census could be organised, a subject that had also been an item on the agenda of the international congresses. For practical and financial reasons he preferred to disseminate questionnaires among heads of households and manufacturers, who would fill in the forms themselves. To encourage the Saxon citizenry, he expressed his expectation that their cooperation would lead to unparalleled results. Engel energetically assumed command by putting three printing houses to work simultaneously to ensure that the forms were sent out in time. He described in detail how many kilograms of paper were used, how much twine and cardboard was needed to package the forms, how the questionnaires were distributed and how many people were involved. He calculated the cost in Thalers of the material, postage and processing. These details show what a colossal intervention a census was in the mid-nineteenth century. The proverbial German *Gründlichkeit* reflected in Engel's descriptions is typical of his assiduity, which is both amusing and alarming when you consider what a well-run bureaucracy is capable of:

> The preparations for packaging 1,600,000 forms began on Sunday 11 November and were in full swing by the 12th. This was a huge operation, requiring considerable concentration and skill from the bureau staff who were given the task of sorting the lists and forms needed for each of the 4,000 towns and cities in Saxony (as determined in advance) and packing them into separate parcels. Task specialisation and cooperation stimulated the staff to work with greater speed. Trained packers combined the parcels into the prescribed post and railway shipping crates, of which there were 434 in total.

At any given time two or three, and in some cases five, people would be busy taking the boxes to the post office or the station. The whole packing operation was managed by a special functionary from the bureau. The entire staff worked from eight o'clock in the morning to eight o'clock at night, and longer if necessary. As a result, this major undertaking was completed in just eight days, on 20 November.[9]

This was the statistical *Schwung* that Engel sought. This reflected a mentality that he would later describe as 'the reckless and unflinching pursuit of truth of a person with order and passion in his blood'.[10]

Engel managed to muster just as much enthusiasm for a seemingly unimportant livestock count. In his journal, he tried to demonstrate that knowledge of the livestock count would indirectly benefit farmers (whose opposition to statistical inquiry was well-known), because it would enable the government to adapt its interventions to the actual state of affairs. To Engel, livestock and feed were indicators of the moral standard of a people. He believed that English workers outperformed their German counterparts because they ate more meat. The evidence came from comparing the performance of German workers who had emigrated to England with that of the English who came to Germany to work. The German migrants were held in high esteem for their diligence and achievements; conversely, the English became lethargic as soon as they began working on the other side of the Channel. In Engel's opinion, something had to be done about the price of meat in Germany, which was kept artificially high by the government.[11]

A similar political statement precipitated Engel's downfall in Saxony. He repeatedly called upon the state to intervene in order to combat social injustices. He emphasised that state intervention could be effective only if it were based on extensive statistical research, and that would require prodigious funding. Business owners and farmers complained about his 'inquisitorial research methods'.[12] Is it any wonder that Engel resigned as director of the Saxon bureau in 1858 a disappointed man? The agency was simply too small to achieve the level of accuracy and effort that he demanded. And the House of Representatives in Dresden was unwilling to help him by increasing his budget. Engel's letter of resignation was bitter. It was offensive to him that in eight years of loyal service he had never been offered a salary rise. He resigned, stating that he preferred to continue his career elsewhere but would remain available for consultation.[13]

Engel knew that he could earn considerably more outside the Saxon civil service. For some time, he had been reflecting on the issue of commercial lending. He was eager to alleviate the uncertainties for small borrowers, which corresponded with the ways in which he wanted to deploy statistics in order to safeguard the morality and standard of living of the middle classes. Bankruptcy was common, especially among small traders, and led to the irreversible sequestration of all the unfortunate person's possessions. Engel wanted to offer a degree of protection against loss of hearth and home, and devised a new type of insurance, the mortgage insurance. In 1858 he established the Sächsische

Hypothekenversicherungsgesellschaft.

His business venture was short-lived. The Prussian statistical bureau had been adrift since the death of its director, Carl Friedrich Wilhelm Dieterici. His replacement would need to be a specialist with considerable organisational skills. Engel had them in spades and was intent on proving it. On 1 April 1860 he was appointed director. Engel immediately began putting together the Prussian presentation for the fourth international statistical congress in London. (Prussia had been noticeably absent in Vienna three years earlier.) He also informed his new minister of his wish to establish a central statistical commission, modelled on the Belgian commission and based on the recommendations of the Paris congress.

Engel's attempts to install such a commission in Saxony had failed, but in Prussia he got a hearing. A coordinating commission was not a superfluous luxury. There were countless government services in Prussia (including the railways) that issued periodic statistical reports. The list for 1863 was 21 pages long and enumerated over four hundred publications.[14] The commission's remit would include eliminating nonessential surveys as well as identifying gaps in statistical research. The commission would publicise its views in the *Zeitschrift des Königlich-Preussischen Statistischen Bureaus*, which Engel – mindful of his experience in Saxony – had rolling off the presses just a few months after his appointment in Berlin. The journal was published on a monthly basis and frequently featured a well-wrought article by Engel himself. He also produced the *Preussische Statistik*, a series of statistical publications with core figures pertaining to the country and the population, and the *Jahrbuch für die amtliche Statistik des preussischen Staates*.

In 1862 Engel launched a statistics seminar that was without precedent. It was intended for civil servants and scientists interested in acquiring a theoretical and practical knowledge of statistics. The programme was impressive, and adjustments were made from time to time. Professors Georg Hanssen and Ernst Helwing gave instruction alongside Engel in the early years; both taught political science at the university in Berlin. Engel regarded the seminar as a step towards a German national statistics. The statistical bureaus in the German states took little notice of each other and even competed whenever there were political gains to be won. It often happened, Engel once wrote in a memorandum, that statistics were used improperly 'by unauthorised persons to set off political or economic fireworks in order to produce such sound and light effects as to obscure the truth'.[15]

Uniformity and scientific method, which underpinned the curriculum of the statistics seminar, were not his only objectives. He also emphasised the importance to Prussia of fulfilling a pioneering role in German statistics. Engel understood that the government was susceptible to arguments of this nature. The Prussian statistical bureau had administrative and scientific significance, but could also be used politically to advance the pursuit of unity under Prussian leadership. The statistics seminar was a strategic instrument but also an unimpeachable one.

The first course in the theory and practice of statistics for civil servants began with eight students at the end of 1862. The theoretical component covered economics, finance and statistics. Engel himself was responsible for the practical component. He organised excursions to large factories, hospitals, prisons and other institutions. He allowed the students to assist in the preparations for the fifth international statistical congress, exposing them to statistical practices in other countries. Engel was the driving force behind the statistics seminar for the remainder of his career in public service. He kept the programme up to date and was always looking for new experts to serve as instructors. Geographer and meteorologist Heinrich Wilhelm Dove and ethnographer Richard Boeckh soon joined the staff. In 1869 economist Adolph Wagner and agriculture historian August Meitzen replaced Helwing and Hanssen. Engel never managed to persuade his superiors to invite the eminent, but liberal, jurists Karl J.A. Mittermaier and Rudolf von Gneist to come to Berlin. Considering his personal interest, it is not surprising that Engel incorporated insurance statistics – or rather statistics concerning areas of insurance cover like health, loss, damage, death etc. – in the programme. Another element, at least as important as content and teaching staff, was the atmosphere that Engel aimed to create. He intended the seminar to provide living proof that statistics was a multidisciplinary affair in which theory and practice went hand in hand. Study trips and, in particular, opportunities for discussion were part of that. Engel wanted the seminar to be open not only to civil servants, but also to graduates and students of political science and the natural sciences, and even for members of occupational groups that had an interest in statistics.[16] The Prussian government felt that this was a bridge too far, but did not forbid Engel to make his proposals in public.

Men who would go on to become famous thinkers, such as Ludwich Joseph 'Lujo' Brentano and Georg Friedrich Knapp, participated in the seminar. The concept of expert training met with enthusiasm abroad, in Jena and in Vienna, where Karl von Czoernig followed the example of his colleague from Berlin. Engel referred to the newly established economics department at the École Pratique des Hautes Études in Paris, but it is doubtful that the French would have ever admitted to copying the Prussian model.[17] The programme's attention to topics like land tax, conditions of ownership, prices, credit and insurance suggests that the Verein für Sozialpolitik, of which Engel was a working member, owed a great deal to the statistics seminar. Engel's successor, Blenck, once referred to his preceptor as the father of Kathedersocialism.[18] In fact, there was not much difference between the mission of the Verein and that of the Berlin-based seminar.

Engel had an ambivalent relationship with the Prussian state. Born in Saxony, he was an outsider. He was not schooled in Prussian-style bureaucracy and, in some respects, he was a self-made man. Like many high-ranking civil servants, he had had a brief career in parliament. Between 1867 and 1870 he served as a member of the Prussian Landtag, a dubious honour that left him, and other Prussian officials, with little room to manoeuvre politically. Ministers could dismiss any civil servant at will whose past voting record displeased them. On the other hand, it bears remembering that in the 1860s and 1870s there were opportunities in the Prussian state apparatus for men like Engel, who positioned themselves in Prussia, Germany and Europe as advocates of a new, progressive social science and had their sights set on an active state with a practical bureaucratic machinery.

Statistics in Germany: the case of Baden

Prussia's power, Berlin's appeal and Engel's authority, though impressive, should not distract us from what was happening in other parts of Germany, where statistics was also flourishing. Most German states had active statistics agencies and they had sent representatives to the congress since 1853. Friedrich von Hermann of Munich, Georg Varrentrapp of Frankfurt, Bruno Hildebrand of Jena, Johann Eduard Wappäus of Göttingen and other prominent scholars came to the congress in Berlin, highlighting Germany's unrivalled position in statistics and related sciences. Since the Napoleonic period, statistics had thrived in Bavaria and the Rhine states. Statistics and state-building went hand in hand, gradually facilitating the periodic publication of national statistics tables about population, agricultural yields and livestock numbers. The liberal 'organisational' politics of the 1830s and the formation of the Zollverein in 1834 accelerated the institutionalisation of statistics in south-west Germany.

The consolidation of the Grand Duchy of Baden, a new medium-sized state in the Rhine Confederation and later in the German Confederation, offered great opportunities for the development of official statistics. In 1835 Wilhelm Ludwig Volz of Rastatt near Karlsruhe, a professor and high government official in Baden, toured Austria, Bohemia, Bavaria, Saxony and Prussia to study how statistical practice was organised. Volz noticed that there was little similarity and that there seemed to be no model for statistics on hand in Baden. There was too little interest to get a private statistical society off the ground and the government considered a full-fledged central statistical bureau too much of a good thing. Volz hoped it would be possible to set up a statistical department at the Ministry of Finance.[19]

Volz's report lay in a desk drawer until 1836 when it was appended to a request from the interior minister Ludwig Georg von Winter to the king. Von Winter wanted to establish a statistical commission, but noted in his request that there was no foreign organisation model that could serve as an example. The aim of the commission, whose membership would comprise experts from science and government, would be to coordinate the collection and processing of statistical data. If the commission functioned well, then further plans could be made for setting up a statistics organisation in Baden.[20]

Von Winter's initiative to improve statistics in Baden was not an immediate success. In 1847 a small budget was set aside to fund a commission, but nothing came of it due to the revolutionary events of the next year. After 1850 a statistical bureau was set up at the interior ministry and transferred to the new trade ministry in 1860. In 1855 the interior ministry began publishing the *Beiträge zur Statistik der inneren Verwaltung des Großherzogthums Baden*. As a middling-sized state, Baden looked 'abroad' for models of organisation for government statistics, though most were found to be unsuitable. Meanwhile, the finance and interior ministries eagerly amassed statistical publications issued in other German states and France and Belgium.

The Verein für deutsche Statistik, founded by Freiherr von Reden in 1846, had some support in Baden. Von Reden wanted to expand the Zollverein's limited statistical activity and was in search of new avenues. Otto Hübner was working on something similar. In the early 1850s he wanted to set up a private international statistical bureau and was keen to receive copies of all the official statistical publications he could get his hands on. The government of Baden was inclined to assist by providing printed statistics. Hübner's 'statistical bureau' was in fact a business, which he ran with his brother Heinrich. Their activities included publishing the *Jahrbuch für Volkswirtschaft und Statistik*, which they launched in 1852. This journal would lead to the periodic publication of global statistical tables, translated into several languages.[21]

If the revolution of 1848–1849 had succeeded, Von Reden's ideas would, no doubt, have gained momentum. At the end of 1848, the Frankfurt Parliament decided to conduct a national census and set up a national bureau for statistics. The government of Baden was favourably disposed towards these initiatives, which were coordinated by an experienced statistician, Johannes Fallati. However, before the project could be launched, the members of the Frankfurt Parliament – including Von Reden – were sent home.[22]

Baden was one of the states that took some interest in the resolutions adopted by the international statistical congress. The Grand Duchy had sent illustrious professors – Robert von Mohl, Karl Mittermaier and Karl Heinrich Rau – to the first congress in Brussels. The Baden government was closely involved in the initiatives introduced at the congresses in Vienna in 1857 and Berlin in 1863 with respect to a common system of statistics in Germany.[23] The German representatives at the Berlin congress adopted a resolution founding an association that would initially be coordinated by the Hessian government. In 1868 the Hessian representative, August Karl Fabricius, drafted a report enumerating the shortcomings of German statistics. A commission was subsequently set up to improve and expand statistical inquiry in the Zollverein. The commission's recommendations ultimately led to the Kaiserliches Statistisches Amt in 1872, after German unification.

The Prussian preparatory commission

Engel's plan for international statistics was similar to his programme for Prussian-German statistics. He even envisaged the two converging. To him, it was obvious that the congresses 'assumed the character of the host country'.[24] This 'national colouring' was in his eyes a logical consequence of the congress moving from capital to capital. Yet, he also believed that there was an element of weakness in the situation. A succession of congresses had failed to generate an organisational tradition or a structure, let alone institutional continuity. Engel wanted to force a breakthrough in Berlin: 'The fundamental and most important subject that the congress needs to address during this sitting is its own organisation.'[25]

Before Engel could give that ambition substance, he had to make two things clear to the Prussian government and bureaucracy: that the congress should be held (at the appointed time) and that it should address organisational issues. The central statistical commission that Engel created soon after his appointment as director of the Prussian bureau had already launched preparatory consultations in 1862. The main topics were quickly selected: the organisation of the congress, land ownership, prices and wages, railway transport, the comparative health of civilians and soldiers, insurance, the role of statistics in mutual assistance and charity, and the standardisation of coinage, weights and measures. Some subjects had already been addressed at previous congresses, while others were new and reflected Engel's preferences.

The central statistical commission did not organise the congress itself. Instead the task was delegated to a preparatory commission of civil servants, scientists, physicians and entrepreneurs. A key priority at the first session in June 1863 was to make it clear that the congress was not political. Ironically, this vain attempt only served to emphasise the unavoidable political aspects of the congress. The discussion about the participation of experts such as Otto Michaelis, Hermann Schulze-Delitsch, Rudolf Virchow and Rudolf von Gneist in the preparatory commission is a case in point. Their involvement was not without controversy. All four represented progressive views which were consistently pushed to the margins in Bismarck's Prussia. Michaelis, an economist, was closely affiliated with the Fortschrittspartei. Schulze-Delitsch was an outspoken proponent of cooperatives as a solution to poverty, sickness, disability, unemployment and other aspects of the social question. Increasing the power of workers relative to capital was not a goal that appealed to the Prussian state. Moreover, Schulze-Delitsch was part of the democratic camp of the Prussian Chamber, which had clashed with the Junker government a year earlier. Virchow, a prominent sanitary reformer, regarded medicine as a social science and was a declared opponent of Bismarck, a position that made him suspect in the eyes of the Prussian aristocracy. Gneist, an expert on constitutional law, was equally unpopular with the Prussian establishment and usually sided with the progressive liberals on political issues.

With the support of interior minister Eulenburg who, though intolerant of political reform, permitted administrative reform, Engel kept the controversy over the composition of the preparatory commission from escalating and managed to seat a few critical experts. They made an important contribution to the draft issue statements that were prepared by the subcommittees.

One of the subcommittees dealt with 'organisational issues'. Richard Boeckh, a census expert and statistical bureau official, Salomon Neumann, a physician,

Rudolf von Gneist and, of course, Engel himself were active members of this subcommittee. Engel had drafted an official constitution and byelaws for the international statistical congress, after the example of the German Juristentag and the British National Association for the Promotion of Social Science. He included a permanent representation, initially seated in Brussels and chaired by Quetelet. The congress membership would henceforth be comprised of individuals and collective bodies (municipalities, associations and other organisations). This new structure would transform what had been a periodic gathering into an international organisation. German, English and French would be the official languages. Decisions of the congress, taken by simple majority voting, would be non-binding. Apart from the congress proceedings there would be a regular newsletter, and an international statistical archive and a library would be established. The subcommittee approved Engel's constitution and byelaws, with no apparent concern for their viability.

Engel's intention was to transform the international statistical congress from a think tank into a genuine board of inquiry, capable of investigating 'matters of great international importance'.[26] He wisely offered no opinion on what those matters were. These ambitions were consistent with the zeal for reform he had shown since his time at the statistical bureau in Saxony. He probably did not anticipate (or simply ignored the possibility) that his scheme would encounter serious resistance in the international statistics community.

The subcommittee also deliberated about the organisation of national government statistics. The previous congresses had urged participating countries to install central statistical committees. Gneist supported this recommendation wholeheartedly, and stressed that a central coordinating body was needed to offset the fragmentation caused by the unavoidable division of tasks within the modern state apparatus. The membership of the central statistical commissions would comprise scientists and representatives of all government bodies that utilised statistics. Furthermore, the commission was to have an advisory function, but also the power to make binding decisions. Acquiring unanimous support for this proposal would not be easy.

The third difficult issue that the subcommittee had to deal with was the census. Neumann, with Engel's support, presented the report. The Berlin census of 1861 was the starting point for several proposals on counting methods. The system involving census agents that had been accepted back in 1853 was rejected because it was too expensive. A more important objection, however, was the implication that the state did not trust the people to provide reliable information. Why were census agents needed if not to verify the data furnished by the heads of households? Neumann and Engel asked rhetorically: 'Should the census be a necessary but feared operation, conducted by strangers, or should it be a great act of national importance, performed by the people themselves, sensibly, willingly and with a sense of patriotic duty?'[27]

The city of Berlin carried out experiments in which citizens filled in the census forms themselves and were responsible for organising the counting work. The idea was that the census should become an act of 'self-government'. The spirit of

Gneist, a great advocate of British forms of self-government, is clearly recognisable in this approach.[28] Free citizens' census committees would be set up, and membership would be an honorary office. The committees would be at liberty to ask questions of local interest in addition to the compulsory questions. It was suggested that a provision be added to the census law to prevent improper use of individual answers. Could this optimism hold its own against the realism of the representatives of states in which the public mood was unreliable, such as the newly unified Italian state or Russia, or against the anticipated scepticism of the French?

Notably, the subcommittee did not endorse Engel's article entitled 'Where do the boundaries of active citizen cooperation lie in the counting and description of the population?' Engel wondered whether a self-administered census system could work if periods between censuses were long and, as a consequence, experience was lost. Because of this problem active cooperation could only really be expected to flourish if there were statistics associations at various levels. Engel therefore called for local, regional and national associations to be established in all the countries affiliated with the congress. The organisers must have sensed that this proposal had no chance of success.

Of all the major themes that would be addressed at the congress, the most innovative theme was the role of statistics in mutual assistance ('sociale Selbsthilfe') and insurance. Engel knew better than anyone that nineteenth-century society was a risk society where everyone – not just the poorest of the poor – faced many more hazards than we can imagine. Economic growth had brought greater certainty and stability into the lives of the middle classes and skilled workers, but the remaining uncertainties were all the greater by comparison. Insurance and mutual assistance funds were safety nets for those who had the means. In 1855 the conferees in Paris had discussed different forms of insurance, but the Germans felt that insurance companies could do a great deal to improve the statistical methods underlying their business. Furthermore, the forms designed in Paris had scarcely been used and the statistical inquiry on this issue had yet to begin. Germany had a highly diverse system of healthcare and insurance institutions. In Prussia alone there were a few thousand worker assistance funds operating in the market. Engel himself owned an interest in a Saxon mortgage insurance company and Otto Hübner, who played an active role in the preparatory subcommittee, was director of a Prussian mortgage insurance company.

Engel presented an elaborate two-part report to the subcommittee. In the first part, he explained in detail what mutual assistance was. Mutual assistance funds had sprung up quickly in the wake of the industrial revolution and the emerging 'social question'. Engel believed that the greatest disadvantage of industrialisation was the mass of dependent lives it created: the proletariat 'living hand to mouth, with no prospect of expanding their capital'.[29] The less capacity a working man had to accumulate capital (he added ominously) the more dangerous he was to the state. Mutual assistance was the only solution and one which had great political significance. Engel defined mutual assistance as a financial reserve in case a household's main income decreased drastically or disappeared altogether. A loss of income had many potential causes, both macroeconomic and moral. 'Social insurance' was only possible if the dynamics of the effects of all those potential causes could be established mathematically.

The fact that many workers' funds did not operate on a mathematical basis was not only socially deplorable, it was also politically unacceptable. Statistics had a multifarious function: studying the fluctuations between good and bad times in industry, monitoring the relationship between wages and prices, measuring the influence of industries on health and mapping the connections between incapacity for work and age. Then it was necessary to calculate statistically how much money had to be deposited in the funds in order to meet every need without the fund going bankrupt.

Mutual assistance was, in Engel's view, a step towards economic autonomy and independence, the common endeavour of most people living in the nineteenth century. The only way to achieve that goal, apart from adopting the dreaded solution preferred by socialists and communists (transferring the means of production to the workers), was through credit. Mutual assistance was primarily a credit facility. Engel was most likely thinking of the cooperative savings banks so warmly favoured by Schulze-Delitsch. In this regard, too, statistics could provide scientific grounding. It was time 'to develop a system that conceptualised the different aspects of the social problem as a cohesive whole and subjected them to statistical wisdom'.[30] It was particularly clear that good statistics opened the door to solutions for a variety of social and political problems. The scope and gravity of the problems depended strongly on the observer's perspective. Engel chose to reduce the social problem to a collection of needs that could be alleviated by mutual assistance funds.

Engel's narrative on the insurance business pointed in the same direction. Here, too, the goal was to facilitate protection against the risks inherent in modern society, and particularly the risks run by manufacturers, entrepreneurs and tradespeople. The first order of business would be to classify each insurance company, a task that statisticians were happy to assume. Then the spectrum of insured risks could be submitted to a logical analysis. As a result, insurance companies could put their operations on a more rational footing and statistics would have to be accepted as a fundamental science.

Engel had raised the ante too high. The subcommittee, whose membership was mainly comprised of civil servants and representatives of insurance companies, had little regard for his statistical aspirations. The members were interested in an accurate overview of the mutual assistance funds, membership numbers and assets, but they were not too keen on statisticians trying to analyse the background of social inequality and poverty. The subcommittee was more magnanimous when it came to the insurance companies. A majority considered it a duty to use statistics to keep both the public and the insurance companies informed. For the rest, they were interested in the differences among the German states in the laws governing the insurance business and the practical environments in which insurance companies operated.

Mutual assistance and insurance had become very popular in Germany and, for political reasons, was of particular interest to the liberal elite. This was the primary reason why these themes were on the agenda. The international dimension was, for many, a secondary consideration. German interests were elevated above others in the preliminary talks concerning all the main themes. The growing threat of wage–price gaps, changes in land ownership, the increase in railway goods transport and the health of the population were subjects that flowed directly from the socio-economic advances in Germany. Each one could be translated into a political reform issue, making consensus all the more difficult.

The way many subjects were treated implied a typically bourgeois view of society. Paternalism, genteel forms of engagement and philanthropic capitalism were the leitmotifs of the day. For example, deliberations on accumulating data on children's health led to the idea of conducting a statistical inquiry of schools. That idea was related to a widely held desire to improve, not just analyse, children's health. Physical education offered possibilities. Gymnastics clubs, which were thriving in Germany, could play an important role, not only by stimulating participation in gymnastics as a physical activity, but also by conducting statistical studies of exercise.[31] Efforts to educate the public, sport, associations and statistics were all components of a broader goal of shaping society, a bourgeois civilising offensive, German-style. Giving an important role to gymnastics clubs in a civilising offensive made the project ill-suited to internationalisation, despite the high expectations of the organisers.

There was great risk in presenting foreign experts with a draft programme laden with such high aspirations. Furthermore, the Prussian government's relentless repressive conduct was provoking resistance among the progressive members of the preparatory commission. Virchow, Neumann and Schulze-Delitsch dropped out after interior minister Eulenburg showed he was serious about ratcheting up censorship of the press.

Statisticians amongst themselves

The congress sessions were held in the Herrenhaus, the Prussian senate building, at Leipzigerstraße 3. An information office and a post and telegraph office were set up especially for the occasion. Police lieutenant Seyfried was the local civil servant in charge and was introduced to all the conferees. Order was the first priority. There was also a recreation programme. Statistical works, maps and tables were on display in the reading rooms. The participants enjoyed free access to all royal museums and the prison in Moabit, the Charité and Bethanien hospitals and several factories and printing offices. On Monday afternoon, King Wilhelm I held an audience at the palace. Visitors were expected to appear in 'Civil-Gesellschaftsanzug', with insignia. Later there was a musical performance by a military band. On Tuesday evening, the participants attended the royal opera. On Thursday evening, there was a banquet at the Krollsches

Etablissement in the Tiergarten. Wilhelm arranged for an excursion to the royal gardens and palaces in Potsdam on the last Saturday. The Prussians were proud of their heritage and eager to show it.

The preliminary sessions were a new feature introduced at the Berlin congress. Attendance was restricted to representatives of official statistics organisations. The sessions were held in the senate building and minutes were taken, but Engel wanted to do business without being bound by ceremony and royal ritual. Officially, the invitations to the preliminary sessions came from Quetelet, whom Europe's statisticians still considered to be the first among equals. It is questionable to what extent he was able to live up to this epithet. He had not yet fully recovered from the stroke he had suffered a few years earlier. Engel shielded him. In a report to his minister, in which he commented on the conferment of honours to foreign delegates, Engel said of Quetelet that he was but a shadow of his former greatness.[32] Nevertheless the Belgian repeated what he had said about a joint statistical project three years earlier in London. With the support of statisticians from several countries he had made progress and was able to present several tables, which were the earliest beginnings of an official European statistics.

Engel's main priority was to discuss the establishment of a permanent commission. This was, in fact, a subject that was normally on the congress agenda, but he wanted to reach agreement with the official representatives in advance. That would prove difficult. Quetelet was in favour of it, but Engel found a staunch opponent in the Austrian representative, Adolf Ficker, who was safeguarding Habsburg interests in Czoernig's absence. Ficker believed that a permanent commission would spell the end of the congress as a forum for government statisticians. A scientific commission, which is what he believed the permanent representation to be, would never have such easy access to government statistics. William Farr supported his position. In Britain, countless societies and institutes organised scientific conferences, but they were all entirely detached from government. What made the international statistical congress special, in his view, was the direct link it generated between initiatives from below and coordination by the state. Legoyt was satisfied with the way the congress was organised and feared that governments would withdraw if it became institutionalised. Engel and the other conferees had little choice but to turn over the matter to a committee, which would present its recommendations at a later date. It was decided that the range of opinion would be best represented by nominating Engel, Ficker, Farr, Legoyt, Visschers, Schubert and Berg to the committee.

Tensions mounted further during the second sitting of the preliminary meeting. Once again the discussion got bogged down in a dispute over language, an issue that had never been resolved. Most Germans spoke their mother tongue and, though there were interpreters present and some speakers gave a summary in French, this ruffled some feathers. On top of that, there was a long list of topics on which agreement needed to be reached. For the first time, an inventory had been made of all the themes and decisions discussed at previous congresses. It was convenient, useful and a step forward organisationally, but at the same time a source of consternation. Engel wanted all the conferees to go through the list and explain to what extent their governments had implemented the agreements. This was a distressing question and touched a raw nerve.

The discussion on this matter was chaotic, perhaps in part because Engel had given Legoyt the chairman's gavel. Some participants were loathe to 'wash their dirty linen' in public. Others were more inclined to report on the state of statistical research in their countries (and provide an unofficial assessment of progress towards compliance with congress decisions and recommendations). A third group called for a quantitative survey. Having to rely on simultaneous translation made things all the more difficult. Compromise was impossible. The second preparatory sitting was a low point in the history of the congress. The participants went their separate ways and would not reconvene until the official opening. Would Engel be able to turn the tide?

The workable compromise: deferral

The official opening session was held on Sunday 6 September. Some 400 people attended; a quarter of them were foreign, i.e. not Prussian. Interior minister Eulenburg delegated the daily management to Engel. Engel was an animated chairman. Gesticulating excitedly, he switched easily from German to French. Statistician and economist Georg Friedrich Knapp recalled how, during the opening, General Albrecht von Roon observed the proceedings from the diplo-matic box with visible scorn and impatience.[33] Present in an official capacity, Roon was the man whom Bismarck had put forward as a candidate for chancel-lor a year earlier. Bismarck had as little appreciation for oration and majority decisions as his protégé.

Engel was more inclined towards open exchange and apologised for the unsavoury commotion during the preparation. He explained the programme and the procedures again. The conferees were assigned to sections, which would begin on Tuesday. Monday was reserved for Eulenburg's opening speech and a word of welcome from King Wilhelm at the royal palace. The words of the minister and the king were perfunctory and could not compare with the speech Prince Albert had delivered in London three years earlier. Albert's recent death was openly mourned at the Berlin congress. Ackersdijck, who had played an active role as a Dutch representative in 1860, had also passed away. Remarkably, it was not the official Dutch delegate, Von Baumhauer, but Auguste Visschers, a Belgian, who gave a brief eulogy in Berlin.

The sessions and plenaries began on Tuesday and ended on Saturday. Foremost on everyone's mind was finding solutions to the organisational issues put forward by Engel. The debate in the section devoted to the topic focused on establishing a permanent commission and the relationship it would have with participating states. There was no international model on which to pattern the commission. Intergovernmental organisations with the authority to make binding decisions were still beyond the horizon. The statistics system in the German Zollverein might have served as a model, except that everybody knew its organisation was very weak.

A few of the participants pointed out that the international statistical congress was no ordinary scientific gathering but a conference of official government delegates. Opponents of Engel's proposal argued that without the support of governments, international statistics would be dead. Gneist remarked that the power of Engel's idea was also its weakness. Statistics thrives when ideas, insights and findings flow freely, but without the contribution of the states there would be no progress: 'Some may say that these congresses are of an amphibious nature, to which I would reply that amphibians have a place in nature, too ... This dual nature is a blessing for statistics.'[34] The plenary concurred, and deferred a decision on the reorganisation of the congress to a future meeting. In the meantime, an international committee was set up to examine the issue. The Prussian government was called upon to inquire as to whether the participating states would be willing to distribute their official statistics publications to the major libraries of Europe and the United States.

The discussion about central statistical commissions proceeded in a similar fashion. The Brussels and Paris congresses had adopted resolutions on this matter. Gneist's proposal, which the congress accepted by and large, added little to the decisions already in effect. The point was to emphasise that besides meeting regularly to exchange ideas, the commissions should be given a certain degree of decision-making authority. This is where the proposal touched on a sensitive issue: ministerial responsibility. Gneist realised that the congress would find it difficult to take decisions that entailed a fundamental change in the structure of national governments. Consequently, no specifics were laid down as to how the proposal should be implemented.

The third component of the organisational issue was the census. The session was opened by Pietro Maestri, the representative of the recently unified Italian state. Within a year of unification, the Italian government had managed to organise a census that largely satisfied the requirements set by previous international congresses, giving the congress movement at least one feather in its cap. A united Italian state had been forged and now the population needed to be counted, preferably in accordance with progressive standards. The census was an act of national self-affirmation. What Quetelet and his colleagues had ultimately achieved through a massive commitment of effort and resources fifteen years after Belgian independence (the 1846 census) the Italian government managed to pull off within nine months, in a country many times the size of Belgium, with virtually no infrastructure and where three-quarters of the population was illiterate. Haughty and proud, Maestri described how the census had been carried out. He emphasised that the people had played an important part by, for example, volunteering to participate in local census committees. This seemed to mirror the course of events in Hesse and Prussia. What he failed to say was that more than eighteen months after the census precise interim results were still not available and there was a chance that the counting process had been seriously flawed.

Ficker and Von Bouschen, the Austrian and Russian representatives, were forthcoming about their serious practical objections to the method proposed by the preparatory commission. Ficker mentioned the problem of the uneducated, who were barely capable of independent participation; Von Bouschen believed that a number of questions were better suited to an ethnographic study than a census, and could not be answered in a self-administered census. Examples included the question concerning language, which was a political issue in Russia. Other questions, such as those on religion and occupation, would 'not be understood' by the agrarian population. The realism of Ficker and Von Bouschen failed to resonate and the session rejected their amendments of the preparatory commission's proposal.

This did not keep Von Bouschen from airing his opinion on the difference between a census and an ethnographic survey again during the plenary. The congress elected to defer discussion on the matter of a precise population description until a later date. Cesare Correnti, who headed the Italian delegation along with Pietro Maestri, made an interesting contribution. He attempted to position his country's recent experience with census-taking in the context of 'European statistics'. He drew attention to the delicate issue of actual versus legal population (the London congress had decided in favour of counting the actual population). The number of available seats in the municipal councils and certain taxes were based on the legal population count, though in many places the numbers were distorted. Many Alpine villages were abandoned in the winter, while the populations of villages in the Maremma region of Tuscany doubled. Correnti posed the practical question of whether 'nations that had implemented liberal administrative practices before modern-day Italy' had found statistical solutions for this discrepancy. By what methods could the size of the legal population be inferred from a count of the actual population?[35] This was a question no one could answer. The congress adopted a resolution expressing the urgency of finding a suitable criterion.

Engel concluded optimistically that the discussion on census-taking at the fifth congress had raised new questions that would have to be answered at the next congress. Peace was maintained, but at a price. No new concrete agreements were made.

Mutual assistance and insurance

The session on mutual assistance and insurance split up into subcommittees, one dealing with mutual assistance funds and five others covering life insurance, fire insurance, transport insurance, livestock insurance and mortgage insurance respectively. Most of the participants by far hailed from German states and many were employed by insurance companies. The private sector's interests were therefore well represented. Considering the many manifestations of mutual assistance funds and the wide range of insurance branches, it is no wonder that a great deal of time was spent classifying the organisations in question. Classification was a favourite activity of statisticians, but the question of what other role statistics could play kept coming back.

Gustav Hopf, the official representative of Saxony-Coburg-Gotha, was nominated to report to the plenary meeting on the proposals concerning insurance statistics put forward during the preparatory session. He had served as director of the Gothaer Lebensversicherungsbank since 1835 and had attended the international statistical congresses since 1855. Hopf began by stating that insurance was a product of the advancing 'civilisation' of the nations and could function as an economic stimulus. In order to meet that goal, the insurance business would have to base its operations on facts. Therein lay the connection with statistics. The statistician's task was to 'register accidents, establish how often and in what circumstances they occurred, determine whether accident prevention was subject to a law and, if so, identify that law'.[36]

There were limits, though, to the matters that statistics should address. Hopf was of the opinion that the some of the proposals Engel had included in his preliminary programme were too ambitious. Hopf believed that statisticians should not concern themselves with consumer requirements concerning the financial accountability of insurance companies, nor with the statutory provisions governing insurance, nor with the oversight activities conducted by the state or by an independent agency. Hopf's restrictions reduced the scope of Engel's proposals significantly. What is more, the members of the preparatory session were unable to reach agreement on mortgage insurance, a subject of particular interest to Engel.

Hopf presented two types of resolution in the end. First, he made a few general points about information sharing between statisticians and insurers; second, he submitted questionnaires on the most common forms of insurance. It was unclear, however, whether the non-German states would be able to use the questionnaires. Nevertheless, the congress adopted the resolutions without substantial comment.

International comparability was less of an issue when it came to the statistics of mutual assistance funds. Auguste Visschers took a keen interest in the matter and provided a French translation of the deliberations. Visschers was able to use the subject of assistance funds as a segueway to a theme that he had raised at the Brussels congress in 1853, namely the statistics of workers' budgets and the general living standard of the working class. The issue of mutual assistance funds was closely related to research into the social condition of the working class and the role of the state in improving it. Proponents of mutual assistance believed that the poor would not have to rely on public relief if the funds functioned well. Again, the resolutions could be divided up into two categories: classification of, and further information about, the various funds, and general preferences with regard to data on the dispersion of the funds, their legal status and their connection with poor relief.

The limits of the statistical component of research into mutual assistance funds remained vague, and it was difficult to draw conclusions about the scope of the funds' activities which varied from city to city and from country to country. Eugène Rendu, an inspector from the French education ministry, was of the opinion that the congress should encourage members of the assistance funds and affiliated organisations to learn foreign languages. This was consonant with the planned inquiry into a special form of mutual assistance, namely 'the acquisition and enhancement of intellectual capital'. Clearly, the self-help theme was part of the civilisation offensive. The questionnaire pertaining to intellectual development was twice as long as all the questionnaires on the other forms of mutual assistance put together. The statisticians thought it was important to map as accurately as possible the intellectual and moral condition of the lower classes.

Continuing in that vein, Rendu had another brilliant idea. He wanted to see international schools established in a number of countries. While his audience applauded this commendable goal, the proposal was not brought to a vote at the Berlin congress, but an international commission was to be set up to explore the matter further. All in all the congress failed to make any real advancements in the area of mutual assistance funds and insurance and little came of Engel's aspirations.

All that remained was to discuss where the next congress would be held. All the great powers, apart from Russia, had hosted the international statistical congress. On behalf of the Italian government, Correnti proposed Turin, Italy's capital at the time. However, not everyone considered Italy a serious contender. A few German delegates were interested in Berne, but Georg Varrentrapp remarked that 'a place in a remote corner of Europe could never be truly international'.[37] Incidentally, he did not consider Turin to be on the periphery of Europe. He thought that the congresses should always be held in 'Central Europe', i.e. along the line running from Britain, through the Netherlands, to Northern Italy. Farr and Engel favoured St Petersburg, the Russian capital. After all, Russia had put in an appearance at two congresses and as a great power was entitled to host such an important scientific forum. By way of encouragement, the congress had adopted a resolution calling upon the Russian tsar to adopt the Gregorian calendar. As before, the final choice was left up to the hosts, in this case the Prussian organisers. Since the Italians had made a concrete offer, the capital of Italy seemed a logical choice. Only Turin was no longer the capital by the time the next congress was held and the honour fell to Florence.

The Berlin congress evoked contradictory interpretations. On the one hand, the Prussians had in Ernst Engel a great organiser. He was the first to produce a printed list of the decisions taken by previous congresses. He had prepared an extensive programme and had major plans for the future of the congress. Engel was also a good strategist. He managed to persuade the Prussian government to support the congress by stressing national interests; he impressed upon the Prussian bureaucracy the administrative benefits of good statistics; and at the congress was scientific neutrality personified. The conferees did not go home empty-handed: the decisions made by the congress took up over fifty pages of the proceedings. As was so often the case, the positive results came from an unexpected quarter. Henri Dunant, Switzerland's official representative, requested and received the attention of foreign governments for the International Committee of the Red Cross, which would hold its first conference in Geneva in October 1863.

Regrettably, the congress's lack of puissance overshadowed the conferees' good intentions. Little remained of Engel's ambitious proposals on organisational matters, the census, self-help and insurance. The time was not ripe for the international standardisation of coinage, weights and measures, a subject that had been on the agenda before. Even efforts to facilitate collaboration among the German statisticians failed to produce results. Serious talks about expanding Zollverein statistics only resumed once German unification was more or less complete. In 1869 Engel attempted to set up a Statistisches Vereinsnetz für die Länder deutscher Zunge, as Von Reden had tried to do over twenty years before. The founding of the Imperial Statistical Service put an end to self-administered statistics in Germany. Engel, too, was forced to accept the dictates of the new state. During the French-German War (1870–1871) he visited Strasbourg and ultimately produced a detailed statistical study of the war.[38] He had found yet another way to channel his passion.

Engel was disappointed in the Berlin congress. He found it intolerable that the local authorities in Berlin had done so little for the congress. The Jewish banker Gerson Bleichröder had organised a banquet for the conferees at his own expense, thus saving the organisers from embarrassment. Engel hoped that the conferment of honours on the official representatives, as France and Austria had done, would go some way to making amends. But there can be little doubt that the hopes of Engel and others who dreamt of an international standard for statistics grew dimmer in 1863.

Notes

1   O. Pflanze, *Bismarck and the Development of Germany*, I, *The Period of Unification, 1815–1871* (2nd edn, Princeton 1990), p. 177.
2   Cited in I. Hacking, *The Taming of Chance* (Cambridge 1990, reprint 1998), p. 34.
3   E. Engel, *Der Werth des Menschen* (Berlin 1883), pp. 1–2.
4   *Zeitschrift des Statistischen Bureaus des Königlich Sächsischen Ministeriums des Innern* 1 (1855), no. 2, 17.
5   *Ibid.*, no. 6, 90.
6   *Ibid.*, no. 9, 143.
7   *Ibid.*, 150.
8   *Ibid.*, 157.
9   *Ibid.*, 160.
10 The concluding words of E. Engel, *System der Demologie* (Berlin 1871).
11 *Zeitschrift des Statistischen Bureaus des Königlich Sächsischen Ministeriums des Innern* 1 (1855), no. 10–11–12, 161–184.
12 Cited in F.-W. Schaer: 'Die Mitwirkung der nationalökonomischen Disziplin bei der Neuorganisation des Preußischen Statistischen Büros im Jahre 1860', *Vierteljahrschrift für Sozial- und Wirtschaftsgeschichte* 56 (1969), 236.

13 Sächsisches Hauptstaatsarchiv Dresden, Ministerium des Innern, no. 689, Bestallungsdekrete beim statistischen Büreau, 1850–1874, Bl. 51–52r.

14 I. Hacking, 'Prussian Numbers 1860–1882', in L. Krüger, L.J. Daston and M. Heidelberger (eds), *The Probabilistic Revolution*, I, *Ideas in History* (Cambridge, MA and London 1987), p. 380.

15 Report of Ernst Engel (9 June 1861), GStA PK, I. Hauptabteilung, Repositur 77, Ministerium des Innern, Abteilung I, Section 13. Titel 94 (Statistik), No. 113 Statistisches Seminar, Bd. 1 (1862–1870).

16 E. Engel, 'Das statistische Seminar und das Studium der Statistik überhaupt', *Zeitschrift des Königlichen Preussischen Statistischen Bureaus* 11 (1871), 186.

17 *Ibid.*, 185.

18 B. Földes, 'Ernst Engel', *Allgemeines Statistisches Archiv. Organ der Deutschen Statistischen Gesellschaft* 11 (1918–1919), 231.

19 Generallandesarchiv Karlsruhe, Abt. 237, Finanz Ministerium, no. 7119, report of Volz, 21 December 1835.

20 Generallandesarchiv Karlsruhe, Abt. 233, Staatsministerium, no. 32766, letter from Winter to the King, 16 June 1836.

21 Generallandesarchiv Karlsruhe, Abt. 233, Staatsministerium, no. 3094, documents related to the statistical bureau of Otto Hübner.

22 Generallandesarchiv Karlsruhe, Abt. 233, Staatsministerium, no. 3094, documents related to the Verein of Von Reden and the Frankfurt Parliament.

23 Generallandesarchiv Karlsruhe, Abt. 233, Staatsministerium, letter from the Ministry of the Interior, 19 December 1857.

24 E. Engel, 'Einleitendes', *Die fünfte Sitzungsperiode des internationalen statistischen Congresses in Berlin vom 4. bis 12. September 1863. I, Bericht über die Vorbereitung des Congresses* (Berlin 1865), p. 6.

25 *Ibid.*, p. 7.

26 *Ibid.*, p. 11.

27 *Ibid.*, p. 19.

28 In 1863 the second edition of one of Gneist's most influential books appeared: *Geschichte und heutige Gestalt der englischen Communalverfassung oder des Selfgovernment* (2nd edn, Berlin 1863)

29 *Die fünfte Sitzungsperiode*, I, p. 57.

30 *Ibid.*, p. 64.

31 *Ibid.*, p. 115.

32 GStA PK, I. Hauptabteilung, Repositur 77, Ministerium des Innern, Abteilung I, Section 13. Titel 94 (Statistik), No. 116, Bd. 1, Engel to the minister of the Interior, 21 September 1863.

33 G.F. Knapp, *Grundherrschaft und Rittergut. Vorträge nebst biographischen Beilagen* (Leipzig 1897), p. 143.

34 *Die fünfte Sitzungsperiode*, II, p. 97.

35 *Ibid.*, p. 470.

36 *Ibid.*, p. 508.

37 *Ibid.*, p. 522.

38 E. Engel, 'Beiträge zur Statistik des Krieges von 1870–71', *Zeitschrift des Königlichen Preussischen Statistischen Bureaus* 12 (1872), 1–320.

6

Unbounded nationalism: Florence 1867

When Florence hosted the sixth international statistical congress in the autumn of 1867, the city had been the capital of the newly united Italy for just three years. In 1864 the Italian government – pressured by the French – had decided to relocate the seat of government from Turin to Florence. In exchange, the French army would withdraw from Rome, a promise it reluctantly fulfilled, but not until 1870. In 1864 many suspected or hoped that 'Firenze Capitale' would be short-lived. If Rome were ever annexed, the Eternal City would undoubtedly become the country's permanent capital. Nevertheless, Florence spared no expense or effort to fashion its image as a true capital city.

The ink was barely dry on the national parliament's decision to relocate when the city government commissioned architect Giuseppe Poggi to design an ambitious expansion plan. The most radical undertaking of all was the demolition of the city walls and creation of a broad boulevard modelled on Baron Georges Haussmann's project in Paris. Several buildings were demolished in the old city centre and construction began on new residential neighbourhoods. The statisticians who made their way to Florence witnessed a massive wave of demolition, as they had in Paris twelve years earlier. An old world was vanishing before their eyes, and the new one was no more than a blueprint. But that was how statisticians saw the world: all at once volatile, threatening and challenging. Statistics was their blueprint.

Florence was eager to position itself as a city of culture and organised several national festivals. In 1861 – soon after unification – it hosted the first national exhibition. The Santa Croce church was gradually transformed into a pantheon of Italian heroes. In 1865 the city council organised a large-scale national festival to commemorate the six-hundredth anniversary of Dante Alighieri's birth, which would enhance the city's stature as the nation's capital. King Victor Emanuel II was there as a guest of honour and – in the presence of the majority of parliamentarians and civil servants – officially took up residence in his new home. Ugo Pesci reported in his chronicle of the *Firenze Capitale* years that the king honoured the statistical congress two years later by inviting the conferees to a gala luncheon at Palazzo Pitti.[1]

In the spirit of the times, Pesci praised the work that Pietro Maestri, organiser of the Florentine congress, had done during the Risorgimento. Like many politicians and civil servants of the new state, Maestri had stood on the barricades for Italian unification. Born in Milan in 1816, he graduated with a degree in medicine from the University of Pavia and was active in the Lombardy democratic movement from a young age. He was a student of the jurist Gian Domenico Romagnosi and the political philosopher Carlo Cattaneo. He was a member of the Committee of Defence in Milan during the revolution of 1848 and later briefly served as a representative to Tuscany of the revolutionary government in Rome. After the Roman revolution was quelled, he fled to Piedmont and then to France. In Turin he published two statistics annuals (on 1852 and 1853) in which his liberal-nationalist agenda is clearly recognisable.[2]

In the foreword to the 1853 annual, Maestri equated statistics with patriotism. Statistical inquiry made it possible to 'determine precisely the true strength of the nation's capacities, and by studying economic unity to reinforce geographical and ethnographical unity and the political ideal'.[3] In 1862 he became the first director of the statistics division of the young state's Ministry of Agriculture, Industry and Trade. His appointment, which was supported by influential friends like Cesare Correnti, was the pinnacle of a life devoted to statistics in the service of a united Italy.

The congress in Florence brought Maestri international fame. The congress venue stirred the imagination of the conferees. It was held in the Uffizi, in the section assigned to the Italian senate two years before. The plenary meetings were held in the impressive Teatro Mediceo, designed by Bernardo Buontalenti and inaugurated in 1586. The space had not been used as a theatre since the end of the Medici family's rule in Florence. It had housed the Tuscan criminal court for a long time and was taken over by the senate in 1865 following unification. Today, only the entrance on the first floor of the Uffizi remains visible.

In addition to the official congress bureau, the organisers set up a committee of distinguished citizens to ensure their guests were received appropriately. The conferees were given a pass allowing them access to museums, libraries, benevolent societies, prisons and printing houses (all regarded as manifestations of modern civic life, for better or worse). And art and culture were available in abundance. The committee offered a programme of special visits and walking tours, including an excursion to a horticulture exhibition near Porta San Gallo, a walk in the Parco della Cascine, a supper at the prime minister's home, an evening visit to the national museum, a dinner at the Pagiano theatre and a concert at La Pergola. Florence made the most of every opportunity to affirm its status as a city of culture.

The Florentine congress was an opportunity for the liberal elite of the new Italian nation to present themselves to the rest of Europe, and to one another. They saw Italian unification as more than the sum of its parts. This unique arithmetic of nationalism did not escape the attention of the Italian statisticians. They proudly presented the series of statistics publications that their newly unified state had managed to produce in a short time, and harked back to the history of statistics in different regions of the Italian peninsula. There was but one outcome to be expected from the study of those historical accounts: a national statistics that would lay the foundation for liberal reform policies.

In the introduction to the overview of statistical productivity since unification, Pietro Maestri looked back at reports written by Venetian ambassadors, Tuscan diplomats and papal nuncios of the early modern period. He gleaned from Niccolò Machiavelli's work, for example, that it was an old Italian tradition for statesmen to base political action on statistical information. Of course Maestri also alluded to more recent heroes of Italian statistics. Like every statistician of his day, he paid homage to the ideas of Melchiorre Gioia (1767–1829) and Gian Domenico Romagnosi (1761–1835), who were invariably cited when it was necessary to underscore the existence of a national statistics tradition. This is perhaps remarkable since Gioia and Romagnosi had died decades before unification and never positioned themselves as dyed-in-the-wool nationalists, but at the same time unsurprising. Nationalism has a tendency to avail itself of mythical traditions.

Gioia earned renown as an eminent statistician back in the time of Napoleonic Italy. In 1806 he became director of the statistical commission, and later the statistical bureau, of the *Regno d'Italia* in Milan. In 1808 he published his detailed 'Statistical tables, or standards for the description, calculation and classification of all elements of private and public administration'. To him, statistics was no more and no less than an administrative science, an instrument used by government to regulate society. In the spirit of the English moral philosopher Jeremy Bentham, whose work he knew well, he stressed the 'true value' of statistics, 'which serves the people, every occupation group, the government and future generations'.[4] After the end of French rule, he continued his work on statistics, though not directly in the service of the government (the Austrian regime in Northern Italy did not approve of Gioia's wish to make statistical data public), but as an independent scholar and journalist.

Gioia published his principal work, *Filosofia della statistica*, in 1826. He defined statistics as an 'economic description of the nations' containing all elements of a country that 'can be of benefit to everyone or a majority of the people, and to the government'.[5] This covered a profusion of subjects: topography, population, agricultural and industrial production, trade, taxation, government, institutions and national customs. Every area could be broken down into countless subcategories. Topography included everything that we associate with geography and meteorology. Gioia believed that wind, for example, was a major factor affecting the economic structure of a country: 'The Dutchman builds a windmill, mounts a rotation and compression mechanism onto it, orders it to drain a swamp and the mill obeys. Behold, a statistical fact that does not cease to be true from one moment to the next.'[6] Intellectual, economic and moral traditions had at least as much continuous influence on the nations and were therefore also statistical facts. Gioia gave as an example the hospitality consistently displayed by all the peoples of Northern Europe, a circumstance from which both the political economist and the traveller benefited. Though the title suggests otherwise, Gioia's *Filosofia della statistica* is not an in-depth analytical work but rather a practical springboard to a full-scale descriptive statistics.

Romagnosi took a more theoretical perspective. He approached statistics from his experience as a jurist, so his ideas about statistics were, in the final analysis, based on his legal background. He deduced the function of statistics from the notion that everything should be subject to an institutional, legal order. Without order, there could be no state and no society. The 'statistica civile' indicated the degree of civilisation, or 'incivilimento', of a people. This went beyond a basic study of economic factors, which is what his influential contemporary, the Frenchman Jean-Baptiste Say, was mainly interested in. For Romagnosi, political and moral progress, as well as economic development, were the marks of true civilisation.

What made Gioia and Romagnosi so interesting to the latter-day architects of the unified Italian state was that an argument for a specific Italian statistics could be gleaned from their work.[7] Where Gioia and Romagnosi saw in statistics the essence or at least a major component of a new kind of political science, later generations interpreted their ideas as a call for a science of a new political entity. Maestri and his peers considered themselves followers of Gioia and Romagnosi. They believed they could bring to fruition what their mentors could only have dreamt of. From that perspective, it was possible to allow the geographical, ethnic and economic diversity of the Italian peninsula to dissolve into a national discourse. The Italian statisticians were arguing precisely the opposite of what Czoernig had tried to show in 1858, from the Austrian perspective: namely that nationalist aspirations in Italy were futile in the face of ethnic differences in the region stretching from the Alps to Sicily (see Chapter 3). This shows just how malleable statistics was in the nineteenth century. In a demonstration of his conciliatory disposition (and political sea change in Austria in 1867), Czoernig addressed the Florence congress in Italian only a year after the war between Italy and Austria, and spoke emphatically about the close relationship between administrative statistics and parliament.[8]

Prior to unification, every state on the Italian peninsula, not just Lombardy, had kept statistics and had its own heroes. In Piedmont, the Napoleonic tradition of 'prefectural' statistics had survived, thanks in part to the fact that it contained elements of the seventeenth and eighteenth-century Piedmontese state. Local officials saw it as their duty to redact the statistics collated by provinces and other entities of public administration in order to support the 'administrative monarchy'.[9] The Venetian geographer Adriano Balbi wrote several 'political-statistical' works about Europe and the world which were used by others to compare the degree of civilisation of various countries and political regimes. Perhaps the most famous geographer to take an avid interest in statistics was the Tuscan Attilio Zuccagni-Orlandini, who published an impressive chorography (a kind of encyclopaedia of geographical statistics) of Italy and its islands between 1835 and 1845. Zuccagni was appointed director of the new statistical bureau of the Grand Duchy of Tuscany in 1848 and attended several international congresses in that capacity. He also took part in the congress of 1867 in Florence, his native city, where he chaired the section on theory and technology.

In the Kingdom of the Two Sicilies in southern Italy, the French revolutionary tradition lived on in the central statistics department for Sicily founded in 1832. Its first director, Saverio Scrofani, had served as Napoleon's statistics and census official in Naples.[10] Despite the efforts of Scrofani, his successors and the staff, the department failed to publish an orderly, long-term statistics series. The population and local elites were unhelpful and wary of greater intervention by the central state, especially in the form of higher taxes. Long after unification, Italian statisticians had difficulty overcoming these prejudices.

The congress in Florence revealed the problems inherent in the Europeanization of statistics like no other congress had before. Or, conveyed more optimistically, the Italian challenge was also the European challenge. Both Italy and Europe sought unity in diversity, a noble goal but – in the context of nineteenth-century political and economic reality – an illusion. Italian statisticians had taken part in the international congresses from the beginning, initially as representatives of the pre-unity states, but now they had the chance to express their national and European aspirations. Never before had the words 'Europe' and 'European' occurred so frequently in the congress proceedings. Without reservation Maestri wrote in the programme foreword that 'the international statistical congress had attained the status and importance of a European institution'.[11]

His friend and patron Cesare Correnti saw the statistical congresses as a harbinger of a European parliament. Correnti's patriotic ideas were interspersed with European references from early on. He was a student of Romagnosi and helped write his *Annali universali di statistica*. Between 1838 and 1844 he worked on the first *Rivista europea*, which was published in Milan. In the second volume of *Annuario statistico italiano*, published in 1864, he wrote about statistics as a 'pacifying science' in close consultation with Maestri. Citing Alexander von Humboldt, he called statistical numbers 'the final arbiters'. As Italy had been and was still being created by numbers, Europe would ultimately be shaped by statistics: 'a time will come when the European Areopagus resolves every problem through voting and numbers'.[12] In this pronouncement lay the beginnings of a European idea and a democratic ideal.

In the 1840s Correnti had an affinity for the ideas of Giuseppe Mazzini, an affinity that never completely left him, even when he became a member of parliament and Minister of Education of a united Italy and had no choice but to renounce the revolutionary aspect of the democratic philosophy. In statistics he saw a possibility of keeping some part of his democratic hopes alive: 'true statistics manifests itself, as it were, by way of a universal vote; it is everyone's confession to everyone; it is the discipline of democracy, and it is the reflexive and experimental consciousness of humanity'.[13]

Under the Austrian regime Correnti had used statistics to avoid censorship and now statistics was giving him another opportunity to devise political projects without being called to account directly for his political convictions. His proposal for organising a municipal-level statistics, which he would promote at the congress in Florence, was another way of conveying his ideas about local autonomy, which clashed with the centralised administrative structure of the unified state.

For Correnti and Maestri, the international statistical congress presented an opportunity to actualise their interpretation of Romagnosi's and Gioia's ideas. Any state with a certain degree of freedom and openness should have an administrative statistics operation. Once a state had attained that level and acquired a statistical overview of the whole society, it would rise automatically to the next level, which entailed identifying the laws and patterns that governed human life. The next step was the highest level of science, 'the prophetic stage'. Attaining this level required international contact, and that was 'the moment of the international statistical congress'.[14] Though the congress movement was still in its infancy, international statistics was the only path to comparisons that would enable statisticians to distinguish general laws from coincidence and outliers. To the Italians, the European dimension of statistics verged on the universal.

Preliminary work

Maestri began his preparations in March 1865 by composing a letter to his fellow statisticians in Europe. He did not want the congress agenda to be determined solely by an Italian committee. His colleagues' replies began arriving in early 1866, and some were published in the congress proceedings. In the meantime, the international commission established in Berlin to study the future of the congress had also discharged some preliminary work by post. It was clear, however, that the commission had not reached a consensus regarding how the congress could be given a more permanent character. The Dutchman Von Baumhauer, for example, feared that a permanent international commission of directors of statistical agencies would not survive. The idea of a supranational commission was a utopian one: no head of department could afford to take annual leave to go abroad and no government would bear the cost. Moreover, the commission would have no means of influencing or pressuring governments or private actors.[15] It was difficult enough to find an organisational form that was congruent with the prevailing framework of international and scientific relations, but even simple, practical problems impeded progress in this area. The rapporteur of the international commission, Auguste Visschers of Belgium, was stranded on his way to Florence and lost his luggage. A trip from Brussels to Florence was no picnic in 1867.

Since the congress was supposed to have taken place in 1866 (but had been postponed for a year due to the war), the programme was finished by spring of that year. There were to be eight sections: theory and technology of statistics, topography, agricultural statistics, municipal statistics, monetary statistics, moral and judicial statistics, military statistics and education. These topics were the cornerstones of 'modern' society, from the Italian perspective at least. Notably, trade and industry were not on the agenda, but municipalities were. We shall see that the selection of the latter had much to do with the political-administrative decisions that the right-leaning liberal elite had made in the early 1860s.

Various Italian and foreign rapporteurs shed light on these topics before the congress began. Correnti wrote a preparatory report on the issue of organising official statistics: how should a modern state structure its statistical research? This topic was incorporated into the theory and technology section. In keeping with Italian convention, Correnti referred to the debate between the realists and the idealists, initiated by Gioia and Romagnosi. The debate played out in the Kingdom of Naples, mainly among philosophers, but Correnti came to the conclusion that all that philosophising had distracted attention from the practical organisation of government statistics. And in his view organisation was the most pressing of political issues. The politics of unification was based on public opinion, and public opinion had to be fed with systematically collected and neatly arranged facts. Statistical inquiries needed to be fast, uniform, comprehensive and, above all, accurate. Like the justice system, statistics had to be fully autonomous and independent, because 'governing is a special way of evaluating or anticipating social data'.[16] What kind of institution would fit these requirements?

Foreign examples were difficult to merge into one format. In Europe, the autonomy of statistical inquiry was regulated differently from country to country. The threat of desegregation was palpable everywhere, which is why Correnti revived the congress's long-standing aspiration to institute a central council or commission for national statistics, which would act like a court ensuring that statistics did not become a bureaucratic plaything and was not used for piecemeal objectives.

Correnti also prepared the section on municipal statistics, a new topic for the international congress. The Paris congress of 1855 had taken a run at urban statistics, but Correnti's choice was, if anything, only tangentially related to that subject. He proposed to establish an international statistics that embraced 'the demographic and economic constitution of municipalities'.[17]

Correnti's approach to municipal statistics cannot be understood without having some knowledge of the Italian state structure and the related debate. The proclamation of the Italian unified state in 1861 was a Bonapartist affair. In a blatant display of contradiction, every male inhabitant of the seized territories was permitted to vote in a referendum on annexation (the official results were without exception 99 per cent in favour and many a town hall has a stone or tablet commemorating the event), while the unified state adopted Piedmont's monarchical constitution of 1848 without parliamentary debate. Subsequently, the administrative laws of 1859, which had applied to Piedmont and Lombardy at the time, were introduced by decree. After an insipid parliamentary debate, Italy's public administration was finally codified in 1865, patterned almost entirely after the Kingdom of Sardinia.

The centralised unified state – which on paper resembled the Belgian state and the Thorbeckian structure in the Netherlands – was thus conceived. Free parliamentary, provincial and municipal elections were held, but the franchise was severely restricted (though it bears repeating that Italy was largely in step with the rest of Europe). The provinces were administered by government-appointed prefects, who reported to the interior minister. Mayors were also government appointees, but were elected by the municipal council first. Although parliament put up no resistance to the package of administrative laws presented to it, issues of centralisation and decentralisation were fiercely debated in newspapers, magazines and books before and after 1865. There was a large group of intellectuals who advocated greater autonomy and were gravely disappointed by the decisions of 1865. Correnti was one of them, and his sentiments were unchanged in 1867.

Correnti's contribution to the municipal statistics section was a special document in which he attempted to integrate theories of political philosophy into the discourse on statistics. Before offering his thoughts on the function of statistics, he explained the nature of the modern municipality. Many statisticians considered the municipality a state in miniature. They studied the land, population, economy and crime at municipal level in the same way they would analyse those variables at a higher administrative and territorial level. According to Correnti, the crucial error was that this method concealed 'the essence of municipal life, its constituting principle, the relationship to other organisational forms'. Political power was ultimately determined by the authorities that every municipality relinquished to the state in the public interest. Politics, therefore, began at the municipal level; the less power relinquished, the better the political system. If the municipalities retained their power, there was true autonomy; if the state intervened in every part of the municipal administration, there was a situation of *tutelle*, or tutelage. There were many intermediate and mixed forms in between these two extremes. In some cases, the status of a municipality vis-à-vis the state was a historical condition, determined by economic circumstances or simply imposed by law.

By using the terms autonomy and tutelage, Correnti made it clear that he intended to keep the debate about Italy's administrative structure alive, although he made no mention of the centralising legislation recently adopted in his country. Correnti showed his hand only indirectly, by referring to administrative liberties that did not exist, or were not exercised, in Italy (such as cooperative partnerships between municipalities, differentiation of municipalities by size and location, appointments of official or semi-official physicians in rural areas). His argument appeared to have little to do with statistics, but he gave it an interesting twist. He demonstrated that statistical research could help ensure that a municipality was granted the most appropriate administrative status. All too often the autonomy conferred on a municipality historically or politically was incommensurate with its true economic, demographic and social potential. Statistics would prepare the way for diversity and flexibility.

The main variables of municipal statistics were, according to Correnti, the municipalities' political, administrative, financial and legal powers vis-à-vis higher levels of government and other organisations in society. He considered public health a special indicator. Statistical inquiry could play a helpful role in society by revealing the ratio of public health officials to population density. This information could then be used to determine whether more civil servants should be appointed or to ensure that more physicians set up practices in a certain area. Inter-municipal cooperation was an option worth considering because it could reduce the need for top-down interference. Correnti's examples show that he envisaged a structure of minimal state intervention at local level. The system in place in Italy in 1865 tended in the opposite direction, particularly in that it did not distinguish between large and small or urban and rural municipalities. Correnti wanted to show that statistics offered a sound scientific basis for making the centralised system more flexible.

How did the international community respond to his appeal? Probably only a minority understood the underlying message of administrative reform in its proper context. And those who did pick up the message were not inclined to burden the congress with it. Correnti's report was presented to all 128 participants of the fourth section. Most were Italians, since as usual the congress was dominated by the host country. Frenchman Maurice Block, who wrote about public administration issues as well as statistics, and understood the finer points of the proposal, was in charge of the discussion. During the first debate on 30 September, two distinct groups emerged: those, like Block, who wanted to begin by compiling a comprehensive questionnaire for the purpose of gathering municipal statistics and those who preferred to discuss the 'philosophical' side of municipal statistics.

Correnti was among the latter group but also realised that the congress had to produce a practical outcome. He defended himself against Block's ideas, which in his view were a throwback to 'the old method of analytical enumeration, which was very tedious and very difficult to complete'.[18] The majority of the section initially supported Block. To avoid offending Correnti, the section opted to have a subcommittee revise his proposal – by then a commonplace procedure for dealing with sensitive matters. In the end, the section decided to present a dual proposal to the plenary, incorporating both the 'philosophical' and practical elements of municipal statistics.

The Romanian delegate, Gregor Vulturesco, was the spokesman for the fourth section in the plenary meeting. Most of the discussion had taken place in Italian, which was illustrative of who was most interested in the subject. Not everyone understood Correnti, though. A departmental director from the Ministry of Agriculture, Industry and Trade, Raffaele Pareto, failed to see the project as anything but a general, national statistical inquiry on a smaller scale. This was precisely what Correnti wanted to avoid. He tried again to explain: 'Acquiring, collating and grouping data pertaining to various aspects of municipal life is different from writing a statistical monograph of a municipality. It is a function, a force, for which we want to find the statistical expression; it is not a form that can be photographed as it appears.'[19] Photography being a recent invention, the metaphor whetted their appetite for discussion but no new insights emerged. Ernst Engel exerted his influence and proposed adopting the fourth section's project unanimously, and so it was done.

Correnti's idea of municipal proportionality was mentioned in the preamble to the congress resolution, followed by a list of twenty questions on topography, public administration, finance and health. The health question was divided into fifteen sub-questions, which illustrates how important this issue was. Hardly any of the questions could be answered quantitatively.[20] A new kind of statistics was born, but could it possibly evolve into a European statistics?

The will to reform

The other topics addressed in the eight sections of the Florence congress expanded on resolutions adopted by earlier congresses. After Engel's example, Maestri had drawn up an overview of previous topics and resolutions in preparation for the congress. It was an impressive, methodical list, so well-ordered that it was immediately obvious that many resolutions had had no follow-up. However much the congress achieved, there was always more to be done.

With regard to language, the rules allowed the participants to choose between French and Italian. In practice, English and German were also spoken, and this was not particularly conducive to mutual understanding. The official opening was presided over by the Minister of Agriculture, Industry and Trade, who spoke briefly and turned over the floor to the statisticians without further ado. The rules of procedure were adopted quickly with little debate. The minister took the podium again on the second day. This time he delved a bit deeper into the significance of the congress for the young state of Italy. He emphasised the power of parliament, which in a short time had pushed through a range of reforms, whereby statistical research had played an important role. He intimated that the results of the parliamentary statistical inquiry were affected to a certain extent by the desired outcome. He urged the congress to find ways to keep the interests of popular representation and government statistics separate.

In an accident of circumstance, it fell to Vice-President Karl von Czoernig, an Austrian, to answer the minister. He spoke in Italian and tried to articulate the recent political changes in the Austrian monarchy. He extolled the virtues of the constitutional monarchy system, which availed itself of 'a national parliament, which being comprised of members from every social class, needs to acquire knowledge by means of statistical inquiry and to find in that knowledge the information and facts that are essential to making good laws'.[21] For someone who had long believed efficiency was more important than participation, these were decidedly remarkable words, which won him the support of the many Italians present.

The first section, theory and technology of statistics, addressed the organisation of the international congress and of government statistics in general, population statistics and nomenclature. Zuccagni-Orlandini, the *éminence grise* of Tuscan statistics, was named chairman of the section. Approximately 180 participants had registered for the section, including most of the foreign official representatives. One key issue was not presented to the section, namely the matter of reorganising the congress. The intended rapporteur, Visschers, was absent due to mishap, so Engel reported directly to the plenary meeting. In Berlin, the congress had decided to delegate responsibility for the issue to an international commission. In Florence, Engel spoke on behalf of the commission and urged great restraint: 'Why should we tie the hands of the nations that will participate in future congresses by imposing on them fixed rules?' The congress in session was proof that every country was capable of organising an excellent gathering of statisticians in its own way. In the end, the Florence congress decided that 'the time was not come to codify the rules of the congress' and deferred the issue indefinitely.[22]

Correnti had written a preliminary report in which he emphatically reiterated the need for a single central statistics bureau and a single coordinating central commission. This was a perennial desire of the congress. On paper, Italy had been in compliance with this obligation since 1861. It had a statistics department at the Ministry of Agriculture, Industry and Trade, led by Maestri, and an advisory body, the *giunta di statistica*, chaired by Correnti. In practice, though, neither the statistics department nor the central commission operated flawlessly. The difficult relationship that existed between the various levels of government (municipal, provincial and national) was an obstacle to government statistics. Correnti used his report to the international congress primarily to re-introduce the organisational principles to his Italian colleagues. As usual, the foreign conferees showed intense interest in the subject, too, though it was unlikely that any of the delegates had sufficient political clout in their home countries to enforce the wishes of the international community.

At one of the meetings, Maestri explained again that in a representative system it was essential for statistics to serve the interests of both the legislative and executive powers. He endorsed a proposal put forward by Pietro Castiglioni, an official from the interior ministry, who like Maestri and Correnti was originally from Milan and had moved to Piedmont after 1848 due to his political convictions. The idea was that the central commission would consist of two sections: one was an advisory body made up of scientists and scholars and would be chaired by a member of parliament, and the other was to be comprised of ministerial officials and chaired by the director of the statistical bureau. The bureau would report directly to the prime minister. The proposal included specific guidelines regarding the activities to be carried out by each body.

Clearly, Maestri and Castiglioni were swept up in their own enthusiasm and consequently failed to see that the more nuanced and detailed their project was, the less viable it became. Experienced congress-goers like Adolphe Quetelet, who incidentally said very little in Florence, and Alfred Legoyt immediately put their finger on the problem: uniform institutions could not be imposed on states.[23] This was a hard-won freedom that the nations of Europe enjoyed. At Engel's suggestion, the section decided it would suffice to inform the official representatives of Castiglioni's ideas and ask them to draw the matter to the attention of the organizing committee of the next congress.

Besides the organisation of the congress, there was one item that had been on the agenda of every congress since 1853: the census. In Brussels in 1853, the congress had spoken out in favour of counting actual population; in London in 1860, a proviso had been added calling for special lists to be drawn up of the legal population, as determined by the local registers. The discussion on this matter in Florence revived the recurring dilemma: should the congress pursue uniformity or accept national diversity in Europe? The Italian census of 1861 revealed that in some provinces the difference between actual and legal population ran into the tens of thousands. It was important to have an exact count of the legal population because many essential rights and obligations of the Italian citizenry (e.g. taxation, conscription, size of representative bodies) were based on the size of the population. That is why Giovanni Anziani, prior to annexation a member of staff at the statistical bureau of the Grand Duchy of Tuscany, proposed full implementation of the system of population registers (another topic addressed in 1853), so that lists of the total population in the various administrative units could be generated at any time.

The deliberations on this matter soon reached a precarious point. The Danish delegate, Christian G.N. David, clarified the distinction: counting the legal population served an administrative and financial purpose, and counting the actual population served a statistical purpose. The conclusion was obvious. The legal population count was contingent on the laws and customs of a particular country and could not, as Engel had correctly said, be deduced. No one dared to ask what categories *could* be determined by deduction. Count everything first, was Engel's straightforward motto. Only then was differentiation possible, as appropriate under national law.[24]

Legoyt pointed out another problematic dimension. Precisely because some unpopular civic duties were dependent on the population count, the information furnished by local authorities in France, for example, could not always be relied on. Mayors of small municipalities, of which France had many, were often inclined to spare their villagers and manipulated the statistics to do so. France was not alone: every country had its idiosyncrasies. Von Baumhauer, the Dutch representative, favoured counting only people with a permanent home, including those who were temporarily absent. The latter proviso was 'especially important in coastal countries'.[25] Friedrich Hardeck of Karlsruhe added that 'temporary' would have to be precisely defined since there were many types of temporary migration.

Engel tried to bring the discussion back to the main issue and warned: 'If we permit every country to implement their own system, we will forego the benefit of uniformity' – the basis of the congress.[26] They decided to put to the plenary that the actual population should be counted first, that censuses should be conducted at the end of the year and that the 'manner and duration of abode of each individual' should be registered.

And then there was the matter of a standardised nomenclature for statistics. Maestri himself had written a preliminary report on this matter. The piece opened with an ominous statement: 'In order to present in international statistics comparisons and assessments of facts rationally, it is essential to verify that words have the same meaning everywhere they are used, that is, to ensure that a given concept is denoted by the same word in every country.'[27] This went to the very heart of diversity: was it human nature, history, the nation or something else that led to differences in the meanings of words?

Maestri suggested compiling a kind of pocket-sized dictionary of terms that could be important for statistical comparisons. But how to go about it? Maestri thought it would not be all that difficult. He selected several subjects (mortality, criminal law, reformatories and prisons, trade, shipping and finance – again, a typical list of nineteenth-century preoccupations), picked out one and explained the significance that Italian statistics and law conferred on aspects of the subject, and then asked whether country X had a similar concept. Sometimes the question was simple. The Italian budget distinguished between ordinary and extraordinary expenditures, based on the duration of the outlay. What was the criterion for this distinction in country X?

In some cases, the question was preceded by a fairly extensive explanation. Italian statistics on reformatories and prisons did not address the causes of crime. No one knew, for example, whether idleness or ignorance led to a particular crime, which in turn resulted in imprisonment. So, it was necessary to ask whether country X had investigated such causes. Maestri was thinking of a country's economic and political situation, general culture, climate, race, epidemics, carnival season and the like. Could the conferees say whether the degree of public control was influential, what impact the intensity of passions had, or what the consequences were of moral decline? These questions were not directly related to a particular national framework but to a bourgeois moral standard, a worldview shared by the middle classes of most European countries.

The section members did not find the problem all that difficult. They mentioned initiatives that had already been launched. Quetelet referred to an international population statistical survey that he and Xavier Heuschling had published in 1865, based on a resolution adopted by the London congress. They had simply translated all the relevant terms into French. He was convinced that it was possible to do the same for other subjects, too. The section wrote a draft resolution proposing that the required definitions be included in each statistical publication. The true extent of the problem became clear when the discussion turned to life insurance and causes of death. Differences in how causes of death were defined led to disparate counts, and those counts led in turn to differences in premiums and payouts. This had an impact on the liquidity of life insurance companies. The subject cried out for further inquiry.

The plenary meeting did not add much to the debate on the themes of the first section. Castiglioni readily admitted that the reorganisation of government statistics had an administrative and political side as well as a scientific one. Yet, given the recent political upheaval in Europe, the inception of the unified Italian state and the establishment of the international congress itself, by comparison a 'very innocent revolution, a revolution in the structure of official statistics' should fall within the realm of possibility. Castiglioni supported Correnti's proposal for an autonomous government statistics configuration, consisting of a central commission and a central bureau. This would institutionally entrench the basic principles of the liberal state: freedom and authority. And with that, the matter was closed until the next congress.

Ernst Engel took the floor to introduce the debate on the census. His speech was technical, apolitical and brief. In his opinion, a census was more than a count of a country's inhabitants. People were asked about their personal circumstances, and their position in the family, the community, the state, the church and society. In other words, a census was an essential building block of demography. The biggest impediment to accuracy was that people moved around for various reasons – seasonal work, military service and illness. Engel proposed counting the actual population, and asking everyone whether they were born in the municipality conducting the count. If not, they would be asked to indicate how long they had been living in the municipality. The worst that could happen was that an inhabitant might 'appear' to be deceased if he was not registered on any census list because he was outside the territory at the time of the count. It was preferable to hold a census in the winter, at the end of the year, since most people stayed 'at home' then. Incidentally, a question about the degree of consanguinity between fathers and mothers was added. Some people could not resist the temptation to ask for more information than was strictly necessary, although admittedly consanguinous relationships had been a legal issue for many centuries and had also entered the debates on public health.

The addition of extraneous questions annoyed Legoyt, the dogmatic French representative. William Farr shared his disapproval, while Engel took a pragmatic approach: governments were not required to adopt every proposal the congress made. This statement, verging on radical, unequivocally exposed the weakness of the congress. His goal was to preserve harmony among the conferees at any cost. Legoyt insisted that his objection be registered in an official report, at the very least. In the end, everyone was satisfied, but no real progress was made on the census.

The fifth section addressed the matter of monetary circulation, a problem that Italy had dealt with in 1862 by making the Piedmontese lira the national currency. In theory, though, the problem required a supranational solution. The underlying issue was the desire to have all governments introduce the decimal system and a standard European system of weights, measures and coinage. The Florence congress, like its predecessors, advocated this change. That the statistical congress willingly took on this set of problems demonstrates its overconfidence, despite many setbacks and failed resolutions. France, Italy, Switzerland and Belgium had concluded a monetary agreement in 1865 and international commissions had met in Paris to discuss this issue in 1867, prior to the congress. The debate in Florence was a bit too technical for the statisticians. The rapporteur of the fifth section, Pascal Duprat (a Frenchman in exile for his republican sympathies), insinuated that his section had arrived at a unanimous proposal.

During the plenary session, however, it turned out that Leone Levi had his own agenda and intended to urge the congress to display greater boldness in the pursuit of monetary union. Levi had been a regular participant since the first statistical congress, and was on the council of the Statistical Society of London. He was born in Ancona but moved to Britain in 1844 and became a naturalised British citizen soon after. Trade law was one of his areas of expertise and he periodically issued a statistical summary of the Parliamentary Papers. At the very least, Levi wanted to put together an international commission to focus exclusively on the monetary issue. Duprat reiterated with emphasis that the international statistical congress was rooted in the pursuit of science and had no political power to speak of. Louis Wolowski believed that the sole purpose of statistical inquiry was to gather data, in this case regarding the production and circulation of precious metals and money. The congress decided to maintain its course and voted in favour of the fifth section's proposal, which was consistent with Wolowski's view.

Les misérables

The sixth section concerned itself with the loaded dual topic of moral and judicial statistics. Justice in the nineteenth century was not infrequently a deeply moral issue, so the combination was not surprising. Two preliminary reports had been drafted: one by Angelo Messedaglia, a statistician and expert on public administration, on the classification of offences, and another by Pietro Maestri, whose topic, 'Les misérables', had been on the agenda back in 1853 but due to its political character had not been addressed as a separate issue since then.

Maestri thought poverty should be studied in two ways. The first approach involved investigating the cause of this 'anomaly', determining whether the cause was permanent or temporary and identifying the legal or moral changes that would need to be made. The second approach was a study of the phenomenon itself. With regard to the latter, Maestri had noticed that the indigent formed a heterogeneous group that included convicts, foundlings and prostitutes, to name but a few: 'Each of these classes of individuals has a special significance but together they form a broad category of suspect cases; dangerous to others and to themselves, and necessarily subject to surveillance ...'[28] Statistical studies of poverty could examine the natural, civil, moral and economic situations of the needy and how they were dealt with (in charitable institutions or prisons). But it was also necessary to seek a remedy for the problem. In Maestri's view, there was an overemphasis on mitigating poverty and too little concern for prevention. There was barely any coordination between charitable institutions. Maestri thought that the congress should advocate the establishment of a general committee for the protection of the underprivileged. The committee's task would be to coordinate public and private efforts to reduce poverty and recommend reforms. Once again the congress found itself confronted by an issue that appeared to be beyond the scope of statistics.

The fact that it was Maestri, the hard-working organiser of the Florence congress, who made this proposal underlined the importance of the issue. Soon after Italy's unification, the government had commissioned a statistical inquiry on poverty, which was in fact more of an investigation into the state (financial and otherwise) of the institutions than a study of the poor. As director of the statistics department, Maestri was responsible for publishing the research, a task he was still working on at the time of the congress.

Poverty was one of the most pressing social issues of the day and thinking about it dovetailed neatly with the statisticians' penchant for classification. In the nineteenth century, countless attempts were made to subdivide the indigent into categories. The fundamental distinctions were between the genuinely unfortunate and the idle, between the deserving and the undeserving poor. This explains Maestri's distinction between temporary and permanent paupers. While he engaged in the debate about the form and usefulness of charity, Quetelet's ideas could be heard echoing in the background. By analogy to the scientific approach to astronomical phenomena, Quetelet was a fierce advocate of tracing the causes of social phenomena. The goal was to eradicate 'temporary' causes and with them social evils. The same could be applied to poverty and pauperism. In that sense, the proposal to establish an international committee for the protection of the underprivileged was an extension of statistical inquiry. Reform-minded intellectuals and civil servants, who were presented in large numbers, found the proposal acceptable in all respects.

Statistics of culture

The statistics of art schools, archives, libraries and museums was an entirely new topic that none of the previous congresses had addressed. A statistical analysis of this kind might seem unusual to us, but it should be clear to the reader by now that in the nineteenth century people attempted to count and categorise just about everything. Moreover, the statistics of culture had everything to do with Romagnosi's idea of 'incivilimento', or at any rate what later generations made of it. The organisers even ventured to suggest that people would not only be interested in collecting data about cultural institutions but would also seek to make organisational improvements. Another reason for Maestri and his colleagues to put this item on the agenda was Florence's mission to uphold its reputation as a city of culture.

Maestri opened the discussion with a piece about art education. Again, moral arguments abounded. Maestri proclaimed: 'Art is the product of the common culture.'[29] Schools were needed not only to make artists aware of beauty and artistic traditions, but also to imbue the working class with taste. The objectives of statistical inquiry ranged from identifying schools to determining what styles they taught, what prizes were awarded and how many students they had. The same kind of broad interest, frequently more qualitative than quantitative, emerged when the proposal regarding the statistics of archives and libraries was put forward. The moral and cultural influence of these institutions was a topic of great interest, and statistics could reveal those influences and enhance them. Attention was also drawn to such matters as bibliography and the training of librarians. The science of bibliography was basically one of classification, a task made for statisticians. The preliminary report drafted by Tommaso Gar, who had recently been appointed director of Venice's state archives, cleverly appealed to this thirst for order: 'The life and soul of all libraries is rational order, the methodical classification of the works they contain.'[30] Every statistician present would have taken this to heart.

Most members of the eighth section, which was responsible for these matters, were Italian. Despite the overlaps in the area of classification, the relationship between statistics and cultural institutions was not clear to everyone, which occasionally led to bizarre discussions. The disagreement about opening hours typified the futilities that preoccupied the conferees. The risk of digression was just as high during the plenary debates. The delegate from Padua, Andrea Cittadella Vigodarzere, delivered an impassioned speech about the decline of Italian painting. If it was possible to study the causes of poverty, he argued, it was also possible to discover why the art of painting was in decline. This must have boggled the minds of many listeners. And the report on the statistics of museums was yet to come. Achille Gennarelli, archaeologist and palaeographer, asked the question everyone had been avoiding: 'Is a statistics of the whole world possible?'[31] He assumed it was. But he also said that statistics of the present had little significance without knowledge of the past. Ethnographic statistics, which had been discussed extensively in Vienna, needed to be viewed from a historical perspective to be fully understood. Museums were an ideal source of historical knowledge, especially if they were acquainted with each others' collections. The task of the statistician was to produce questionnaires that would yield a clear survey and accessible catalogues.

The Italians appeared to be oblivious to the fact that their infatuation with these topics was causing the cohesion of the congress to erode further. Those who regularly attended the statistical congresses remained reticent during these discussions, preferring not to engage in a debate about the domain of statistics. Obviously, there was a great deal of uncertainty about where the boundaries lay. There was also a lack of consensus on statistical methods. One minute, statisticians were calling for the theory of probabilities to be given greater precedence, and the next they were satisfied with a questionnaire that would yield nothing more than a museum catalogue. The only thing everyone agreed on (in silent consensus) was that statistics had the potential to address every issue and was an essential first step towards progress.

The final plenary was devoted to discussing the location of the next congress. On behalf of the Netherlands, Von Baumhauer had already expressed an interest in organising the event. His offer was received with gratitude, but he had competition. William Farr made a case for Russia, the only great power that had not had a turn at hosting the congress. Farr gave two reasons: first, Russia was a vast country and an enormous producer in many industries, and was therefore rich in statistical potential; second, Russia had recently implemented major political and social reforms. Farr stressed that by abolishing serfdom, the tsar had made a giant step forward on the road to modernisation, a step that should be acknowledged by the congress. If Russia was not in a position to organise the next congress, the alternatives were, according to Farr, Sweden, Denmark, the Netherlands and Switzerland.

Von Baumhauer defended the Netherlands' candidacy in German. With no discernable hesitation, he praised the land of Rembrandt, a seafaring nation liberated by means of the Eighty Years' War and since then the standard-bearer for a free and enlightened Europe. The Dutch economics and statistics association, the Vereniging voor de Staathuishoudkunde en Statistiek (1849), had enough capable members to put an organising committee together. He added that the location and climate of The Hague made it an excellent venue.

The French representative Wolowski supported the Netherlands' bid with a formal argument (one does not reject an invitation) and a substantive argument: '… everyone knows that Holland gave the world its first example of what can be accomplished by persevering in the love of freedom and making the sacrifices that love demands'.[32] The discussion continued in a similar vein. Engel sang the praises of the private statistics associations in Switzerland: official statistics was, after all, ultimately reliant on the cooperation of the citizenry. The Swiss representative, Giovan Battista Pioda, happily continued along these lines and explicitly confirmed his country's candidacy. Von Baumhauer could not refrain from responding that the Netherlands was no less free than Switzerland, stating 'our King rules over a free nation, he does not rule over her as if she were a slave; and we love our King as one loves a father, not as one loves a master'.[33]

This was the kind of language statisticians used when they abandoned the domain of numbers. The platitudes betrayed their preoccupation with the threats to, and refuges of, bourgeois civilisation. The congress in Florence demonstrated that dual concern like no other, with its debates on the statistics of migration flows, crime and poverty on the one hand and research into charitable institutions, land registries or cadastres (protection of property!), uniform weights and measures, art and culture on the other.

The proceedings concluded with the usual words of praise for the organisers, and Maestri in particular. It is doubtful whether the congress was considered a success afterwards. It was a gathering that had coupled reformist thinking with lacklustre compromises and European aspirations with national interests. Concrete results were few and far between. It was clearer than ever that no resolution would ever have a direct impact on statistical practice, and the official representatives voiced this observation with increasing frequency.

The European ambitions of some of the Italian delegates were a relic of early liberal nationalism but were out of touch with the realism that began to dictate international relations after 1860. Italy's vision of Europe was very different from that of other countries. In its enthusiasm, Italy had reverted to an obsolete ideology, as if it could shore up its own legitimacy by making a bold appeal for a European future. Most of Europe's governments had long considered that notion passé.

Notes

1   U. Pesci, *Firenze Capitale (1865–1870)* (Florence 1904), p. 387.

2   P. Maestri, *Annuario economico e politico dell'Italia per l'anno 1852* (Turin 1852) and Id., *Annuario economico-statistico dell'Italia per l'anno 1853* (Turin 1853).

3   Maestri, *Annuario economico e statistico dell'Italia per l'anno 1853*, V.

4   Cited in F. Sofia, *Una scienza per l'amministrazione. Statistica e pubblici apparati tra età rivoluzionaria e restaurazione* (Rome 1988), p. 320.

5   M. Gioia, *Filosofia della statistica* (Milan 1826), III.

6   *Ibid.*, XI.

7   S. Patriarca, *Numbers and Nationhood. Writing Statistics in Nineteenth-Century Italy* (Cambridge 1996), p. 41.

8   *Compte-rendu des travaux de la sixième session du Congrès International de Statistique réunie à Florence les 30 Septembre, 1, 2, 3, 4 et 5 Octobre 1867* (Florence 1868), p. 349

9   U. Levra, 'La "statistica morale" del Regno di Sardegna tra la Restaurazione e gli anni Trenta: da Napoleone a Carlo Alberto', *Clio* 28 (1992), 353–378.

10 For an account of pre-unitary statistics, see Patriarca, *Numbers and Nationhood*, and G. Favero, *Le misure del Regno. Direzione di statistica e municipi nell'Italia liberale* (Padova 2001).

11 *Compte-rendu des travaux de la sixième session*, 8.

12 *Annuario statistico italiano* 2 (1864), XXIII.

13 *Ibid.*, XXV.

14 *Ibid.*, XXVII–XXVIII.

15 *Compte-rendu des travaux de la sixième session*, p. 37.

16 *Ibid.*, p. 50.

17 C. Correnti, 'Statistique comunale: constitution démographique et économique des communes', *Compte-rendu des travaux de la sixième session*, pp. 111–124. His argument is also discussed, albeit with a different emphasis, by Patriarca, *Numbers and Nationhood*, pp. 210–232, and Favero, *Le misure del Regno*, pp. 97–113.

18 *Compte-rendu*, p. 234.

19 *Ibid.*, p. 381.

20 *Ibid.*, pp. 483–484.

21 *Ibid.*, p. 349.

22 *Ibid.*, p. 393.

23 *Ibid.*, p. 201.

24 *Ibid.*, pp. 204–205.

25 *Ibid.*, p. 206.

26 *Ibid.*, p. 207.

27 *Ibid.*, p. 58.
28 *Ibid.*, p. 131.
29 *Ibid.*, p. 145.
30 *Ibid.*, p. 153.
31 *Ibid.*, p. 446.
32 *Ibid.*, p. 461.
33 *Ibid.*, p. 463.

7

Small gestures in a big world: The Hague 1869

Karl Baedeker's travel guide to Belgium and Holland said of The Hague that no other Dutch city had so many pretty, broad streets, tall stately homes and large open squares.[1] A person who had not visited any other major European city might well think that The Hague was a resplendent place, comparable to the grand capitals of nineteenth-century Europe. But people arriving from Paris, London, St Petersburg, Vienna, Brussels, Rome or Berlin – like the foreign guests of the seventh international statistical congress – would have thought they had landed in a provincial town. The city centre must have made a modest, even small-town, impression. According to the census conducted at the end of 1869, The Hague had a population of just over 90,000, far less than the cities where the congress had been held before.

You could walk across the entire city in a good quarter of an hour. In those days, Hollandsche Spoor railway station lay outside the city limits. One side of Stationsweg, the road that ran straight to the city centre from the station, offered 'a free and unobstructed view … charmingly alternated with taste-fully planted pleasure gardens, straight leafy lanes, fertile orchards and opulent fields, ornamented with handsome, gambolling livestock.'[2] So much green in and around the city was an important feature of the urban landscape at a time when the pleasure of the respectable bourgeoisie depended on beauty, refined entertainments and fresh air. The Hague was the appropriate setting for the seat of government of a nation that proudly displayed its conventionality and self-restraint, preferably within view of the neighbours. Anno 1869 the city was worthy of its stately full name, 's-Gravenhage.

The population of The Hague grew steadily throughout the first half of the nineteenth century, not because local trade and industry had any particular pulling power but because of the influx of civil servants, diplomats and servants of the Royal Household. From 1830 onward, the government was no longer divided between The Hague and Brussels, so the Royal Household and the government bureaucracy were moved to The Hague permanently. Until well into the second half of the nineteenth century, newcomers were able to find homes within the old city limits. With the construction of the Willemsparkbuurt and Stationsbuurt districts in the 1860s the city began a conservative expansion, initially only for the benefit of the wealthy. There was certainly nothing comparable to the spate of demolition and construction in many other European cities. At the time of the congress, a national monument – Batavia with a flag, a sheaf of arrows and the Dutch lion at her feet – was under construction on Plein 1813. It was the only structure in the city that was in the same league as the architectural and sculptural lieux-de-mémoire being erected in the countries neighbouring the Netherlands. No one had yet heard of the young Vincent van Gogh, who was hired for a position at The Hague branch of Goupil & Cie art dealers in 1869.

The social programme for the congress was in keeping with the entertainment conventions of the upper middle class: a visit to the zoo founded in 1863, free admission to the local museums (including the temporary exhibition of the Red Cross in the drawing academy building on Prinsessegracht), admission to gentlemen's societies like De Witte and the Besognekamer (when in female company, the conferees repaired instead to the Tent, an establishment in the Haagsche Bosch, a wooded parkland in the city), an evening concert in the Haagsche Bosch, dinner at Badhotel at the beach in Scheveningen and an excursion to Amsterdam by chartered train. It is remarkable how accommodating the programme, even the official part, was to women. The congress newsletter reported that a large number of ladies had attended the ceremonial opening of the congress in the Ridderzaal (Knights' Hall). The members of the congress would have had to order tickets for them in advance. 'Unaccompanied' women were not welcome everywhere, and when women were unchaperoned they had to make it blatantly obvious that they had no improper intentions.[3]

The Hague was modest in its hospitality, as a correspondent remarked: 'The city does not have a festive appearance, as it did during the literature congress, the marksmen's' congress and the official welcoming of The Hague's victorious marksmen.' But that was no great matter: '... the statisticians have not come to make merry and most of the local inhabitants understand little of what the gentlemen have come to do'.[4] We must count King Willem III among 'most of the local inhabitants', as he had no interest whatsoever in the congress or its participants. In the monarchical states that had hosted previous congresses, members of the royal house had put in an appearance. Willem III, known for his occasional breaches of decorum, had absolutely no desire to attend the statistical congress. The rules of international courtesy, though, required him to grant an audience. The reception he hosted at Noordeinde Palace interrupted the opening session on Monday 6 September. The king received his guests at one o'clock, but disappeared not ten minutes later, having spoken to no one. The official chairman of the congress, the energetic minister of the interior Cornelis Fock, later wrote that the king's behaviour 'did not leave the delegates with a

147

favourable impression'.

The subsequent reception at Huis ten Bosch, Queen Sophie's summer residence, was quite different. She 'spoke to most individuals in their own language about their field of study and the interests of their country'. The audience lasted for over an hour and was highly appreciated by those present. Sophie announced later that she hoped to attend a few of the sessions. The next day the conferees had an opportunity to pay their respects to the Prince of Orange, the honorary chairman of the congress, but he had no more time for the guests than the king. Fock – a liberal – decided that the Family of Orange had cut 'a pathetic figure in the presence of the foreigners'.[5]

The plenary sittings took place in the Ridderzaal, better known at the time as the Loterijzaal, the office of the national lottery. The renovations carried out by Willem Nicolaas Rose, the government architect, in 1861 had done nothing to improve the hall, at least not in the opinion of the public press. Replacing the wooden coping with a cast-iron structure was seen as the ultimate manifestation of the 'artifice of faux Gothic'.[6] Moreover, the rest of the building was left in a pitiful state: 'The decaying and grimy condition of the building is a vexation for many, and now on this occasion when so many distinguished foreigners are to be received, they thought to beautify it by sweeping the exterior stair, repairing a few broken panes and hanging a new, peculiarly-shaped oak door'.[7]

The sessions were held in the rooms surrounding the chamber of the Tweede Kamer, the lower house of parliament, and the pre-congress meetings took place in the hall of the 'Vereeniging' on Willemstraat. A 'highly remarkable exhibition of statistical maps and drawings and a collection of books by Nijhoff were assembled together' in the antechamber of the Tweede Kamer. The local correspondent mentioned above, who mingled with the statisticians, observed that there were 'so many decorated – and such abundantly decorated – gentlemen'.[8] What he did not know was that every host country, where the custom existed, had conferred honours on the conferees on a large scale, which meant that each of the congress veterans had a whole collection of medals.

The two faces of Dutch statistics

Simon Vissering and Marie Matthieu von Baumhauer were familiar faces to the regular participants of the international statistical congress. After the death of Jan Ackersdijck in 1861, they became the torchbearers of Dutch statistics in Europe. The Dutch government had good reason to put Vissering and Von Baumhauer in charge when the congress came to The Hague. Vissering was acting chairman of the preparatory commission and Von Baumhauer was responsible for organisational matters. They knew each other from various learned societies and had served together on the Rijkscommissie voor Statistiek (State Commission for Statistics, 1858–1861), a failed attempt to establish a permanent central commission of scientists, scholars and civil servants in the Netherlands, as recommended by the congress.

Vissering distinguished himself as a liberal thinker well before the political revolution of 1848. He was involved in the founding of the Amstel Sociëteit, the precursor of the liberal party in the Netherlands. Von Baumhauer belonged to a group of liberal reformers intent on improving the moral condition of the nation. He and Willem Hendrik Suringar established a Dutch agricultural colony in the manner of Mettray and participated in the first prisons congress of 1846 in Frankfurt.[9]

It is difficult to tell whether Vissering and Von Baumhauer got along. They shared a fundamentally liberal mindset and a passion for statistics, though their opinions about nature and method differed at times. This had more to do with the nebulous state of the science than with any deep intellectual differences they may have had. Where Vissering and Von Baumhauer differed most was in their professional background: Vissering was a law professor and Von Baumhauer was a civil servant at the Ministry of Foreign Affairs, where he served as direc- tor of the statistics department established in 1848. They were dependent on each other because statistics had never been an exclusively state affair in the Netherlands. Given his subordinate position at the ministry, Von Baumhauer was unlikely to ever become the Netherlands' undisputed senior spokesman for statistics, like Engel in Prussia or Czoernig in Austria. Vissering was repeatedly rebuffed in his attempts to improve the way statistical inquiry was organised in the Netherlands, as evidenced by the dissolution of the Rijkscommissie in 1861. Together they had more leverage than on their own.

Until the Centraal Bureau voor de Statistiek (Central Statistics Office) was established in 1899, Dutch statisticians had been virtually ignored by govern- ment. Admittedly, some ministries had departments that conducted counts, but without any efficient coordination. Throughout the nineteenth century, various statistical bureaux, departments and commissions came and went, none of them surviving for very long. A unique state tradition of strategic restraint and deliberate intervention was part of the reason why efforts at institution-building consistently failed. The Netherlands was not a weak state but rather an accom- modating one, which steered a middle course between concession to social forces – the legacy of the Republic – and a strong tendency towards organisa- tion, a Batavian–French impulse. Statistics flourished under both approaches, though in different ways. Vissering and Von Baumhauer represented the two organisational structures of statistics in the Netherlands: one shaped by the state and the other supported by society's elites.

Without denying the pre-revolutionary roots of statistics, it can be said that the Batavian–French Revolution ignited the development of government statistics.[10] Once the organs of public administration and, to a lesser extent, parliament had sampled the benefits of statistical information, they could no longer go without. What had been introduced in the Batavian–French period survived in one form or other after 1815. That is to say, the statistics remained, but organisation and methods of collecting data tended to change. The politi- cal climate was not conducive to increasing and centralising statistical activity within the government bureaucracy. A powerful central statistics bureau would have been inconceivable immediately after 1815. The spectre of French centralisation haunted those in power and public opinion. Nevertheless, the provincial agriculture commissions continued to submit their annual statistics report to the ministry. Charity boards, provincial executives and school inspectors continued to write their reports on poor relief and education. And with conscription in force, municipalities kept up-to-date statistics on residents who were eligible for military service.

There were two problems impeding the usefulness of all these figures: insufficient systematisation and a lack of openness. If both were to be dealt with, government statistics would at a stroke meet the criteria that Gijsbert Karel van Hogendorp had formulated back in 1819 regarding the necessity of good statistics: publicity, participation and an informed public opinion. There was also some pressure from the academic world – specifically from Hendrik Willem Tydeman (the translator of Schlözer's *Theorie der Statistik*) – to lift the veil of secrecy shrouding statistics.

In 1826 the regime of King Willem I responded to their call by establishing a statistical bureau and a commission. This small but specialised system began as an energetic operation (see Chapter 1). With specialists like Édouard Smits, Rehuel Lobatto and the young Quetelet collaborating, it seemed as if government statistics in the Low Countries had carved out a niche for itself. The census of 1829 was an impressive achievement. But with Belgian independence and the subsequent brain-drain of prominent statisticians, statistical activity at the central government level in the Northern Netherlands virtually ground to a halt. It was as if the Dutch government wanted to differentiate itself from the Belgian government, which was directly involved in statistical activity.

So, once again, it was up to the academic elite and the provincial and local authorities to keep the fires burning, a difficult task at best. Only after the political sea change of 1848 was there scope for setting up a new statistical bureau. Johan Rudolph Thorbecke, the new Prime Minister and Minister of the Interior, had taught statistics for two decades as a professor of law. He was not fond of 'arithmeticians' like Quetelet but, like most liberals in Europe, believed that statistical information was essential for public administrators and citizens. Von Baumhauer was put in charge of the bureau, which was made an autonomous department in 1857. In 1849 Von Baumhauer published an article in *De Gids*, in which he laid out the function of statistics. He defined statistics as 'the science of reality, which attempts to express in numbers that which has come to pass.'[11] He was obviously not considered to be an 'arithmetician' of the kind so loathed by Thorbecke (who would never have employed such a person at his ministry). Statistics, Von Baumhauer continued, 'is not about theory, but about practice and history'. This was, of course, a sensible point of departure for a civil servant. Furthermore, he stressed how powerful statistics ('the truest friend of humanity') was, despite the apparently weak position it had occupied for nearly two decades: 'No individual, however inconsequential in influence and power, can elude statistical inquiries. From the moment he first sees the light of day, statistics confers on him a place in the record of births.' Von Baumhauer then demonstrated how many times in a human life statistics registered an individual's actions, concluding in an almost threatening tone: 'Statistics does not leave he whom it recorded in its registers on the first day of his life to his death bed without one last time chronicling the terminus of a full course of life and the hour of death'.[12]

Soon after the Netherlands had undergone far-reaching constitutional reform in 1848, Jeronimo de Bosch Kemper began publishing an annual entitled *Staatkundig en Staathuishoudkundig Jaarboekje*. He continued in the same vein as Tydeman and Van Hogendorp and emphasised the voters' obligation to stay abreast of what was happening in the country with the help of statistical information. Various associations, such as the Provinciaal Utrechts Genootschap voor Kunsten en Wetenschappen (Utrecht Provincial Society of Arts and Sciences), the Nederlandsche Maatschappij tot bevordering der Geneeskunst (Netherlands Medical Society) and the Landhuishoudkundig Congres (National Agriculture Congress), pressed for a statistical society, modelled on the Statistical Society of London.

In the same volume of *De Gids* in which Von Baumhauer published his defence of statistics, Vissering wrote a searing piece about the necessity of promoting statistics in the Netherlands. Openness was his guiding principle, too: 'The time of secrecy in state government is over; the altered structure of our public institutions compels the government to greater openness and the nation to cognizance. Statistics is the foundation of that openness, and as each day passes the need for statistical information will be felt more and more strongly'.[13] Universities were urged to present the discipline of statistics more distinctly, and the government to make funding available for that purpose, but also – primarily – for the establishment of an independent statistical bureau. The first task the bureau should undertake was the compilation of a comprehensive *Statistiek des Rijks* (Statistics of the State). In the meantime, Thorbecke had set up a statistical bureau at the ministry, but it met only a few of Vissering's criteria. In 1857 Vissering managed to consummate his plan for a Vereeniging voor de Statistiek (Statistical Society) which in 1862, after the Rijkscommissie proved unviable, functioned as a kind of central statistical commission.

Yet, Dutch statisticians were not entirely satisfied. Though they enjoyed a good reputation internationally and were always prominently represented at the international congress, they were unable to implement important decisions adopted by the congress, especially those relating to organisational matters. When, in 1863, Vissering looked back at his own article in the *Gids* of 1849, his optimism was measured. The number of statistical documents issued by both the Vereeniging voor de Statistiek and the government had increased significantly, but the loss of the Rijkscommissie after just three years was a serious setback. Vissering, who had served as acting chairman of the Rijkscommissie for a time, blamed the failure on two problems, one being geography – the members had to travel from all over the country to attend the meetings – and the other, parliament's lack of appreciation for statistics. 'The only possible result of parliament's precipitous decision [to abolish the Rijkscommissie],' Vissering

wrote with foresight, 'is that this country will be without an effective arrangement for statistics for a very long time.'[14] From our vantage point, we can see
that they continued to deliberate about an effective arrangement, but decades
would pass before it came to fruition.

Idées-mères

Vissering and Von Baumhauer had vast experience of Dutch and European
statistics by the time they were asked to organise the seventh international
congress. Both men were members of the state commission set up at the end
of 1868 to plan the congress. In addition, several members of both houses of
parliament, the Raad van State (Council of State) and other government institutions joined the preparatory commission. In January 1869 the commission's
ranks were expanded with the addition of another ten people, most of them
professors and senior civil servants 'whose help and advice on the development of a programme for the congress' were considered essential.[15] A few more
secretaries were brought in as time grew short. The organisers were given a total
budget of 20,000 guilders for the congress.

Much of the brainpower came from Von Baumhauer, who presented the
preparatory commission with an Idées-mères, a grand scheme encompassing
organisational matters and congress topics. Following the example of Engel
and Maestri, who had compiled an overview of topics treated by previous
congresses, Von Baumhauer wrote a reasoned commentary on what had gone
before, accompanied by suggestions for further discussion. His plan had two
main objectives. The first was to enhance the international character of the
congress. In Florence, nine in ten participants had been Italian, while about
half the conferees in Brussels and Paris had been foreign. Von Baumhauher
wrote in his epilogue that the grandest idea of all was the 'denationalisation' of
the congress.[16] Secondly, he favoured limiting the number of sections to ensure
there would be time to address the items on the agenda thoroughly and avoid
fragmenting the expertise. He proposed five themes: methodology, statistics
of the justice system, financial statistics, fisheries statistics and statistics of
overseas territories. With the latter two, he obviously intended to incorporate
specific Dutch interests into the programme.

Von Baumhauer believed that this configuration would increase the effectiveness of the congress. The role of the official representatives would also need
to be enhanced. As suggested earlier by the Danish statistician Christian David,
the representatives would stay on for a few days after the congress to go over
the section and plenary reports and distil the information into final decisions,
which they would then present to their respective governments. They could
expect their decisions to be received favourably and constructively only if there
was uniformity in the organisation of government statistics. Von Baumhauer
endorsed the proposal about streamlining national statistics put forward by
Pietro Castiglioni in Florence, which until then had been ignored. There were

also several practical matters, such as franked international mailings of statistical publications, which had yet to be arranged.

In the introductory section on methodology, Von Baumhauer reiterated his vision on statistics, showing himself to be a faithful adherent of Quetelet. He emphasised the close relationship between statistics and legislation: 'A lawmaker without statistics is like a steersman without a compass; a statistician who knows nothing of the law and nothing of national customs is like a man in a rowboat on a desolate coast without lighthouses.'[17] It was vital to have knowledge of differences and changes in legislation in order to make accurate interpretations. The figures for stillbirths or children born out of wedlock, for example, could vary widely from country to country for the simple reason that the phenomena were defined differently. Von Baumhauer also asked his audience to give special attention to the subdivisions of statistical categories. Borrowing from Quetelet, he said 'The more subcategories there are, the closer one comes to identifying the cause'.[18] He also shared Quetelet's interest in numbers, tables and mathematical calculations. He even adopted Quetelet's position on probability – that it should receive more attention at the congress – though he knew this was a controversial issue. It is very likely that his stance was connected with a dual desire to limit the number of outsiders and build a bridge between statistics and actuarial mathematics. Moreover, the theory of probabilities was for Von Baumhauer to return to the foundations of nineteenth-century statistics, the theory of constants and the law of periodicity, i.e. the idea that all manner of natural and social phenomena increase and decrease according to fixed patterns.

The next proposal concerned judicial statistics, an area of inquiry that served administrative interests, but also provided insight into a country's moral condition. Quetelet owed his fame to his analysis of criminal tendencies, based on crime statistics gleaned from court records in various countries. However, national differences in legislation tended to restrict comparative statistical inquiry. Existing statistics on civil law and commercial law – the two areas Von Baumhauer wished to concentrate on – were a mixed bag, though this subject had been on the agenda at the congresses in Paris, Vienna and London. By way of illustrating the importance of this topic, he talked about the consequences of the surge in international migration. Marriages between people of different nationalities were becoming much more common, but the legal ramifications were virtually unknown. Statisticians could help map the differences between countries in order to bring lacunas to light more quickly to facilitate a system of 'best practices'.

The third theme, financial statistics, had been treated exhaustively at the Vienna congress in 1857, but few concrete results had been achieved in international statistics. Von Baumhauer unleashed such a barrage of questions his audience must have wondered whether it was possible to make any progress at all in this area.

Fisheries statistics was the fourth topic. Various North Sea countries had hosted international exhibitions on fishing methods and fish products. It was thought that the statistics of offshore and river fishing would provide valuable information about the most effective fishing methods. This subject was also important for regulating fishing areas.

The final major topic was the statistics of overseas territories. Von Baumhauer admitted that he was not a specialist in this area. One of the more important objectives of this type of inquiry was to obtain information regarding the revenues of the system of forced farming in the Dutch East Indies. Remarkably, his overview contained hardly any references to existing colonial statistics of other countries, though the London congress of 1860 had introduced this issue.

The commission which was in charge of preparing the congress, attempted to shape the programme along the lines set out by Von Baumhauer. The pre-congress of official representatives addressed just three topics: the congress's decision-making process, the rules of procedure and franked mailings of statistical publications. Only the first topic was likely to arouse disagreement, since it was related to the overall organisation of the congress. One of the questions that had to be resolved was whether every invitee was permitted to vote on resolutions. Professional statisticians were growing more concerned that the congress would lose influence if every interested person had a vote. As we have seen, in Florence the invitees included several hundred Italians, many of whom were not well versed in national statistics.

With regard to the rest of the programme, too, the preparatory commission built on Von Baumhauer's *Idées-mères*, completing it with commentary provided by Dutch and foreign experts. Vissering, who had been teaching statistics as part of the law curriculum at Leiden University since 1850, was eager to join in the ongoing debate about the nature of statistics as a science. Like the lecturer he was, he systematically recounted the different movements that made up the multifaceted field of statistics. Statistics intersected with other areas of scholarship such as history, geography and ethnography and various natural sciences, but ultimately it was an independent discipline. He compared statistics to Proteus, the son of Poseidon, who had the power of prophecy but assumed different guises to avoid being asked to tell the future. Vissering agreed with Moreau de Jonnès, who had said: 'Statistics is the science of social facts, expressed in numerical values.'[19] But like so many who wished to have the last word about statistics as a science, Vissering did more to increase the confusion than to resolve it, as the ensuing discussion would reveal.

Von Baumhauer sought a path to consensus. With his essay on the methodology of statistics, he hoped to foster solidarity among professional statisticians by appealing to them at the level of their technical, practical capacities. However, his remarks were as incisive as Vissering's. Von Baumhauer believed that methodology was a cover for the problem of defining statistical categories. He showed that official statistics commonly lacked empirical rigour because of the haphazard way in which categories were defined. For example, the German states divided up the population into age groups for no other purpose than to show how many people were available for military service. There were various subcategories for men aged 14 to 60, but not for women in the same age group, which made it impossible to do other kinds of analysis, for example comparing the age distribution of the population with mortality tables. An ordinary civil servant could simply rearrange figures and units that had been defined in advance, while a civil servant specialising in statistics would first need to have detailed knowledge of the material in order to present the figures in the best possible light. For that reason alone, Von Baumhauer argued, a central commission was needed to provide scientific oversight.

Von Baumhauer continued in this vein, using the seemingly undisputed topic of methodology to put forward his ideas about accuracy. He proposed to minimise the number of subjects that could be investigated in a single statistical inquiry: 'The more we ask, the more likely it is that inaccuracies or lacunas will occur in the answers to each question.'[20] He had a strong aversion to simultaneous counts of population, livestock, agricultural production and industrial production. Moreover, he claimed that it was not just necessary to differentiate by subject, but also by season so that data about specific topics could be collected at the proper time. Occupational surveys would be more accurate if they took more account of the possibility that members of a single household might have different occupations. Precision was possible only if statisticians counted exactly what was meant to be counted, no more and no less.

For the same reasons Von Baumhauer also favoured restricting the scope of statistics. The mere fact that a phenomenon was quantifiable did not make it a legitimate object of statistical inquiry. Only the very best statisticians – giants like Humboldt and Quetelet – were capable of integrating the natural sciences into statistics. Von Baumhauer believed it was more realistic to limit statistical inquiry to matters pertaining to the physiology of human beings and society. After all, he argued, in the natural sciences a law is the point of departure and facts are the goal; in statistics, facts are the point of departure and identifying a law or pattern is the goal. He insisted that there was no other way to approach social phenomena.

His 'neutral' discourse on the methodology of statistics was actually a fairly obvious attempt to bring about professionalisation, centralisation of competences and decentralisation of implementation. Von Baumhauer made three recommendations. First, work should be organised systematically; specifically, there should be continuous contact between the central level and implementing bodies. Second, detailed documentation should be produced and should include conversions to percentages and references to the legislation in question to facilitate international comparison. Third, probability theory should be applied, as Quetelet had proposed in Florence. He also suggested that greater attention be paid to fluctuations and tendencies, especially in the context of moral statistics. With regard to crime, for example, it was easy enough to make generalisations based on the number of crimes committed, but this was of little use if the circumstances of the crime and the perpetrator were not included in the narrative. He explained that he did not interpret Quetelet's 'propensity for crime' at the level of society as a whole, but always at the level of the individual. It would be absurd to compare a person of poor upbringing and education with a cultivated individual and derive from that comparison an average inclination towards criminal behaviour. Slightly bending Quetelet's teachings, Von Baumhauer presented an ambitious programme that was consistent with the trend towards professionalisation seen at previous congresses. However, it was so specific that it was likely to incur opposition.

The programme included a few shorter pieces for the statistical theory section. Johan Marinus Obreen, director of the repository of maps, plans and models and the library at the Department of the Navy, revived the discussion of the graphics method initiated at the Vienna congress in 1857. Johannes Adrianus Boogaard and Lucas Jacob Egeling, both physicians, took up the problem of registering stillbirths, another vintage topic that was tied to the larger issue of registering causes of death, a matter that was regulated by law in the Netherlands (in the Burial Act of 10 April 1869). Von Baumhauer himself addressed the topic of mortality tables and age distribution, a matter of great interest to life insurance companies as well as statisticians and sanitarians. In 1868 he had published an article in the *Journal des Economistes* proposing a new calculation method that had as much to do with accurate registration as with mathematics.

The conferees were given a chance to respond to aforementioned papers before the congress began. Georg Mayr, the coming man from Bavaria and Friedrich von Hermann's successor, was eager to make his mark. As his later writings would show, Mayr had a predilection for theory. He proposed to define statistics as quantitative 'Massenbeobachtung', or mass observation. In the spirit of Quetelet, he stated that mass observations would be useful only if they were then subjected to logical classification and patterns and laws were identified. Though in theory all human circumstances the world over were potential objects of statistical inquiry, Mayr admitted that the state was usually the best unit within which to conduct statistical research. This implied that statistical laws would apply primarily within national boundaries. At the same time, Mayr acknowledged that the statistics of administrative units such as provinces and municipalities were frequently inadequate when it came to representing 'natural territorial groups'. Mayr did not specify how these natural groups were to be identified, but insisted they could be presented graphically. Another advantage of graphic representations was that they were accessible to a broad public. In Mayr's opinion, maps and diagrams were easier to understand than numbers alone.

Mayr's ideas about statistics as a universal method appeared to correspond well with the overseas territories theme. The topic of colonial statistics was given more attention in the programme overview than in Von Baumhauer's *Idées-mères*. A provisional committee was formed, comprising former governor-general Ludolf A.J.W. baron Sloet van de Beele, ichthyologist Pieter Bleeker, member of the Council of State Wolter Robert baron van Hoëvell, and Pieter Johannes Veth, a professor of geography and ethnology of the Dutch East Indies – all experts on the Netherlands' overseas territories but none of them known for their statistical talents. Nevertheless, they had big plans. European ideas were often applied more systematically and effectively in the colonies than at home, at least initially. According to the committee, colonial statistics should be made to serve the administrative project in the colonies, which consisted in the 'sacred guardianship' of the subjugated peoples. The mother country 'is bound to respect, to a certain degree, the special genius of the subjugated races and, on pain of one day being accused of crimes against humanity, is obliged to justify its dominion by effecting social progress'.[21] Statistics would be an excellent instrument in this pursuit. Furthermore, the committee continued, statistics – in the form of population and tax registers – was already gaining acceptance in Muslim and – to a lesser extent – Hindu regions of Asia. The committee then discussed statistical material pertaining to the colonies that various European powers had produced. In the end, the committee agreed on a set of recommendations regarding the organisation and substance of colonial statistics.

Not on Sunday

The five proposed themes were accepted by the international statistics community, with one minor addition: it was decided that the fisheries statistics section would also discuss import and export statistics. It was clear from the start that – despite Von Baumhauer's call for denationalisation and efficiency – the congress in The Hague would be burdened by national interests (and not least by Dutch interests) and the unpredictable implications of the topics on the agenda. The assembled statisticians would find it difficult to take authoritative decisions on matters like migration policy, fishing quotas and colonial policy. However, Von Baumhauer did succeed in increasing the share of foreign guests to a quarter of the total, thus reversing the decline in international participation.

As was now customary, the official delegates gathered for a meeting prior to the opening of the congress. On the evening of Friday 3 September the gentlemen met at the 'Vereeniging', on the invitation of the minister of the interior and the mayor of The Hague. Deliberations began the next day. In attendance were 47 delegates (including 18 members of the Dutch preparatory commission) from 26 countries (the eight German states were counted separately). They aimed to complete their talks on Saturday, since Anders Nicolai Kiaer of Norway objected to meeting on Sunday on religious grounds.

Quetelet, who was elected chairman, came straight to the point and asked what specific activities had been undertaken to meet the congress's long-standing goal of establishing an international statistics regime. The answer was disappointing. Though the commission set up specifically to address this matter had not convened even once, it was determined that no decision on new appointments would be possible for the time being. Another suggestion aimed at professionalisation and increasing efficiency came from Christian David, the Danish delegate. He proposed convening a post-congress meeting of official representatives to take real decisions. Not surprisingly, there was opposition to this idea. Maestri suggested the congress was taking an 'aristocratic' turn and showing a tendency towards 'liberticide'.[22] But his congress in Florence had been exceedingly liberal with respect to the participation of Italians. Most looked favourably on taking action to professionalise the congress. Engel anticipated a conflict and suggested finding out how other congresses structured their decision-making processes. After a second and third ballot, Engel's proposal was adopted. For the rest, the pre-congress dealt with a few motions of order that did not give rise to any lengthy discussion. There was no need to reconvene on Sunday, and the delegates attended a banquet held in their honour at one of the halls of The Hague Zoo. Probably without Kiaer.

The official opening took place in the Ridderzaal on Monday 6 September. Prince Willem of Orange did not attend, but conveyed his apologies through interior minister Fock (in light of what would happen during the royal reception, this is hardly surprising). Fock's opening address was less than inspiring. Predictably, he looked back at a long tradition of statistics in the Low Countries, which – by his timeline – began with a census in 1514. He recalled the work of Jan de Witt, Willem Kersseboom and Nicolaas Struyk, eventually arriving at the nineteenth century, which he described as if statistical research was the country's main occupation. He diverted attention away from the plodding progress of government statistics in the Netherlands by focusing on a few isolated achievements. When he was finished, Vissering took charge of the meeting. The first order of business was to pay tribute to the deceased, including the Bavarian statistician Friedrich von Hermann, Professor Friedrich Wilhelm Schubert of Königsberg and Édouard Ducpétiaux of Belgium, all of whom had attended the congresses from the very beginning. Their generation was dwindling, and this was a great drain on the international statistical movement and contributed to the gradual decline in enthusiasm.

Theory and methodology

The conferees dispersed for their section meetings immediately after the opening session. The next plenary was not scheduled until after the sections – on Friday afternoon. Some ninety participants, including many official representatives, attended the section on statistics theory. This was the section that people had come for. Von Baumhauer opened the meeting with an homage to Quetelet, who had recently published a new edition of *Sur l'homme* under the title *Physique sociale*. Quetelet reciprocated by having Von Baumhauer appointed chairman of the section. Von Baumhauer, who had anticipated that the participants would speak various languages (and did nothing to impede them), appointed minutes secretaries for English, French, German and Italian.

The Belgian Xavier Heuschling, who had always operated in Quetelet's shadow, polarised the debate straight out of the starting block. This was somewhat unconventional and provoked some consternation. Heuschling was worked up about Vissering's stance on the dichotomy between the historical and mathematical schools of thought. He was irritated by the observation

Vissering made in his paper that the mathematicians had overtaken the historians and perhaps even made them redundant. Heuschling, who was an adherent of the historical school, believed that the mathematical approach was a matter for professors and other learned men, while historical statistics, which he identified with administrative statistics for argument's sake, should be entrusted to statesmen and statisticians in government service.

Quetelet intervened immediately. He was not interested in polarities. 'Statistics can be found everywhere', he said defiantly. He invoked great men like Laplace and Fourier, whom he had known personally. There was no point in having one party create the tables and the other explain and use them. 'One can do no greater harm to statistics than failing to apply a sufficiently scientific approach in the statistical bureaus.'[23]

Engel supported this position. He told the section that he had found 180 different definitions of statistics and held up the very case in which he kept them all. In his opinion, there was little point in trying to settle on a single definition. But then he complicated matters by trying to cobble together a definition of sorts. Statistics was, he said, the 'physics of human communities' of which there were four: first, the community of blood, 'the family, the race, the nation'; second, the community of co-existence (the way people lived together), from municipality to the state; third, the community of faith; and finally, the community of common interests – 'society' – though no one knows 'where it begins or ends'.[24] This was not a terribly helpful classification system. Engel concluded that the congress should not take a decision on Vissering's article but should leave the task of defining the limits of statistics to those engaged in the practice. Other prominent statisticians, including Farr, Legoyt and Semenov, concurred, bringing the discussion of Vissering's contribution to a close with the writer's assent.

In the discussion about Von Baumhauer's paper on methodology the same problem returned in a different guise. Again, the debate centred on the relationship between science and public administration, but this time against the backdrop of Von Baumhauer's annoyance about the frequent excess of questions asked in the context of statistical inquiries. This defect could be remedied with some scientific guidance. Fundamentally, everyone agreed with this principle. The question was how to articulate it in a resolution. Attempts to this effect soon sparked a debate on a recurring and sensitive theme: establishing a central commission and determining its remit. In France, Legoyt said, all too often ministries conducted surveys padded with extraneous questions because there was no oversight. Contrary to preconceived notions, centralisation was rare in his country.

According to Engel, where there were central commissions, their performance was mediocre at best. They were no more than an extension of executive power. Rarely was a central commission made up of an efficient mix of scholars and scientists and representatives of the legislative and executive powers. And even those that met this criterion were unable to accomplish much. With the increase in private-sector organisations with a public function, such as railway companies, insurers and banks, and the trend towards local autonomy, the only way that statistical societies could achieve anything was by pooling their resources. Clearly, Engel was thinking of the German situation and reintroduced a proposal that he had put forward in Berlin.

Digressions such as these threatened to turn the discussion into a litany of proposals based on national preferences. Engel wanted both centralisation and decentralisation: centralisation in order to harness scientific, political and administrative forces and decentralisation in order to ensure that political and economic realities were taken into account. Others, such as Britain's Lord Houghton, wanted nothing to do with centralisation, even if only in the service of science. The conferees eventually agreed on the formulation of a vague resolution calling for both scientific and administrative interests to be considered when statistical research was being prepared. And once again states that did not already have a central statistical commission were urged to establish one.

The second meeting of the section was also devoted to Von Baumhauer's article. He proposed to count only that which was directly related to the 'physiology of human beings and society'. He defined his terms later in the debate as all knowledge pertaining to the nature of human beings, from the physical, medical, intellectual and moral perspectives, and knowledge of human beings in all conceivable social circumstances. This was a dubious definition. Where precisely should the line be drawn? Quetelet took meteorology as an example. He had famously hypothesised that since temperature had a major influence on disease and death, it should be incorporated into statistics. Alfred Legoyt agreed and informed the section that the Paris Academy of Sciences had recently commissioned a study to determine whether the nearby forest had any effect on the intensity of hailstorms. In Legoyt's opinion, the positive findings of the study underlined the value to meteorology of the statistical method. Engel responded by pointing out that the issue at hand was the methodology of statistics: as a method, statistics was applicable to many things, but it would be wise to limit the scope of statistics as an autonomous science. Von Baumhauer believed that statistics was being confused with its methods. He said that statistics had many methods, of which the numerical approach was just one. His primary goal was to limit the congress agenda to topics that served the interests of public administration, and he felt there was no need for the congress to vote on this.

The discussion moved on to the training of junior statistics officials. In some countries, like Britain and the United States, completed questionnaires were simply sent to a central office where the counting took place. Farr explained that civil servants were paid 'by the piece' as in a factory. In many other countries, lower levels of government were responsible for processing the forms, and the officials working for these agencies needed to have some knowledge of statistics. Engel and Ficker explained that the statistics seminars in Prussia and Austria prepared civil servants for statistical work. But, Engel remarked, universities did not produce statisticians: 'people become statisticians by doing the work'. He compared his bureau to a laboratory where people learned hands-on.[25] There was no disagreement about the need to train statistics officials or about the other methodological issues. Nor did the section have any difficulty reaching consensus about the usefulness of multilingual commentary, the incorporation of percentages, the desirability of teaching statistics at various levels or the need to make birth registrations more precise.

A greater degree of controversy was expected during the session held the next day, Wednesday 8 September, which was largely reserved for a discussion of the graphics method. The last discussion on this topic, in Vienna in 1857, had yielded few concrete results. The author of the introductory paper, Johan M. Obreen, opened the debate. He presented a draft resolution and proposed to incorporate maps and diagrams in government statistics reports to improve education in, and simplify, the science of statistics. The contributions to the debate show that statisticians were not yet accustomed to assessing the value of graphical representations, though the British chemist Joseph Priestley had described the advantages precisely one hundred years before – in 1769. He was perhaps the first to use a timeline to illustrate the rise and fall of empires. In any case, he did his best to show his readers that it was possible to represent time as a line.[26] One might well assume that this idea caught on quickly and was soon being widely imitated, but apparently it was not that simple. After 1830 graphics started to appear regularly in academic periodicals and books, but even then the method was not widely accepted by statisticians.

The Austrian Adolf Ficker examined further the various ways in which figures could be presented, as if he was proposing a new idea. He rejected the notion of presenting absolute numbers graphically because it would require assigning a unique symbol to each figure, which would only add to the confusion. It made more sense to use relative numbers, which would make it possible to colour in geographical maps and create diagrams. However, it was unclear precisely how that was to be done. For example, what geographical unit could best be used? Ficker's answer was that the size of the geographical unit would be dependent on the level of homogeneity of the conditions underlying the data. This line of reasoning was difficult to follow but apparently required no explanation since everybody seemed to accept that it ensued from Quetelet's theories.

Following Ficker's lead, Engel referred to the wide variety of graphical representations that had been produced since the middle of the century. His thinking on the subject had clearly progressed since 1857. He remarked that many were no more than pictures. Before the congress could address this matter seriously, attempts would have to be made to standardise the graphics method for statistics. Ficker pointed out that the classification of series of observations posed another problem. Quetelet took up this issue. The objective was to discover the law underlying the observations. Dividing the waist measurements of a large group of people into four groups would yield little information. But examining twenty or thirty groups above and below the average would reveal patterns. This applied not only to body measurements, Quetelet pontificated, but also to human behaviour, such as crime. Despite Quetelet's intervention, the resolutions concerning the graphics method were insubstantial. The congress decided that graphs were useful for the popularisation of statistics, and should therefore be added to official statistical documents. As for other matters, it was up to the next congress to take further action.

Next the section addressed the matter of stillbirths, another long-standing issue. It seemed so simple but was in fact extremely complicated because the statisticians wanted to measure something that could not be measured in many countries due to inadequate registration. It would be difficult for statisticians to reach an agreement in this regard because that would require the medical and legal professions as well as local authorities in different countries to come to an understanding. Had the child lived for a time? If the mother died in childbirth, did the child die before or after her? Could it actually be considered a child (or merely a foetus)? These were matters that had a direct bearing on inheritance law and could not be resolved simply because statisticians wanted them to be. Regardless, their deliberations on the subject were impassioned. Several conferees explained how stillbirths were dealt with in their countries. The colourful descriptions revealed a great deal about the role of local government, the clergy, the justice system, physicians and midwives. Had the statisticians forgotten, as they often did, what their field of expertise was, or does this example demonstrate how serious they were in their desire to count – and observe – everything? Legoyt probably would have said the latter. When everyone had had their say and turned their attention to drafting a resolution, he said: 'The real question, the great question, that preoccupies us is this: how do we define a stillbirth?'[27] They were back where they had started on this issue.

It appears that the statisticians were looking for common ground on the matter of stillbirths, but unanimity vanished like snow in summer when the issue of mortality tables arose. Various conferees claimed expertise in this area and quarrelled about their use. Quetelet had to assert his authority to end a 'tis-'tisn't argument, after which the conferees were able to calmly discuss ideas on the best way to structure a mortality table. The private sector had a major interest in this matter. Life insurance companies were important actors in Great Britain and the United States, and as such were represented at the congress by influential actuaries such as Samuel Brown, Thomas Bond Sprague and Sheppard Homans. However, they were forced to yield to the assembled statisticians, who had little faith in the calculation methods employed by the insurance companies. Statisticians were able to align themselves, but only when they found a common adversary.

The most remarkable moment in the discussion about mortality statistics came when Quetelet admitted openly that he had compiled his comparative mortality tables from the national tables generated by Farr, Berg and others, without accounting for the way in which the original figures had been produced. He had detected regularity and so was not much interested in the method underlying the statistics. Legoyt, Farr and Engel felt that he was going a bit too far. Without contradicting Quetelet directly, they pointed out the marked differences between various countries in the average age of death. As with many other subjects, the way in which European countries registered their populations had a direct effect on the accuracy of mortality statistics. But the intractable difference of opinion on the best method of compiling mortality tables was also the result of contrasting arithmetic insights and a lack of criticism with regard to the sources of information.

At the close of the meeting, Engel took the floor. He expressed his wish to evaluate all the congresses, including the gathering in The Hague, before the final plenary session began. He acknowledged that too little had been achieved in terms of standardisation but also identified points of progress, such as the 'large association' of statistics directors that had evolved and the sharp increase in the production of statistical publications. It was imperative to make wise use of this situation. He suggested improving the congress's approach to the idea of international comparative statistics. Each central commission or statistical bureau would choose one subject on which to publish an international statistical report, in French since The Hague congress had proved it was the lingua franca of statistics. The official representatives would need to make separate agreements on this matter.

The official representatives discussed Engel's proposal on Monday 13 September – after the congress ended. He had divided up his project on international and comparative statistics into twenty-five themes and assigned one to each country. Little was accomplished in the way of implementation during the life span of the congress, but the project showed where consensus had been reached: French as the official language, the metric system and the franc as the unit of currency, though conversion would not take place until the final phase of the project. Always one for thoroughness, Engel also suggested that the national statistical bureaux compile a catalogue of statistical works. Speaking for the French, Legoyt and Wolowski insisted it would be an impossible task for French statisticians if they were expected to go back to the start of the international congresses. France, they argued, was not sufficiently centralised and, unlike Germany, it did not have a consolidated book trade catalogue. Others were less pessimistic and thought it would be fairly easy to compile a national statistical bibliography. In the end, the section agreed to publish a joint catalogue in 1870. Though it was beyond the power of the international statistical congress to implement Engel's ideas, they had illuminated the path to a new future. In 1869 the statisticians could not have known that the end of their congress movement was nigh, and that they would soon redirect their efforts to establish the International Statistical Institute in 1885.

Engel introduced the first section's draft resolutions at the plenary on Friday 10 September. He candidly informed the conferees that the section had rejected Vissering's original proposals and Heuschling's alternatives, and decided to propose to the congress that the object and boundaries of statistics were best left to the field to define. He believed that the solution to the factional conflict lay in a new science, 'demology', which would unite all the statistical schools of thought. In essence, this science concerned itself with the goals of every human being on earth. These goals could never be served through individual exploits but only through association and cooperation. In other words, the purpose of every human community was to make sure that any individual that was part of it could achieve his aims. The first aim was to be healthy, but thereafter all other aspects of life – physical, intellectual, moral, economic and political – were relevant. At this point, he also addressed the women in the room. In Engel's view, consumption was the measure of well-being and prosperity, and hence of man's purpose on earth. A statistics of consumption – focusing in particular on household expenditure, the province of the woman of the house – was the next great challenge.

Wolowski disagreed with Engel. He thought it was not necessary to invent a new science. He believed that statistics as it was known should be defined, and that it should be defined as a science that made 'social facts' comparable. Statistics was 'decidedly peculiar to the propensities and needs of our time', not only because it was the age of positivism, but also because statistics and democratisation were mutually reinforcing.[28] With such great differences of opinion among leaders of the congress it was evident that the plenary meeting had no choice but to decide to let the matter of defining statistics rest.

Semenov took the floor to inform the meeting about Von Baumhauer's methodology proposals. He was more concise than Engel and made only a few remarks about each draft resolution, all of which were subsequently adopted. The congress managed to reach agreement on several proposals which, though far from radical, were certainly substantial. They agreed to balance the needs of government, society and science, foster conformity between the various levels of statistical enterprise (in particular, between the envisaged central statistical commissions and the statistical bureaucracies), provide adequate training and instruction for officials, translate essential sections of national statistics publications into German, French or English, incorporate percentage conversions and calculate averages and standard deviations. The decisions concerning the internal organisation of statistics agencies were perhaps difficult to implement since the congress had no power to enforce compliance, but the technical agreements brought standardisation and professionalisation of official statistics a step closer.

Statistics overseas

The fifth section, the statistics of European overseas territories, drew many Dutch participants, a few Britons, two Spaniards and a Frenchman. It was obvious to everyone that this theme was of particular interest to the host country, but as a courtesy the young Englishman Thomas John Hovell-Thurlow, secretary of the British embassy in The Hague and author of the book *The Company and the Crown* (Edinburgh 1866), was appointed chairman. The idea of conducting the discussion in English was rejected, also out of courtesy. More problematic was the proposal to appoint former Minister of Colonies Guillaume Louis Baud as vice-chairman, to serve alongside Lieutenant-General Jan van Swieten and Professor Pieter Johannes Veth, who had likewise been appointed vice-chairs.

The nomination came from Graaf D.C.A. van Hogendorp, who acknowledged that the congress had no political interests but nevertheless his fellow member of the conservative party would have to be given an official function. The section agreed, but it had become clear that the topic of colonial statistics had an unmistakable political dimension. This was true, to a certain degree, of all the congress themes, only on colonial issues it was acceptable to admit it.

Rather than actually debating issues, the members of the section primarily exchanged information. Hovell-Thurlow surprised the section participants by presenting a recent statistical publication by Mooldie Abdool Sutief, an enlightened Muslim, whom he described as a member of the 'Young Bengal' party, which sought to foster the integration of European and cosmopolitan customs, ideas and laws. Several more publications by Europeans or more or less original inhabitants of the colonies were reviewed. The conferees wanted to know how reliable was the information that could be obtained locally. Some were concerned about the religious prejudices of Hindus and Muslims, others believed that – as in Europe – the respondents gave false information for fear of incurring higher taxes. For this reason, it was proposed to add a reliability indication to all colonial statistics reports. With the same scepticism, combined with a thirst for knowledge, they discussed the proposals for creating registries of births, deaths and marriages, and enlisting indigenous locals to help gather statistical data. The participants gave one example after another illustrating how primitive and backward indigenous populations were, but no one knew how to overcome this obstacle other than by paying locals well and showing appropriate respect.

The section attempted to use statistics to evaluate the abolition of slavery, and the participants were especially interested in the increase and decrease of population and production. In other words, they wanted to know whether the ethical decision also made economic sense, or at any rate whether it would work out for the best in the end. Lacking the desired statistical precision, they advanced ideas for acquiring more information about the status and composition of the population. However, the discussion yielded no feasible solutions for their predicament. In the plenary session, the draft resolutions of the fifth section passed without further discussion. On the one hand, the topic of colonial statistics was too far removed from the direct interests of European statisticians to merit the same attention as 'domestic' themes. On the other, the subject had the capacity to satisfy or even fuel the statisticians' urge to promote civilisation and development. They applauded the abolition of slavery, but failed to keep the 'Dutch' theme on the agenda in later years.

The plenary meetings adopted a series of section decisions that are not covered in detail above. These decisions concerned topics such as statistics pertaining to property in mortmain, pro bono legal services, bankruptcy and partnerships limited by shares, cadastral statistics (eighteen pages of questions and tables), the statistics of land credit, national income, taxation, issuing houses, municipal finances, trade and fish catches. As usual, the congress addressed a dazzling array of topics. The Hague congress, like those before it, spoke out in favour of implementing the metric system universally and making preparations to introduce a common currency.

The last item of business was to choose the location of the next gathering. The Austrian Ficker designated Switzerland, Russia and Hungary as the prime candidates. Von Baumhauer informed the conferees that during the banquet in Scheveningen the Russian delegate, Semenov, had rhapsodised about the good relations that the Netherlands and Russia had enjoyed since Peter the Great and that he was pleased to support Russia's bid. At the same time, he felt that every country was free to offer itself as a candidate. Victor Balaguer, the Spanish representative, eagerly announced that his country was in the running. Semenov followed suit and officially announced Russia's candidacy. Von Bouschen supported his countryman, resolutely calling upon Europe to do its utmost to finally discover the great unknown. Jules Schreyer, a delegate from the Imperial Free Economic Society in St Petersburg, made Russia's bid more attractive by offering free train journeys from the Prussian border. Though the decision would not be made until later, St Petersburg was the clear favourite.

Von Baumhauer and Vissering achieved in The Hague what they had set out to accomplish: to limit the number of topics, limit the number of participants from the host country, give ample attention to theory and methodology and create a place for colonial statistics. Nevertheless, it was apparent that the international congress needed to do more. There was a pervading sense that no real progress was being made. During the post-congress meeting of official representatives – an organisational innovation that would be discussed as such in St Petersburg – fervent attempts were made to launch a collective project. Tasks were assigned but no guarantees could be given. Some participants, including the Danish delegate Christian David, feared that The Hague would be the last congress. An unfamiliar sentiment had taken possession of the statisticians: doubt.

Notes

1   *Baedeker's Belgien und Holland. Handbuch für Reisende* (12th edn, Koblenz and Leipzig 1873), p. 223.
2   F. Allan, *De stad 's-Gravenhage en hare geschiedenis* (Amsterdam 1859) 5, as cited in H. Schmal, *Den Haag of 's-Gravenhage. De 19de-eeuwse gordel, een zone gemodelleerd door zand en veen* (Utrecht 1995), p. 92.
3   J.H. Furnée, 'Beschaafd vertier. Standen, sekse en de ruimtelijke ontwikkeling van Den Haag, 1850–1890', *Tijdschrift voor Sociale Geschiedenis* 27 (2001), pp. 1–32.
4   'Uit 's-Gravenhage', *Utrechtsch Provinciaal en Stedelijk Dagblad*, 7 September 1869 (I would like to thank Jan Hein Furnée for this reference).
5   Nationaal Archief, The Hague, Collectie 426 Familie Fock, 1842–1976, Mémoires over de jaren 1828–1901, inv. no. 4, pp. 441–442.
6   Carel Vosmaer cited in A. van der Woud, *Waarheid en karakter. Het debat over de bouwkunst 1840–1900* (Rotterdam 1997), p. 91.
7   'Uit 's-Gravenhage', *Utrechtsch Provinciaal en Stedelijk Dagblad*, 7 September 1869.
8   'Uit 's-Gravenhage', *Utrechtsch Provinciaal en Stedelijk Dagblad*, 9 September 1869.
9   M.M. von Baumhauer, Verslag der beraadslagingen op het Poenitentiair Congres, gehouden

te Frankfort a/M. 28, 29 en 30 September 1846 (Leeuwarden 1846); De landbouwkolonie te Mettray (in Frankrijk), een voorbeeld voor Nederland (Leeuwarden 1847).

10 N. Randeraad, 'The Dutch Path to Statistics (1815–1830)', in P. Klep en I. Stamhuis (eds), *The Statistical Mind in a Pre-Statistical Era: The Netherlands, 1750–1850* (Amsterdam 2002), pp. 99–123.

11 M.M. von Baumhauer, 'De statistiek', *De Gids* 13 (1849) I, 80.

12 *Ibid.*, 86.

13 S. Vissering, 'De statistiek in Nederland', *De Gids* 13 (1849) II, 17.

14 S. Vissering, *Herinneringen*, II, *Politische vertoogen* (Amsterdam 1863), XIV.

15 Nationaal Archief, The Hague, Tweede afdeling, Ministerie van Binnenlandse Zaken, Afdeling statistiek en voorgangers, inv. no. 8, draft resolution 2 January 1869.

16 M.M. von Baumhauer, *Idées-mères ou plan motivé d'un programme pour la septième session du congrès international de statistique* (The Hague 1868), p. 81.

17 *Ibid.*, p. 11.

18 *Ibid.*, p. 17.

19 S. Vissering, 'Limites de la statistique', Congrès International de Statistique à la Haye, *Compte-rendu des travaux de la septième session. Première partie. Programme* (The Hague 1869), p. 13

20 *Ibid.*, p. 18.

21 *Ibid.*, p. 180.

22 Congrès International de Statistique à la Haye, *Compte-rendu des travaux de la septième session. Seconde partie* (The Hague 1870), p. 10.

23 *Ibid.*, p. 38.

24 *Ibid.*, p. 39.

25 *Ibid.*, p. 55.

26 J. Priestley, *A New Chart of History* en *A Description of a New Chart of History, Containing a View of the Principal Revolutions of Empire that Have Taken Place in the World* (London 1769), cited in D.R. Headrick, *When Information Came of Age. Technologies of Knowledge in the Age of Reason and Revolution 1750–1850* (Oxford 2000), pp. 124–125.

27 *Compte-rendu des travaux de la septième session, Seconde partie*, p. 88.

28 *Ibid.*, p. 438.

8

'Sadder and wiser': St Petersburg 1872 and Budapest 1876

Russia and Hungary, the hosts of the last two editions of the international statistical congress, worked hard to prepare and execute the task entrusted to them. The St Petersburg congress was probably the most stylish of all the congresses, and that had everything to do with the city itself. In the course of the nineteenth century St Petersburg acquired the qualities of a European capital. Between 1800 and 1850 the population grew from 220,000 to 487,000. By 1869 the city had 550,000 inhabitants and by 1890 over one million. Infrastructural improvements were made as the city industrialised. Railway connections established with Warsaw and Tallinn in 1862 intensified St Petersburg's economic and cultural contacts with north-western Europe.

The cityscape assumed an international elegance. Théophile Gautier noted in his account of his travels in Russia that Nevski Prospekt was teeming with carriages, and the scene even surpassed the bustle of Paris at times.[1] The 'Passage', a magnificent two-storey arcade housing a theatre, shops and cafés, and featuring a glass roof, opened on Nevski Prospekt at the end of the 1840s. The enormous St Isaac's cathedral was completed in 1856. At the time, its dome was the third largest in the world. The nobility and the nouveau riche had mansions built in eclectic styles in a departure from the harmony of the eighteenth century. Tranquillity gave way to excitement. Musicians, painters and dancers sought and found access to the ultimate in European modernity. Max Nordau, a correspondent from the *Pester Lloyd* who visited the city to cover the creation of the Three Emperors' League in 1873, was overwhelmed by the contrasts between Budapest, his city of birth, and the Russian capital. In his eyes, St Petersburg in the 1870s was comparable to Vienna before the revolution of 1848 and Paris in the heyday of the Second Empire: the city 'revels in enjoyments with an intensity of which even the hedonistic Romans were incapable'.[2]

The participants of the St Petersburg congress stayed in the best hotels in the city at the city's expense. Coaches were made available to drive them to their meetings each day. The conferees and their families were invited to receptions and offered excursions nearly every day. Right before the opening session, they were treated to a boat trip to the botanical gardens and the islands. Afterwards, they were received at the Kamenny Ostrov (Stone Island), the palace of the Grand Duchess Helena Pavlovna, and were welcome there throughout their stay in the city. During the congress, they had free admission to the museums of St Petersburg; the Hermitage was of course the favourite. Near the end of the congress, the programme offered a visit to Kronstadt's Forts: 280 people boarded 16 boats flying national flags. The newspapers wrote of a magnificent procession.[3] Congress participants were given free passage on the Russian railways during their journey to and from St Petersburg. The contrast between this and the simplicity of the congress in The Hague could not have been starker.

The congress in Hungary was similar to the gathering in Italy nine years earlier in that the host was a young nation eager to introduce itself to the world. Budapest became a single city when Buda, Pest and Óbuda were unified in 1873. The city's population increased from 54,000 in 1800 to 140,000 in 1850 and 370,000 in 1880, following the trend of rapid growth in European capitals in the nineteenth century. Budapest experienced a period of large-scale modernisation. The city government commissioned designs for new boulevards, bridges and public buildings. Between 1850 and 1890 the German–Austrian culture was gradually supplanted and Budapest became a Hungarian city.[4] In 1865, the Academy of Sciences moved to a brand new building in Lipótváros, the government district. The monumental neo-Renaissance building marked the transition to a new national architectural style, and it was the most obvious location for the international statistical congress.

The conferees were offered an extensive social programme in Budapest too. The closing dinner was held in Svábhegy, in the hills of Buda. The Hungarian winegrowers invited the participants to their vineyards to taste over eighty wines. The statisticians were overwhelmed by so much hospitality. Engel hoped that the tenth congress (which never took place) would be held in a smaller, less imposing place so that it would be easier to concentrate on statistics. Afterwards, the British health inspector Frederic J. Mouat wrote: 'The balls, banquets, excursions, receptions, and other entertainments were organised on a princely scale, and had but one defect, if it be permissible to use such a term in relation to arrangements which were perfect in themselves. They were, if possible, too numerous, and too great a strain upon the mental and physical capacities of those engaged in the serious work of the congress.'[5]

While Europe's statisticians gathered at their international statistical congresses, the continent was in a constant state of unrest. After the Franco-Prussian War of 1870–1871, the turbulence subsided, but this did not bring better times for the congress. Indeed, the new balance of power in Europe was strengthening the nation-state at the cost of international cooperation. Not since the Congress of Vienna had the countries of Europe been so focused on finding means to shore up their own states and so heedless of good international relations. The long economic depression that began in 1873 fostered national self-interest and protectionism, which was not conducive to the free circulation of statistical data. The attempts made by the international statistics community to streamline their organisation by, for example, establishing a 'supranational' permanent commission, were at odds with the inward orientation of national governments.

Moving the international congress to Eastern Europe was a logical step. Russia had implemented sweeping reforms in the early 1860s, and it was no longer possible to pass over this great power. And the 'new' state of Hungary was determined to present itself as a progressive nation eager to integrate into modern Europe. Eastern Europe, however, was no more united than Western Europe. Relations between Russia and Hungary had been anything but strong in the recent past. The Hungarians had not forgotten the tsarist intervention in their revolution of 1848–1849. Russia's interference had thrust them back into a period of neo-absolutism that lasted until 1867. Since then, Hungary had been pursuing liberal policies under Ferenc Deák's leadership. The Austro-Hungarian Compromise of 1867 transformed the Habsburg Empire into a dual monarchy, in which only defence, foreign relations and the financial aspects of these two policy areas were managed jointly. Hungary's parliament immediately introduced new legislation on ethnic minorities, education and criminal law. It was prepared to pursue a more liberal course than the tsarist empire. Despite the reforms implemented by Alexander II, Russia continued to represent old Europe politically and economically. A tsarist autocracy was not a particularly fertile environment for liberalism, the rule of law and political participation. Further reforms had no chance of success without the support of the machinery of state. As we have seen before, statistics was a faithful and versatile servant to both regimes.

Statistics in Eastern Europe

There were three traditions of statistics in tsarist Russia: descriptive statistics (based on the ideas of German scholars), political arithmetic and administrative surveys, all of which had flourished to a certain degree back in the eighteenth century. The ministries that replaced the collegial administrative bodies in 1802 were charged with the task of producing regular statistical reports. This marked the beginning of official statistics in Russia and very nearly coincided with the rise of Napoleonic statistics in Western Europe. A statistics department was set up at the Ministry of Police in 1811 and transferred to the Ministry of the Interior in 1819. The Russian state developed an ambivalent attitude towards statistics. In the 1830s and 1840s, the work of prominent statisticians like Karl Hermann, Dmitri P. Zhuravskii and Konstantin I. Arseniev was censored. Hermann and Arseniev were even removed from their chairs at the University of St Petersburg for publishing numbers that presented an unfavourable picture of conditions in the countryside.

Under the careful management of Ivan Vernadski – a participant of the congresses in Vienna, London and Berlin – statistics came to be seen in a better light. He convinced the Russian bureaucracy that statistics was a useful instrument for state-building.[6] The statistics department at the Ministry of the Interior underwent a gradual process of professionalisation, primarily as a result of the major reforms of the early 1860s. In 1863 Russia established the Statistical Council and Central Statistical Committee in compliance with the congress's decisions concerning the organisation of national statistics. Petr Petrovich Semenov was appointed director of the Committee. In 1869 he organised the first 'modern' census in St Petersburg, which resulted in a headcount correction of nearly 25 per cent.

Following the abolition of serfdom, the zemstvo system was promulgated in 1864. A zemstvo was an elected provincial body vested with a certain degree of autonomy. Zemstvos conducted regular statistical inquiries, which together formed 'the largest collection of statistics on an agrarian society'.[7] The zemstvo statisticians were well versed in Quetelet's ideas and the German Historical School's criticism of it. The first Great Russian statistical congress took place in 1870, assembling hundreds of statisticians from all parts of the empire. Notwithstanding Western Europe's impression that Russian statistical practice was weak – an opinion shared by many Russians – the statistical apparatus of the vast Russian empire was probably much more advanced in the nineteenth century than many people thought.

Hungarian statistics had a less illustrious history but the Hungarian statisticians, under the leadership of Károly Keleti, were determined to change that. Keleti had first proposed a national statistics for Hungary at the congress in The Hague – two years after the formation of the dual monarchy and Hungary's partial independence. Following the short-lived experiment of 1848–1849, Hungarian statistics was entirely subordinated to Austrian absolutism: 'The statistical publications of the day, in a foreign language, could be but of little importance to us.'[8] The Hungarian Academy of Sciences, which had fought for the national language and culture since 1825, established a statistical committee in 1860 to foster a national statistics that 'could no more be the work of strangers than a national history'.[9] The Academy's statistical committee independently organised a census with the assistance of churches and private citizens and published the results in 1864. After the Austro-Hungarian Compromise a statistics department, managed by Keleti, was set up at the Hungarian Ministry of Agriculture, Industry and Trade. In 1871 the department became an autonomous agency. Keleti looked to Europe for examples of organisation and implementation practices, which were based on the decisions of the international statistical congress. The young Hungarian state was in the advantageous position of being able to build new state institutions from scratch. Keleti also sought an audience for his statistics. Shortly after independence, he organised a series of public courses which drew some three hundred people from all levels of public administration and society.

Keleti was a member of a new generation, though he was only a few years younger than his Russian colleague Semenov. Keleti would go on to play an important role in the establishment of the International Statistical Institute in 1885, by which time Semenov had retired from administrative statistics. Statistics was just one of Semenov's many pursuits. He was born in 1827 on the country estate of Urusovo in what is now the province of Lipetsk, 400 kilometres south of Moscow.[10] Like many members of the Russian nobility, Semenov attended cadet school in St Petersburg as a first step towards a career in government service. His exceptional examination results secured him an exemption from military service.

He studied science at the University of St Petersburg in its early days when there were relatively few students and intensive contact between lecturers and students was possible. Semenov graduated in three years rather than the usual four. As a student he moved in progressive circles with people who were highly critical of the tsarist bureaucracy and serfdom. He became friends with Nikolai Danilevski, a utopian socialist in his younger years who would later gain renown for his pan-Slavist work *Russia and Europe* (1869). Semenov kept any tendencies he may have had towards radicalism under control and focused his energy on science instead. The arrest and imprisonment of his friend Danilevski in 1849 reinforced his desire to always strive for compromise and a positive outcome. This is not to say that he always sought the path of least resistance. His ideal was the neostoic notion of 'constantia', or constancy, a virtue that was fed by an unwavering fortitude unmoved and unperturbed by random circumstances. From the vantage point of that ideal, he felt a sense of affinity with Quetelet's ideas of the average man.

In 1849 Semenov became a member of the Russian Geographical Society, which had been established four years earlier as one of many initiatives taken under Tsar Nicolas I to enhance the prominence of science. The society attracted many progressive scientists and scholars who would make a name for themselves in the reform years under Alexander II. Semenov came into contact with young intellectuals and civil servants with whom he would prepare the decree abolishing serfdom in 1860.

To aid his recovery from a serious illness Semenov decided to make a tour of Central and Western Europe in 1853. After travelling for several weeks in Central Europe and France he attended a course of lectures by Gustav Rosé and Carl Ritter in Berlin in the summer of 1853. He was translating and annotating Ritter's standard work, *Die Erdkunde von Asien*, for the Russian Geographical Society. To his delight, he had an opportunity to speak to an ageing Alexander von Humboldt, who encouraged him to undertake a study expedition to Tian Shan in Central Asia that he been planning. He practiced by trekking on Mount Vesuvius on various occasions in 1854 and 1855.

Back in St Petersburg, Semenov began the preparations for his trip to the Tian Shan Mountains, a virtually unexplored area. Semenov had to conceal his true destination from the Russian government since even military expeditions had not penetrated that far and private initiatives were discouraged; it was the time of the Crimean War and its aftermath. Semenov was in the Tian

Shan region, a remote corner of the Russian empire, close to the north-western border of China, in 1856 and 1857. On several occasions he encountered Fyodor Dostoyevsky, an acquaintance from his university days, who spent the final years of his exile there in Semipalatinsk. But the highpoint for Semenov was undoubtedly his expedition into the heart of Tian Shan, where no European had set foot before. He refuted several assumptions of Ritter's and Humboldt's concerning the composition of the soil in the region, measured the snow-line in the mountains and discovered uncharted glaciers. The trip solidified Semenov's reputation as a geographer. In 1860 he was appointed chairman of the physical geography department of the Geographical Society and vice-president of the Society in 1873. He organised several more expeditions to Central Asia and in 1906 was permitted to officially add 'Tian-Shanski' to his surname.

Semenov was known primarily as a geographer, but he had more than one string to his bow. After his career in public administration he became a senator in 1882, which allowed him to devote time to his other passion, the fine arts. He had been collecting paintings by Dutch and Flemish masters of the sixteenth and seventeenth centuries since the 1860s. In 1910 – four years before his death – he donated the entire collection (600 paintings and 3,500 engravings) to the Hermitage.

In addition to being an explorer, art collector, civil servant and politician, Semenov was a statistician. In the nineteenth century these areas of interest were more closely related than we can imagine today. The director of Austrian statistics, as we have seen, was a proficient painter; Vissering must have had an extraordinary collection of photographs; Quetelet was happiest associating with writers and artists, and had even composed an opera. The Russian Geographical Society assisted and inspired Semenov in all his areas of endeavour (during his expeditions he was always accompanied by a painter, who recorded the landscapes and people they encountered along the way). Chorography – the describing and mapping of geographic regions – was closely related to statistics. Semenov spent over two decades working on a monumental dictionary of geography and statistics of the Russian Empire, which was published in volumes between 1863 and 1885.

When Semenov returned from his first trip to Tian Shan, St Petersburg was engrossed in a debate about major reforms, including the abolition of serfdom. Many of the key figures involved in the debate were people he knew from the Geographical Society. The Society gave the progressive position a voice, while the majority of landowners took a reactionary stance. Semenov, himself a large landowner with serfs working his estates, was in favour of transferring land to freed farmers. He supported the ideas of the enlightened bureaucrat Nikolai A. Milyutin, who was pursuing far-reaching reforms from inside the Ministry of the Interior.

Semenov was a distant cousin of General Jakov I. Rostovtsev, a conservative, who had been put in charge of the committees responsible for drafting the new legislation. Rostovtsev was impressed by Semenov's reputation for neutrality. Rostovtsev believed that because Semenov had managed to stay out of the heated debates raging in St Petersburg he was in a position to help ease divisions. Semenov's statistics expertise was a key factor in Rostovtsev's decision to add him to the committee of reformers, because once serfdom was abolished it would be necessary to calculate how much rent farmers would have to pay landowners and how much tax landowners would owe the state. This was a thorny issue because both payments had to be based on rational grounds, the cadastre, or land registry, while the Russian agrarian economy was geared towards 'sufficiency' and subsistence rather than profit maximisation. These were quantities that were difficult to record in a cadastre.

Semenov was well-versed in these matters, not only as a landowner but also as a statistician. He was familiar with the international debate on cadastral description, but also knew that the Russian cadastre poorly reflected the realities of the agrarian economy. Nevertheless, for many decades it had been the primary source of information about the state of agriculture in Russia, but that information generated an incomplete picture of Russian farmers that was considerably more pessimistic than reality warranted.[11]

Rostovtsev died before the emancipation process was completed, so Semenov's role grew significantly. He was the linchpin of the committee for most of 1860, and acquired a good position at the State Chancellery for his efforts. In 1863 he was appointed to the statistical council of the Ministry of the Interior and sent to the international congress in Berlin. At the same time, he was made director of the statistics department, a position he would occupy for nearly twenty years. For those two decades, he would serve as the 'first ambassador' of Russian statistics in Europe.

The final congresses

The congress in St Petersburg was delayed by the Franco-Prussian War of 1870–1871, but in August of 1872 representatives of every country in Europe made their way to the Russian capital.[12] Despite recent events, there was no sign of animosity among the delegates. The plenary meetings were held in the great hall of the Noblemen's Assembly, which – according to a description in the *Sankt-Peterburgskie Vedomosti* (St Petersburg Gazette) – was beautifully decorated. At the entrance was a banner bearing the coat of arms of the Russian empire, surrounded by various national flags. The names of the cities that had hosted previous congresses were engraved onto two shields. Twenty-two shields containing the French names of the countries that had sent representatives were placed around the hall.[13]

Reorganisation was the intractable issue facing the congresses of St Petersburg and Budapest (and the meetings of the permanent commission held in between). The first problem was the choice of language. As always, the organisers had to agree on the languages that participants would be allowed to speak at the congresses in Russia and Hungary. The Russian preparatory commission proposed French and Russian as the official languages. The use of other languages in debates would be tolerated if the bureau (i.e. the minutes secretaries) agreed. Engel and Farr insisted that everyone had a right to speak his national language, whether or not the bureau approved: this was 'not an issue of politics but of statistics'.[14] The Russians had no choice but to concede.

The Hungarian preparatory commission tried to steer a middle course by adopting a rule stating that in addition to French and Hungarian, every language would be tolerated. Engel protested that this was too weak and maintained that everyone had the right to speak another language. This gave rise to a discussion about whether the proceedings should be translated into French immediately. They decided that was a step too far and settled for a summary. The reports show that French was the dominant language at both congresses, but German was widely spoken. Displaying a good sense of humour, the Italian delegate Cesare Correnti addressed the conferees in Latin at the close of the Budapest congress.

The census was a fixture at every congress, and other topics such as population registers, migration, nationalities and mortality tables were frequently discussed in relation to it. In St Petersburg the issue of actual population versus legal population came up again, though the congress had decided years before to count the actual population. Rather than proceeding along the path they had chosen, the statisticians backtracked and introduced a third option: the effective or regular population (whether or not '*de séjour habituel*', people who lived at a particular address but were absent during the headcount, were deemed members of the legal population depended on the type of registration that a country or city maintained). With his usual enthusiasm for definitions, Engel remarked that he could come up with a few more alternatives and that there were even categories of persons who eluded every definition.

It gradually became clear that each country had slightly different aims for their population counts and had adopted different methods. For example, Russia's primary interest was in the headcount for each administrative unit rather than a total population count. Ernst Engel wanted to know everything and had introduced individual, multilingual census cards in Prussia. To make the operation even more efficient, Engel had instructions for filling in the cards distributed two weeks before the count. The census officials gave every household envelopes in which to keep their cards until they could be retrieved. Not wanting to be outdone by Engel, the others explained the ways in which their countries were professionalising the census process, though many had to admit that high illiteracy rates made individual census cards practically useless. It was obvious that previous congresses had affected the way censuses were held, but there was still disagreement on some of the vital issues, such as precisely who should be counted. Engel was not surprised. 'The population is about as unstable as the atmosphere', he said.[15] Granted, it was difficult to make agreements on standardisation, but the world was not standing still and statisticians appeared to have trouble keeping up. The congress adopted a resolution that permitted diversity and stood in stark contrast to the original objectives. They elected to abandon the uniform rules concerning the legal and regular population, 'given the time- and country-specific variations in legislation.[16] Quetelet must have heard this with sorrow in his heart.

And so it went with most of the topics addressed in St Petersburg and Budapest. It gradually dawned on the statisticians that in their search for uniformity they had discovered diversity. In fact, they had laid the foundations for diversity to a certain extent themselves. Every few years they got each other excited about a wide range of statistical research but all too often they lacked the means to fully harmonise their data. Sometimes, though, there were surprising exceptions. Crime statistics, for example, had been on the agenda since Brussels and discussed in detail in Paris, Vienna, London and Florence. The moral dimension of crime statistics appealed to statisticians. Prior to the congress in St Petersburg, Georg Mayr of Munich indicated that little progress had been made in the area of international crime statistics and he knew why. Because crime statistics were closely connected to national criminal law, they were more difficult to generalise than, say, the number of births or deaths.[17] The Russian preparatory commission agreed. M. Rajevski and J. Oetin wrote in the congress programme that though national statistics provided some insight into the state of a country, they had little comparative value.[18] The St Petersburg congress was able to build consensus on detailed forms which apparently could be used to standardise the registration of crimes and sanctions, irrespective of the criminal justice system involved.

Was it easier to reach agreement on topics that seemed to have no impact on national interests? The congresses in St Petersburg and Budapest again tackled the issue of using graphics in statistics. The advantages and disadvantages had been discussed at length in Vienna and The Hague. One of the experts, Georg Mayr, sent Semenov a report before the St Petersburg congress in which he elegantly and lucidly contrasted his cartographic method with Quetelet's averages. This was a minor revolution in the international statistics community. If they wanted statistics to play a significant role in society, Mayr argued, statisticians could not settle for large averages and abstractions but would need to define the spatial and temporal dynamics of social phenomena with as much precision as possible. The 'geographical method', based on a detailed territorial classification, was the appropriate instrument. According to Mayr, 'for each concrete statistical problem [this method] abandoned the easy use of large averages applied to large administrative units, and instead sought the precise geographical boundaries of natural groups of facts'.[19] A proper spatial unit was defined as the area in which an average could reasonably be calculated. These units were very different from states or provinces. By this method, Mayr was able to calculate child mortality in Southern Germany with greater precision than ever before by taking local averages as his starting point rather than national or regional averages. Mayr's smallest possible 'natural' units came to replace Quetelet's averages.

Semenov was taken with this method, and had employed it in a survey of the Russian population. He believed that Russia's administrative units were ill-suited to drawing connections between population figures and the 'underlying causes'.[20] Zones shaped by natural forces were a much better place to start. Semenov's background in physical geography made him highly receptive to Mayr's ideas. Those ideas, however, increased the complexity of the statisticians' task. The impossibility of counting everything was matched by the difficulty of determining the appropriate natural environment for obtaining usable averages.

Other experts, like Adolf Ficker of Vienna and Hermann Schwabe, director of the statistical bureau in Berlin, also submitted proposals on cartography and diagrams to the Russian preparatory commission. Schwabe believed that the use of diagrams was essential to the advancement of statistics: 'Anyone who considers the massive, pompous calculations which, unfortunately, are commonplace in statistical publications cannot possibly be amazed by the unpopularity of statistics, but must be inspired to cultivate an appealing form of presentation that is different from, and supplementary to, the tables. We must not forget that our generation more than any other is striving for a *natural representation of all things*, because that is the starting point of nearly all political and social reforms'.[21]

Ficker's and Schwabe's main points related to chorographic mapping (descriptive mapping of countries or regions), identifying discontinuities in statistical series and shading (practice had shown that differences could be depicted only by working with gradations of light and dark). In Schwabe's opinion, graphical representations were ideally suited to illustrating correlations, provided that the underlying numbers were made comparable by, for example, converting absolute numbers into percentages. Harmonising cartographic symbols was a more difficult task. Even thornier was the question of whether diagrams and maps could be used together. Draft decisions concerning all of these problems were drawn up and would be discussed at the congress. Semenov added a draft decision calling for every subsequent congress to set up an exhibition of graphical representations of statistics, complete with explanatory text.

The subcommittee that prepared the final decisions on graphics methods presented modest proposals in the end. Schwabe introduced the topic at the general meeting. With little optimism, he said the problem was not unlike trying to square a circle. Gesturing towards the diagrams that the participants had put on display, he concluded that full comparability should not be the goal. He explained to his audience that 'every diagrammatic table has a highly individual character ... In this domain, the mind and the imagination should have complete freedom. Uniformity may be applied as appropriate, but our statistical diagrams should be allowed to reflect national customs and individual practices'.[22]

The French economist Émile Levasseur came to the same conclusion regarding statistical maps: 'Each map should be made by different means, in accordance with the diversity of objectives'.[23] Those were heavy-handed conclusions at a congress that set such great store by standardisation. Engel was troubled. Semenov, also a member of the old guard, rushed to his aid, suggesting that the congress should decide that the time was not ripe for uniform rules on this matter. Everyone was satisfied that this was a good compromise.

The topic came up again in Budapest in the form of a report on the exhibition of graphical representations at the congress (at least one proposal *was* put into practice). Semenov, Ficker, Mayr and Levasseur saw the 686 catalogue numbers and could only conclude that the quantity was impressive despite the lack of guidance from the congress on this matter. Every country had submitted samples of maps and diagrams. Maps of all descriptions were a speciality of the dual monarchy and Russia, while Britain had always had a preference for diagrams. In the commission's view, graphical representations could be useful in popularising statistics and help representatives of the state and the private sector understand statistical overviews.

It would be unfairly limiting to assess the successes of the international statistical congresses merely on the basis of their stated objectives. The Budapest congress continued to explore contemporary mass society and initiated new statistics covering such areas as large cities, public limited companies, industrial accidents, railways, epidemic diseases, spring water, agriculture and forestry, cottage industries, institutions for factory workers etc. As specialisation increased, it became decidedly more difficult to maintain unity and ever more important to streamline the decision-making process. But that was somewhat problematic.

What was the best way to organise international cooperation at the interface of science and public administration in the nineteenth century? Statisticians had been trying to answer this question since their first gathering. Without a mandate, they could promise each other very little and there was as yet no model for European integration. The most they could do was try to make their decision-making process as efficient as possible.

The permanent commission: beginning of the end

Each congress attracted large numbers of participants from the organising country. On the one hand, this was good for the congress's image in the host country. On the other, the experts felt that the large turnout diminished the quality of the debate. Since Berlin, the official delegates had been meeting in advance at what they called the *avant-congrès*. The proposal to establish a permanent commission dated from the Berlin congress too, but nothing had come of it. The official representatives had convened after the congress in The Hague to try to come up with a new organisational structure. With his experience in large-scale reform, Semenov must have thought he had what it took to facilitate a solution at his congress. Not surprisingly, reorganisation of the congress was a priority during the preparations.

Semenov distinguished between conferences of 'free' scientists and scholars and conferences of statisticians. Statisticians needed the direct cooperation of their governments to actually implement their joint decisions. This scenario was virtually unknown in international law, which made the statistical congresses both unique and complicated. They combined private and public elements, making it all the harder to develop an adequate decision-making procedure. Semenov summed up the main problems: first, official representatives formed a small minority in the plenary meetings, which meant that technical matters received too little attention; second, the congress agenda was drafted by the national preparatory commissions, which were not particularly well-versed in international issues; third, a thorough inventory had yet to be made of the political, administrative, legal and social state of affairs in participating countries; fourth, there was too little continuity in the activities of the congress; and finally, the congress had no way of verifying whether its decisions had been implemented.

Semenov believed that the solution was to improve the distribution of tasks among 'producers' and 'consumers' of statistics. He believed that the best results could be achieved by establishing a permanent commission, based on the ideas put forward by Ernst Engel in Berlin in 1863. The permanent commission would comprise the directors of national statistics agencies and official representatives who had attended at least five congresses. The commission's remit would include monitoring compliance with congress decisions, producing the congress agenda and facilitating international statistics projects. The commission would convene at least twice between congresses, and one such meeting was to be scheduled in the run-up to the opening session. Future congresses would be held once every five years.

The proposal was discussed at the pre-congress meeting of official representatives. Von Baumhauer, who spoke first, raised serious objections. He thought that the five-year interval was much too long and that an excess of rules would place too great a burden on the organising countries. He also had concerns that a permanent commission would lack authority if its membership was constantly changing, a scenario he envisaged and feared based on his experience in the area of crime statistics. By contrast, Engel endorsed the proposal wholeheartedly. The majority of the delegates fell in line with Engel and Semenov.

It soon became clear that determining the make-up of the commission was going to be an awkward problem. The debate that ensued foreshadowed the innumerable discussions and negotiations that would take place within the context of European integration nearly a century later. Should all parties be represented proportionally or was a functional approach preferable? Should they take a political or a technical line? Should membership be restricted to government officials, or could scientists and scholars who, for example, had a seat on a national central statistical commission be seconded to the permanent commission? No one wanted to cause affront, but it was obvious that membership would have to be limited. And who would preside over the permanent commission?

Constant Bodenheimer, a Swiss delegate, suggested limiting the size of the commission to five members in order to maximise its effectiveness. Despite his proclivity towards compromise, Semenov fiercely opposed this restriction. How could five members adequately represent countries of which they were not citizens? How would they acquire the knowledge they needed about those countries? Bodenheimer answered: 'The argument that some countries would be unrepresented in the permanent commission is of secondary importance to me. What we do is not politics, it is science, and science is not Russian, not German, not English, not Spanish.'[24] And he noted examples of international committees for telegraphy and calculating the meridian. Incisive as ever, Engel observed that statistics – given its thousands of objects – was not comparable to telegraphy or identifying the precise location of the meridian.

Professor Émile Worms of the University of Rennes, one of five official French representatives, and the Swedish statistician Fredrik Berg wondered how permanent the permanent commission was to be. A single meeting would not be sufficient to guarantee continuity. Without realising it, they were anticipating the arrangement that would replace the congress ten years later: a permanent institution.

Since the *avant-congrès* was unable to reach a decision, Semenov, Engel, Émile Yvernès, Max Wirth and Von Baumhauer formed a subcommittee and agreed to work out a detailed proposal. They made the following suggestions: the permanent commission would lay the groundwork for international statistics; it would meet at least once between congresses; the organiser of the congress held most recently would chair the permanent commission. Sensibly, the subcommittee did not provide any specifics as to membership. However, the subsequent discussion of their proposal revealed that the five men had given it some thought. Most countries would be represented, provided all the participants in the international statistics project launched at the congress in The Hague submitted nominees. Unrepresented countries could delegate their director of national statistics. This arrangement was adopted at the St Petersburg congress. Twenty-seven representatives (eight from Germany) attended the first meeting of the permanent commission in Vienna in 1873. There was no one there from Britain. Karl von Czoernig, by then retired from active service, was one of the ten guests of honour. The commission attended to several pending matters and assessed the progress on the international statistics project. Like the congress, the permanent commission was unable to achieve any major breakthroughs in Vienna or at its second meeting in Stockholm in 1874.

The permanent commission met again immediately before the congress in Budapest. Initially, there was some confusion as to the purpose of their meeting. Had they convened in their capacity as the commission or was their meeting actually the pre-congress? It was also unclear precisely who the rightful members of the permanent commission were. This uncertainty signified a lack of unity and efficacy, which was compounded when the permanent commission, having finally disentangled itself from other bodies, evaluated its priority project – international statistics. Little progress had been made on the international statistics series commissioned at the congress in The Hague, as the first inventory of results taken at the St Petersburg congress showed.

Levasseur had developed a system of geographical divisions for Europe and the rest of the world that the authors would be expected to abide by. His division of Europe into four zones is somewhat remarkable from a modern-day perspective: North-Western Europe comprised Britain and the Nordic Countries; Eastern Europe was actually just Russia; Central Europe included Austria-Hungary, Switzerland, Germany, the Netherlands, Belgium and France; and Southern Europe covered the remaining Mediterranean countries. At least on this point there was agreement. The rest of the project posed a much greater challenge, as would become clear when the time came to evaluate it again in Budapest, seven years after the congress in The Hague. The French were making headway with their statistical overviews of the agriculture industry and civil and commercial law in Europe. Not to be outdone, the director of the statistical bureau of the city of Budapest, Joseph Körösi, announced that he had completed an international statistical survey of large cities. Luigi Bodio presented a survey of savings banks, which he himself described as deficient. Anders Nicolai Kiaer of Norway had published the first volume of commercial shipping statistics, but he never completed the work.

The permanent commission met again in Paris in 1878, but this meeting would be the last. It appears that they had plans to continue, because they made yet another attempt to define the remit and composition of the commission. The statistics service of the German empire was strongly opposed to a provisional charter, and the fact that the commission would be based in Paris, where an international library and the editorial office of the planned newsletter would be housed, was an insurmountable obstacle. By all appearances, Chancellor Otto von Bismarck personally forbade the Prussian statisticians to attend any new meetings of the commission. The commission cancelled a scheduled meeting in Rome in 1879 without setting a new date and Keleti resigned as chairman.[25] The line of continuity was severed. Without a permanent commission, there would be no more congresses, and with that an era ended, as the poet says, 'not with a bang but a whimper'.

Quetelet's legacy

The end of the international statistical congress cannot be attributed solely to the utopian visions of uniformity or organisational impotence. After a quarter of a century, a generation of statisticians had disappeared from the scene. For various reasons many of the key figures who had been involved from the very beginning – Quetelet, Visschers, Von Baumhauer, Czoernig, Maestri, Legoyt and Dupin – were not in Budapest. The Budapest congress paid tribute to the statisticians who had passed away since the previous congress. Charles Dupin, already a man of advanced years when he managed the Paris congress, had died in 1873. Louis Wolowski, one of the many Poles who had fled to France in 1831 and acquired French nationality, died shortly before the congress. Semenov gave a brief eulogy for Christian David, who had represented Denmark since 1853. Others paid homage to Samuel Brown, Hermann Schwabe, director of the Berlin statistical bureau, and Edouard Horn, who had only recently returned to

Hungary, his home country after roving around Europe.

But the man who was missed most of all was, of course, Adolphe Quetelet. He made his final appearance in St Petersburg, where he tried one last time to explain the principles of probability to his most faithful supporters: 'In our science things are probable, but some probabilities are more evident than others; take life expectancy – you could say that a man aged 77, like myself, is unlikely to have more than two or three years to live and you would seldom be mistaken.'[26] However many errors we can attribute to Quetelet, he was right about that. In 1874, he succumbed to illness.

Ernst Engel, considered by many to be his most fervent student and likely successor, delivered a long speech on the achievements and the shortcomings of the father of international statistics. He admitted that his words were more polemic than eulogy, but that was fitting to the memory of Quetelet. Putting Quetelet's life into a broader context, Engel quoted what Franz Xaver Neumann-Spallart had written in the Vienna *Neue Freie Presse* immediately after Quetelet's death: 'Erudite Europe has grown old.' With the passing of giants like John Stuart Mill, Justus von Liebig, David Friedrich Strauß, Jules Michelet and now Quetelet 'the best branches of European intellectual life had fallen leaf by leaf'.[27]

Following Neumann, Engel explained that before Quetelet man believed that, as the culmination of Creation, he was the centre of the universe and everything around him was subject to laws from which he alone was exempt. Building on Vico and Laplace, Quetelet developed the idea that laws controlled human life, too. If this was the case, then the mathematical method Quetelet knew so well from astronomy could be used to analyse social phenomena. From this ensued the familiar metaphor of the average man, who like any tribe or state was subject to the law of averages.

Engel used this metaphor to explain the innovation that Quetelet had brought to the world. 'In essence,' said Engel, 'he was a determinist. The search for causal links in what appeared to be voluntary acts of individuals was at the core of all his studies.' With his approach, he made moral statistics and the mathematical method mainstream. But would his contribution withstand the test of time? Had statistics become an autonomous discipline? Was the 'average man' a useful concept?

Engel answered these questions with great caution. He wondered why Quetelet had remained so passive in the face of growing criticism of his work, especially from Germany. Engel pointed out that many thought Quetelet had never fully recovered from the stroke he suffered in 1855. He published nothing of consequence after 1855, only revised editions of his earlier work. Should the statisticians assembled at the congress take the criticism of the master to heart? 'Are we pursuing the wrong goals?' Engel wondered aloud.[28] It was irrefutable that statistics had failed to acquire the autonomous status that Quetelet had so passionately advocated. More and more voices were saying that statistics was nothing more than an auxiliary science. Even in Belgium statistics had become 'science's Cinderella'.

But Quetelet's statistics, his 'social physics', stimulated the development of a science 'which has still not been properly named'. Some called it 'sociology', some 'mass psychology', and others 'demography' or 'demology'.[29] The latter was coined by Engel himself and would be as unsuccessful as Quetelet's 'social physics'. It was up to Quetelet's followers to continue his work, and strive for an overall 'system of human interactions'.

Engel acknowledged indirectly that he was troubled by the tenacity with which Quetelet sought the natural laws that controlled human interaction. In his opinion, Quetelet took too little account of the political laws that were sometimes the product of compelling circumstances but usually the outcome of a battle between political parties. Consequently, the object of moral statistics, 'that which presents itself for quantification', is the result of political arbitrariness, so how can abiding laws be at its root? Engel revealed a similar reservation with respect to the 'average person'. What would an average of all physical, mental and moral characteristics look like? And even more important, what use would it be? In practice, facts that reflect special circumstances were more useful than an average of everything and everyone.

With that, the bottom dropped out from under the international statistical congress, or at least Quetelet's version of it. Engel could only conclude that statisticians would never be able to make the same observations at the same time, like meteorologists and hydrographers. The international statistics project was well on its way to becoming a waste of time: '... despite two decades of congress decisions on the use of identical census and summary forms for all branches of statistics, no such forms are being used in any area of statistics in any of the civilised states'.[30] Nevertheless, the congress could leave a legacy behind if statisticians upheld the objectives formulated in Berlin in 1863 by standardising statistical publications, generating statistics reports on state and society so that questions of international consequence could be answered, promoting appreciation of statistics and organising regular meetings of statisticians from all over the modern world. Engel found it regrettable that issues like the living standard of the working class, which had been on the agenda in 1853, had not been given more attention. He referred to the work of Édouard Ducpétiaux in Belgium and Frédéric Leplay in France, and hoped that small-scale precision studies of that kind would be conducted more frequently. 'It should be possible to construe the volumes and patterns of production and consumption from the actual income and expenditure of workers (*of whom only an adequate number of typical and characteristic representatives are observable*) with a level of precision that import and export statistics could never provide'[31] (emphasis added). This was a cautious step towards sampling, a method that would not be widely accepted until the twentieth century. Despite his good intentions, Engel had set forces in motion that would erase the name of Adolphe Quetelet from the collective memory.

Engel would have liked nothing better than to set up an international Quetelet foundation to award prizes and travel grants and subsidise international statistical publications. Quetelet was, after all, the 'embodiment of internationality'.

He immediately added that the international legal rules needed to accomplish this were nonexistent. What Europe could not offer statistics, it could not give one of its champions either.

Engel's realism must have been discouraging. Neither the congress nor the permanent commission was viable – that much was already clear in 1876. Was there any scope for progress and, if so, what shape would it take? What was left of the optimism that had drawn the first conferees to Brussels in 1853? By the end of the 1870s the statistics community was certainly sadder, but was it also a bit wiser? Though the congress movement did not survive, it is not unreasonable to suggest that the statisticians had actually achieved a great deal. Statistics had become an integral part of public administration. The epilogue attempts to evaluate the benefits of the statistical congresses.

There is no call to end on a negative note. According to the *Oxford English Dictionary*, 'sad' originally meant 'orderly and regular in life; of trustworthy character and judgement; grave, serious', which explains the combination of 'sad' and 'wise' in the expression. In that sense, the statisticians were undoubtedly sadder and wiser after nine international congresses. They had made a serious attempt to elevate statistics to a higher plane, but the uniformity they sought remained elusive. For the time being, statistics would continue to develop along national lines. Europe may have become more orderly, but in many respects it was still an unknown quantity.

Notes

1   T. Gautier, *Voyage en Russie* (Paris 1866–1867) I, p. 116.
2   M. Nordau, *Erinnerungen Erzähtt von ihm selbst und von der Gefährtin seines Lebens* (Leipzig and Vienna n.d.), p. 56.
3   *Peterburgskie vedomosti*, 18/30 August 1872.
4   C. Horel, *Histoire de Budapest* (Paris 1999), p. 160; K. Bakker, *Boedapest. Metropool in het hart van Europa* (Amsterdam 1996).
5   F.J. Mouat, 'Preliminary Report of the Ninth International Statistical Congress, held at Buda-Pesth, from 1st to 7th September 1876', *Journal of the Statistical Society of London* 39 (1876) no. 4, 642–643.
6   E. Kingston-Mann, 'Statistics, Social Science, and Social Justice: the Zemstvo Statisticians of Pre-Revolutionary Russia', in S.P. McCaffray and M. Melancon (eds), *Russia in the European Context 1789–1914. A Member of the Family* (New York 2005), pp. 117–118.
7   D. W. Darrow, 'The Politics of Numbers: Zemstvo Land Assessment and the Conceptualization of Russia's Rural Economy', *The Russian Review* 59 (2000), 54.
8   Ch. Keleti, 'Hongrie', in: Congrès International de Statistique à la Haye, *Compte-rendu des travaux de la septième session du 6 au 11 septembre 1869, Troisième partie* (The Hague 1871), p. 46.
9   *Ibid.*
10 W. Bruce Lincoln, *Petr Petrovich Semenow-Tian-Shanskii: the Life of a Russian Geographer* (Newtonville, MA, 1980).
11 D.W. Darrow, 'Statistics and "sufficiency": toward an intellectual history of Russia's rural crisis', *Continuity and Change* 17 (2002), pp. 63–96.
12 *Rossiiskii gosudarstvennyi istoricheskii arkhi,v St Petersburg*, Historical Archives of the Russian State (St Petersburg), Ministry of the Interior (MVD), Central Statistical Committee,

1290 (1870) reg. 2, dossier no. 62, letter from the minister of the Interior to the Ministry of Finance, 25 April 1871.

13   *Petersburgskie vedomosti*, 9/21 August 1872.

14   Congrès International de Statistique, *Compte-rendu de la huitième session à St-Pétersbourg. Deuxième partie, Travaux du congrès* (St Petersburg 1874), p. 6.

15   *Ibid.*, p. 101.

16   *Ibid.*, p. 113.

17   Congrès International de Statistique, *Compte-rendu de la huitième session à St-Pétersbourg. Première partie, Programme* (St Petersburg 1872), fifth session, p. 1.

18   *Ibid.*, p. 7.

19   *Ibid.*, first session, p. 53.

20   *Ibid.*, p. 55.

21   *Ibid.*, annexes, p. 62.

22   Congrès International de Statistique, *Compte-rendu de la huitième session à St-Pétersbourg. Deuxième partie, Travaux du congrès* (St Petersburg 1874), p. 383.

23   *Ibid.*, p. 387.

24   *Ibid.*, p. 41.

25   J.W. Nixon, *A History of the International Statistical Institute 1885–1960* (The Hague 1960), p. 9.

26   *Ibid.*, p. 139.

27   Cited in Congrès International de Statistique, *Compte-rendu de la neuvième session à Budapest. Deuxième partie, Travaux du congrès* (Budapest 1878), p. 89.

28   *Ibid.*, p. 100.

29   *Ibid.*, p. 102.

30   *Ibid.*, p. 108.

31   *Ibid.*, pp. 109–110.

Afterword

The series of international statistical congresses ended somewhat abruptly with the Budapest gathering in 1876. The participants were unwilling to admit that they would not meet again in that context, but it soon became clear that they would have to temper their usual optimism. A tenth congress, should it ever be convened, would have to be based on a different model. That very debate had already played out at recent congresses but without concrete results. The congress expected a great deal of the permanent commission it had established in St Petersburg, but in four sessions the commission failed to make any significant headway.

Articles published in international statistics journals conveyed the urgency of the need for organisational reforms. Frederic J. Mouat, a British health inspector, was critical of the Budapest congress. In a report for the Statistical Society of London he claimed that too little had been achieved because there had been too much on the agenda. This was a shortcoming that had impeded progress at several previous congresses. British businessman and journalist William Newmarch, a long-time member of the board of the Statistical Society of London, scornfully referred to the congresses as 'international picnics' which had accomplished next to nothing in twenty years.[1] British scepticism about unity in Europe is nothing new.

Anyone who has followed the debate about the future of the European Union will have seen many parallels between contemporary events and the dealings of the international statistical congresses. A Eurosceptic would have written off Quetelet's international statistics project as an obvious failure, and he would be inclined to regard the congresses as an attempt to reconcile incompatible interests, which is the reason he would consider the process of European integration a hopeless task. He would liken the rotating presidency of the European Union and the resulting succession of national priorities to the practice of setting successive congress agendas in the capitals of Europe. Quetelet and Jean Monnet were members of the same moribund breed. The comparison seems obvious but it is inaccurate. We don't know what the future has in store for the European Union, but we do know that the field of international statistics continued to evolve along various lines after the international statistical congress met its end.

The International Statistical Institute (ISI), which was established in London in 1885 and still exists today, was in many ways the congress's natural successor. The founders of the ISI had faithfully attended the final congresses and learned that politics and scholarship, states and statistics were not compatible. The drafters of the ISI statutes and by-laws were careful to avoid establishing close connections between national governments and the new institute. The first president, Sir Rawson W. Rawson, stressed that the institute was 'purely a private and scientific body. While the direct object of the Congresses and the Permanent Commission was to influence Governments, that of the International Statistical Institute is to acquire and perfect statistical knowledge and to furnish information which may be useful to those Governments who may pay attention to its proceedings'.[2] He could hardly have been more cautious. The congresses had demonstrated that statisticians would have to professionalise in order to meet their goals. The founders of the ISI emphasised the professionalism of the institute and limited membership to 150 to keep out the 'free-floating intelligentsia', who in the opinion of many experts had had a disruptive influence on the congresses. Membership did not reach 150 until the end of the century. Professionalisation was a broad goal encompassing many areas of activity. ISI publications, in particular the Bulletin de l'Institut international de statistique, addressed the subjects and methods of statistical research more systematically and with greater precision than the congress reports. In addition to the internationalisation process, a process of 'localisation' was taking place: more and more large cities were establishing their own statistics bureaus, and the directors of those bureaus made their way to the ISI.

The project launched by Quetelet and his contemporaries transcended Europe's borders. From the start it was universal, or at any rate a project for the 'civilised world'. This universalism – though not particularly typical of the nineteenth century – manifested itself in many new ways. Following Britain's example, governments attempted to promote trade through international exhibitions modelled on the first world's fair, the Great Exhibition in London in 1851. Pope Pius IX transformed Catholicism into a transnational, centrally administered political force to resist liberalism and anticlericalism. With the First International, Marx and his followers attempted to promulgate socialism worldwide.[3] But universalism could also be found on a smaller scale in the standardisation of weights and measures, free postal traffic and the gold standard. Statisticians sought to combine the large and the small. They had cosmopolitan ideals but were also interested in the details. The congress met Quetelet's universalist aspirations in one respect: non-Europeans attended each successive congress in increasing numbers. The United States, Brazil, Egypt and

Japan sent representatives to Budapest. The ISI continued this trend.

Evaluating the 'technical' achievements of the congress poses a greater challenge. In Budapest, Engel admitted that the congress had accomplished only a fraction of the objectives its resolutions were intended to fulfil. But in making this observation Engel had overlooked the law of unintended consequences, perhaps the only law that nineteenth-century statisticians were loathe to understand, but it applied to them nonetheless. Though standardisation remained elusive, government statistics organisations in European countries were undergoing a process of convergence. Statistics experts formed an international network and maintained contact with one another through journals, correspondence, exhibitions and conferences. More and more countries established their own central statistical commission comprised of civil servants, scientists and scholars. Though styles of implementation varied and not every country had a commission, clearly a European standard was emerging.

The Netherlands finally got its commission in 1892 (the Rijkscommissie had failed in 1861 and the statistics department at the interior ministry was shut down in 1878), but the source of inspiration was the consensus that statisticians had reached in the early days of the congress.

Graphical methods gradually caught on and came to be widely used. There was still no uniformity in the design of maps and diagrams, but everyone realised that the advantages outweighed the disadvantages. Statisticians would henceforth exchange and compare methods and procedures of census-taking and other forms of demographic inquiry.

The international statistical congress was a typical example of a conduit for the transnational transfer of scholarship and political and technological ideas, a form of communication that would take off over the course of the nineteenth century. The international statistics community was one of many overlapping networks at the crossroads of science and public administration.[4] The records show that many of our 'statisticians' attended other conferences at the time, on prisons, public health, demography and poverty reduction. They were also to be found at meetings of idealist societies, such as the Friends of World Peace. A majority of the participants in the international statistical congresses shared a moderate liberal vision of social reform within the existing political and economic system. The congress gave the liberal movement a more powerful voice, and though there were subtle variations of message, that voice was heard in nearly every country in Europe.

The statisticians reinforced in each other the idea that statistics was an essential part of the solution to social and economic deprivation resulting from population growth, industrialisation and urbanisation. Despite the opposition that the champions of statistics encountered and persistent scepticism regarding figures and tables, statistics came to play a more important role on the public stage. To a certain extent statistics stood in for democratic reform in authoritarian states such as tsarist Russia and the Habsburg monarchy. If the truth was to be found in numbers, the opinions of the people's representatives were secondary or even superfluous. In Germany, statistics was the refuge of liberals, even in conservative Prussia. Social legislation enacted in the late nine-teenth century reflects the ideas that Ernst Engel and his peers were developing back in the 1850s and 1860s based on, for example, their statistical studies of credit facilities offering relief to the poor. Statistics – in its old and new forms – became a vehicle of social reform in the states that pursued democracy early on. The practice of studying workers' budgets, first introduced in Belgium back in the 1840s and then discussed at the first congress in 1853 (though not without controversy), became widely accepted in France, Britain, the Netherlands and other countries before the First World War. Quetelet's holistic approach was abandoned for targeted inquiries and sampling.[5]

There was yet another unintended consequence. Quetelet needed the help of the national state to meet his goal of universal standardisation. For their part, states were devoting all their administrative energy to building the nation: railways, schools, social legislation and statistics contributed to the inter-nal 'unification' of the European nation-states. Paradoxically, Quetelet's goal became less and less achievable as the national state assumed greater control over statistics. The evolution of national statistics was driven forward by a barrage of incentives – a process in which the international congresses played a role – and became inextricably linked to the modern administrative state. Every European state was undergoing its own processes of modernisation, so statistics was serving perpetually changing goals and evolving along different institutional lines. The international statistical congress had little success in consolidating the range of styles that emerged as a result of these processes.[6]

The nineteenth century was an age of lists and classifications, of encyclopae-dias, bibliographies and lexicons. Many of those projects were unviable from the start. Many towers of Babel were erected only to meet the same fate as the first. *The Allgemeine Encyclopädie der Wissenschaften und Künste in alphabetischer Folge von genannten Schriftstellern bearbeitet und herausgegeben von Johann Samuel Ersch und Johann Gottfried Gruber* (Leipzig 1818–1889) was discon-tinued though 167 volumes had been published.[7] Statistics as practiced by Quetelet and his contemporaries was an expression of the nineteenth-century desire for general, well-ordered knowledge. For many of the participants, the international statistical congress was symbolic of an endeavour to measure and know everything. To them, statistics represented the possibility of understand-ing and resolving all of the problems that plagued society. The mid-nineteenth century was characterised by a restless search for an adequate science of society that would also serve as a guide for government action.[8] It must have seemed for a brief time that statistics could bridge the gap between the natural sciences, which already had a solid structure, and the social sciences, which were still taking shape. If only society would conform to the same laws as nature … For a while there was hope that statistics would make objective policy and unchal-lenged state intervention possible. This testing of the boundaries of science and politics was a circuitous process that led to new definitions (remember Engel's 180 definitions of statistics), new terminology (sociology, demography) and new explanations for socio-economic changes (class struggle). In the end, statistics did not emerge the big winner, at least not in a way that the pioneers had envisaged. Statistics had become an auxiliary science, essential perhaps, but ancillary rather than primary.

As boundless as Quetelet's enthusiasm had been, his undertaking was doomed from the start due to its nature and structure. The international statistics project was impeded by problems of implementation in the context of the emerging nation-states and by the impossibility of accumulating statistics on everything and everyone, though that was the overriding objective of the statisticians. Moreover, the social laws that they imagined would emerge from the numbers remained largely obscure. The history of international statistics in the nineteenth century is a tragic narrative. The utopian idea of an active and successful international congress movement was a miscalculation of enormous proportions. The power of numbers proved to be finite.

Notes

1 Cited in the discussion following F.J. Mouat, 'Second and Concluding Report of the Ninth International Statistical Congress, held in Buda-Pesth, in September 1876', *Journal of the Statistical Society of London* 40 (1877) no. 4, 555.

2 J.W. Nixon, *A History of the International Statistical Institute 1885–1960* (The Hague 1960), pp. 14–15.

3 W. Kaiser, 'Transnational Mobilization and Cultural Representation: Political Transfer in an Age of Proto-Globalization, Democratization and Nationalism 1848-1914', *European Review of History* 12 (2005), 403–424.

4 M. Herren, '"Die Erweiterung des Wissens beruht vorzugsweise auf dem Kontakt mit der Außenwelt." *Wissenschaftliche Netzwerke aus historischer Perspektive*', *Zeitschrift für Geschichtswissenschaft* 49 (2001), 197–207.

5 A. Desrosières, *La politique des grands nombres. Histoire de la raison statistique* (Paris 1993).

6 L. Schweber, 'Manipulation and Population Statistics in Nineteenth-Century France and England', *Social Research* 68 (2001), 547–582.

7 Herren, 'Die Erweiterung des Wissens', 204.

8 J. Heilbron, *Het ontstaan van de sociologie* (Amsterdam 1991).

Bibliography

Archives

Archives de l'Académie royale de Belgique, Brussels
Archives Quetelet

Archives départementales des Hautes-Alpes, Gap
Série M: Administration générale et économie 1800–1940 (Répertoire numérique 1984)

Biblioteca Nazionale Braidense, Milan
Carteggio Luigi Bodio

Bibliothèque royale de Belgique/ Koninklijke Bibliotheek van België, Brussels
Archives Auguste Visschers

Geheimes Staatsarchiv Preußischer Kulturbesitz, Berlin
I. Hauptabteilung:
Repositur 77, Ministerium des Innern, Abteilung I, Section 13, Nr. 99, Bd. 1 Statistische Generalversammlungen des In- und Auslandes (1853–1859)
Repositur 77, Ministerium des Innern, Abteilung I, Section 13. Titel 94 (Statistik)
Repositur 77, Ministerium des Innern, Band 5, Abteilung Z (Zentralabteilung), Preußisches Statistisches Landesamt
Repositur 90, Staatsministerium, Titel 51

Generallandesarchiv, Karlsruhe
Abteilung 76, Staatsdiener
Abteilung 233, Staatsministerium
Abteilung 236, Ministerium des Innern
Abteilung 237, Finanz Ministerium

Nationaal Archief, The Hague
Tweede afdeling, Ministerie van Binnenlandse Zaken, Afdeling statistiek en voorgangers

Collectie 426 Familie Fock, 1842–1976, Mémoires over de jaren 1828–1901

Rossiiskii gosudarstvennyi istoricheskii arkhi,v St Petersburg
Ministry of the Interior (MVD), Central Statistical Committee, 1290 (1870) reg. 2, dossier no. 62

Sächsisches Hauptstaatsarchiv, Dresden
Ministerium des Innern, no. 689 (Bestallungsdekrete beim statistischen Büreau, 1850–1874)

Stadsarchief, Bruges
Hedendaags Archief, Bevolking en burgerlijke stand, Statistique – recensement de population 1846, no. 1; Statistique – Population 1856

Universiteitsbibliotheek, Utrecht
Collectie Ackersdijck

Reports of the International Statistical Congresses, 1853–1876

Compte rendu des travaux du congrès général de statistique réuni à Bruxelles les 19, 20, 21 et 22 septembre 1853 (Brussels 1853)
Compte rendu de la deuxième session du congrès international de statistique réuni à Paris les 10, 12, 13, 14 et 15 septembre 1855 (Paris 1856)
Rechenschafts-Bericht über die dritte Versammlung des internationalen Congresses für Statistik, abgehalten zu Wien vom 31. August bis 5. September 1857 (Vienna 1858)
Report of the Proceedings of the Fourth Session of the International Statistical Congress held in London July 16th, 1860, and the Five following Days (London 1861)
Die fünfte Sitzungsperiode des internationalen statistischen Congresses in Berlin vom 4. bis 12. September 1863. I, Bericht über die Vorbereitung des Congresses (Berlin 1865); *II, Bericht über die Verhandlungen des Congresses* (Berlin 1865)
Compte-rendu des travaux de la sixième session du Congrès International de Statistique réunie à Florence les 30 Septembre, 1, 2, 3, 4 et 5 Octobre 1867 (Florence 1868)
Congrès International de Statistique à la Haye, *Compte-rendu des travaux de la septième session. Première partie. Programme* (The Hague 1869); *Compte-rendu des travaux de la septième session. Seconde partie* (The Hague 1870); *Compte-rendu des travaux de la septième session du 6 au 11 septembre 1869. Troisième partie* (The Hague 1871)
Congrès International de Statistique, *Compte-rendu de la huitième session à St-Pétersbourg. Première partie, Programme* (St Petersburg 1872); *Compte-rendu de la huitième session à St-Pétersbourg. Deuxième partie, Travaux du congrès* (St Petersburg 1874); *Compte-rendu de la huitième session à St-Pétersbourg. Troisième partie, Travaux présentés au congrès* (St Petersburg 1874)
Congrès International de Statistique, *Programme, avant-propos* (Budapest 1876); *Compte-rendu de la neuvième session à Budapest. Deuxième partie, Travaux du congrès* (Budapest 1878)

Publications

150 Jahre amtliche Statistik in Baden Württemberg (Stuttgart 1970)

Adolphe Quetelet 1796–1874. Exposition documentaire présentée à la Bibliothèque Royale Albert Ier à l'occasion du centenaire de la mort d'Adolphe Quetelet (Brussels 1974)

Allan, F., *De stad 's-Gravenhage en hare geschiedenis* (Amsterdam 1859)

Anderson, B., *Imagined Communities: Reflections on the Origins and Spread of Nationalism* (2nd edn, London 1991)

Anderson, O., *Suicide in Victorian and Edwardian England* (Oxford 1987)

Annals of the Royal Statistical Society 1834–1934 (London 1934)

Annuario statistico italiano 1 (1857–1858); 2 (1864)

Armatte, M. 'Une discipline dans tous ses états: la statistique à travers ses traités (1800–1914)', *Revue de synthèse* 112 (1991), 161–205

Baedeker's Belgien und Holland. Handbuch für Reisende (12th edn, Koblenz and Leipzig 1873)

Bakker, K., *Boedapest. Metropool in het hart van Europa* (Amsterdam 1996)

Baumhauer, M.M. von, *De landbouwkolonie te Mettray (in Frankrijk), een voorbeeld voor Nederland* (Leeuwarden 1847)

Baumhauer, M.M. von, 'De statistiek', *De Gids* 13 (1849) I, 79–88

Baumhauer, M.M. von, *Idées-mères ou plan motivé d'un programme pour la septième session du congrès international de statistique* (The Hague 1868)

Baumhauer, M.M. von, *Verslag der beraadslagingen op het Poenitentiair Congres, gehouden te Frankfort a/M. 28, 29 en 30 September 1846* (Leeuwarden 1846)

Beaud, J.-P. and J.-G. Prévost (eds), *L'ère du chiffre. Systèmes statistiques et traditions nationales / The Age of Numbers. Statistical Systems and National Traditions* (Québec 2000)

Behnen, M., 'Statistik, Politik und Staatengeschichte von Spittler bis Heeren', in: H. Boockmann and H. Wellenreuther (eds), *Geschichtswissenschaft in Göttingen. Eine Vorlesungsreihe* (Göttingen 1987), 76–101

Blum, J., *In the Beginning. The Advent of the Modern Age. Europe in the 1840s* (New York 1994)

Bonß, W., *Die Einübung des Tatsachenblicks. Zur Struktur und Veränderung empirischer Sozialforschung* (Frankfurt a.M. 1982)

Boschloo, T.J., *De productiemaatschappij. Liberalisme, economische wetenschap en het vraagstuk der armoede in Nederland 1800–1875* (Hilversum 1989)

Boterman, F., *Moderne geschiedenis van Duitsland* (Amsterdam 1996)

Bourguet, M.-N., *Déchiffrer la France. La statistique départementale à l'époque napoléonienne* (Paris 1988)

Bracke, N., *Een monument voor het land. Overheidsstatistiek in België, 1795–1870* (Gent 2008)

Brian, E., 'Bibliographie des comptes rendus officiels du congrès international de statistique (1853–1878)', *Annales de Démographie Historique* (1990), 469–479

Brian, E., *La mesure de l'État. Administrateurs et géomètres au XVIIIe siècle* (Paris 1994)

Brian, E., 'Observations sur les origines et sur les activités du congrès international de statistique (1853–1876)', *Bulletin de l'Institut International de Statistique. Actes de la 47ème session*, Tome LIII, Livraison I (Paris 1989), 121–139

Brian, E., 'Statistique administrative et internationalisme statistique pendant la seconde moitié du XIXe siècle', *Histoire & Mesure* 4 (1989), 201–224

Brown, L., *The Board of Trade and the Free-Trade Movement 1830–1842* (Oxford 1958)

Bruce Lincoln, W., *Petr Petrovich Semenow-Tian-Shanskii: The Life of a Russian Geographer* (Newtonville, MA 1980)

Bulletin de la Commission de Statistique and *Algemene volks-, nijverheids- en handelstelling op 31 December 1947*, I (Brussels 1949)

Bulmer, M., K. Bales and K.K. Sklar (eds), *The Social Survey in Historical Perspective, 1880–1940* (Cambridge 1991)

'Carl Freiherr von Czörnig', *Statistische Monatsschrift* 15 (1889), 545–554

Chadwick, E., 'On the best Modes of representing accurately, by Statistical Returns, the Duration of Life, and the Pressure and Progress of the Causes of Mortality amongst different Classes of the Community, and amongst the Populations of different Districts and Countries', *Journal of the Statistical Society of London* 7 (1844), 1–40

Chaline, J.-P., 'Louis-René Villermé: l'homme et l'œuvre', in: L.-R. Villermé, *Tableau de l'état physique et moral des ouvriers employés dans les manufactures de coton, de laine et de soie* [1840] (Paris 1989)

Correnti, C., 'Congressi di statistica', *Annuario statistico italiano* 2 (1864), XLIII–LIV

Correspondance mathématique et physique(1825–1839)

Cullen, M.J., *The Statistical Movement in Early Victorian Britain: The Foundations of Empirical Social Research* (New York 1975)

Czoernig, C. von, *Ethnographie der oesterreichischen Monarchie* (3 volumes, Vienna 1857)

Czoernig, C. von, *Oesterreichs Neugestaltung 1848–1858* (Stuttgart and Augsburg 1858)

Czoernig, C. von, *Systematische Darstellung der Budgets von Grossbritannien (1862), Frankreich (1862) und Preussen (1861), nebst einer Uebersicht der Budgets von Baiern, Belgien, den Niederlanden, Portugal, Spanien und Russland* (Vienna 1862)

Darrow, D.W., 'The Politics of Numbers: Zemstvo Land Assessment and the Conceptualization of Russia's Rural Economy', *The Russian Review* 59 (2000), 52–75

Darrow, D.W., 'Statistics and "sufficiency": Toward an intellectual history of Russia's rural crisis', *Continuity and Change* 17 (2002), 63–96

Denkschrift der k.k. statistischen Zentralkommission zur ihrer fünfzigjährigen Bestandes (Vienna 1913)

Desrosières, A., *La politique des grands nombres. Histoire de la raison statistique* (Paris 1993)

Diamond, M. and M. Stone, 'Nightingale on Quetelet', *Journal of the Royal Statistical Society* 144 A (1981) part 1, 66–79; part 2, 176–213; part 3, 332–351

Dieterici, (C.)W.(F.) *Über preußische Zustände, über Arbeit und Kapital. Ein politisches Selbstgespräch seinen lieben Mittbürgern gewidmet* (Berlin and Posen 1848)

Drobisch, M.W., *Die moralische Statistik und die menschliche Willensfreiheit. Eine Untersuchung* (Leipzig 1867)

Dufau, P.A., *Traité de statistique ou théorie de l'étude des lois d'après lesquelles se développent les faits sociaux suivi d'un essai de statistique physique et morale de la population française* (Paris 1840)

Dupâquier, J. and M. Dupâquier, *Histoire de la démographie: la statistique de la population des origines à 1914* (Paris 1985)

Dupin, C., *Forces productives et commerciales de la France*, 2 vols (Paris 1827)

Eastwood, D., '"Amplifying the Province of the Legislature": The Flow of Information and the English State in the Early Nineteenth Century', *Historical Research* 62 (1989), 276–294

Eastwood, D., 'Rethinking the Debates on the Poor Law in Early Nineteenth-Century England', *Utilitas* 6 (1994), 97–116

Engel, E., 'Beiträge zur Statistik des Krieges von 1870–71', *Zeitschrift des Königlichen Preussischen Statistischen Bureaus* 12 (1872), 1–320

Engel, E., 'Das statistische Seminar und das Studium der Statistik überhaupt', *Zeitschrift des Königlichen Preussischen Statistischen Bureaus* 11 (1871), 181–211

Engel, E., *Der Werth des Menschen* (Berlin 1883)

Engel, E., *System der Demologie* (Berlin 1871)

Eyler, J.M., *Victorian Social Medicine. The Ideas and Methods of William Farr* (Baltimore, MD and London 1979)

Fallati, J., *Einleitung in die Wissenschaft der Statistik* (Tübingen 1843)

Farr, W., 'Inaugural Address', *Journal of the Statistical Society* 34 (1871), 409–423

Farr, W., 'Vital Statistics; or the Statistics of Health, Sickness, Diseases, and Death', in: J.R. McCulloch (ed.), *A Statistical Account of the British Empire: Exhibiting Its Extent, Physical Capacities, Population, Industry, and Civil and Religious Institutions* (London 1837) II, 567–601

Favero, G., *Le misure del Regno. Direzione di statistica e municipi nell'Italia liberale* (Padova 2001)

A. Ficker, 'Die dritte Versammlung des internationalen Congresses für Statistik zu Wien om september 1857', *Mittheilungen aus dem Gebiete der Statistik* 6: 3 (1857) 1–162

Fischer, W. and A. Kunz (eds), *Grundlagen der historischen Statistik von Deutschland: Quellen, Methoden, Forschungsziele* (Opladen 1991)

Fletcher, J., 'Moral and Educational Statistics of England and Wales', *Journal of the Statistical Society of London* 10 (1847), 193–233; 11 (1848), 344–366; 12 (1849), 151–176; 189–335

Földes, B., 'Ernst Engel', *Allgemeines Statistisches Archiv. Organ der Deutschen Statistischen Gesellschaft* 11 (1918–1919), 229–245

Furnée, J.H., 'Beschaafd vertier. Standen, sekse en de ruimtelijke ontwikkeling van Den Haag, 1850–1890', *Tijdschrift voor Sociale Geschiedenis* 27 (2001), 1–32

Gautier, T., *Voyage en Russie* (Paris 1866–1867)

Geschichte und Ergebnisse der zentralen amtlichen Statistik in Österreich 1829–1979. Festschrift aus Anlaß des 150jährigen Bestehens der zentralen amtlichen Statistik in Österreich (Vienna 1979)

Geyer, M. and J. Paulmann (eds), *The Mechanics of Internationalism. Culture, Society, and Politics from the 1840s to the First World War* (Oxford 2001)

Gigerenzer, G. et al., *The Empire of Chance: How Probability Changed Science and Everyday Life* (Cambridge 1989)

Gioia, M., *Filosofia della statistica* (Milan 1826)

Gneist, R. von, *Geschichte und heutige Gestalt der englischen Communalverfassung oder des Selfgovernment* (Berlin 1863²)

Goldman, L., 'The Origins of British "Social Science": Political Economy, Natural Science and Statistics, 1830–1835', *Historical Journal* 26 (1983), 587–616

Goldman, L., 'Statistics and the Science of Society in Early Victorian Britain. An Intellectual Context for the General Register Office', *Social History of Medicine* 4 (1991), 415–434

Gossart, E., 'Adolphe Quetelet et le prince Albert de Saxe-Cobourg (1836–1861)', *Bulletins de l'Académie Royale de Belgique, Classe des Lettres et des Sciences Morales e Politiques* (1919), 211–254

Guerry, A.M. *Essai sur la statistique morale de la France* (Paris 1833)

Guerry, A.M. and A. Balbi, *Statistique comparée de l'état de l'instruction et du nombre des crimes dans les divers arrondissements des académies et des cours royales de France* (s.l. 1829)

Guillard, A., *Éléments de statistique humaine ou démographie comparée* (Paris 1855)

Hacking, I., *The Taming of Chance* (Cambridge 1990, reprint 1998)

Halbwachs, M., *La théorie de l'homme moyen. Essai sur Quetelet et la statistique morale* (Paris 1912)

Hankins, F.H., *Adolphe Quetelet as Statistician* (New York 1908)

Headrick, D.R., *When Information Came of Age: Technologies of Knowledge in the Age of Reason and Revolution, 1700–1850* (Oxford 2000)

Heilbron, J., *Het ontstaan van de sociologie* (Amsterdam 1991)

Herren, M., '"Die Erweiterung des Wissens beruht vorzugsweise auf dem Kontakt mit der Außenwelt." Wissenschaftliche Netzwerke aus historischer Perspektive', *Zeitschrift für Geschichtswissenschaft* 49 (2001), 197–207.

Heuschling, X., 'Des naissances dans la ville de Bruxelles, considérées dans leur rapport avec la population', *Bulletin de la Commission de Statistique* 1 (1843), 165–205

Heuschling, X., *Manuel de statistique ethnographique universelle, précédé d'une introduction théorique d'après l'état actuel de la science* (Brussels 1847)

Higgs, E., *A Clearer Sense of the Census. The Victorian Censuses and Historical Research* (London 1996)

Higgs, E., 'A cuckoo in the nest? The origins of civil registration and state medical statistics in England and Wales', *Continuity and Change* 11 (1996), 115–134

Hilts, V.L., 'Aliis exterendum, or, the Origins of the Statistical Society of London', *Isis* 69 (1978), 21–43

Hilts, V.L., *Statist and Statistician: Three Studies in the History of Nineteenth Century English Statistical Thought* (Ph.D. thesis, Harvard University, Cambridge, MA 1967)

Hogendorp, G.K van, *Bijdragen tot de huishouding van staat in het koninkrijk der Nederlanden* (2nd edn, edited by J.R. Thorbecke, Amsterdam n.d.)

Horel, C., *Histoire de Budapest* (Paris 1999)

Horváth, R.A., 'Le concept de statistique internationale et son évolution historique', *International Statistical Review* 40 (1972), 281–298

Houwaart, E.S., *De hygiënisten. Artsen, staat & volksgezondheid in Nederland 1840–1890* (Groningen 1991)

Hunfalvy, P., *Magyarország ethnographiája* (Budapest 1876)

Jessen, R. and J. Vogel, *Wissenschaft und Nation in der europäischen Geschichte* (Frankfurt and New York 2002)

John, V., 'Quetelet bei Goethe', in: H. Paasche (ed.), *Festgabe für Johannes Conrad. Zur Feier des 25-jährigen Bestehens des staatswissenschaftlichen Seminars zu Halle a. S.* (Jena 1898), pp. 313–334

Journal de la Société de Statistique de Paris (1860–)

Journal of the Statistical Society of London (since 1886 Royal Statistical Society) (1838–)

Jubilee Volume of the Statistical Society (founded 1834), June 22–24, 1885 (London 1885)

Kaiser, W., 'Transnational Mobilization and Cultural Representation: Political Transfer in an Age of Proto-Globalization, Democratization and Nationalism 1848–1914', *European Review of History* 12 (2005), 403–424

Kaufhold, K. and W. Sachse, 'Die Göttinger "Universitätsstatistik" und ihre Bedeutung für die Wirtschafts- und Sozialgeschichte', in: H.-G. Herrlitz and H. Kern (eds), *Anfänge Göttinger Sozialwissenschaft. Methoden, Inhalte und soziale Prozesse im 18. und 19. Jahrhundert* (Göttingen 1987), pp. 72–95

Kendall, M.G. and R. L. Plackett (eds), *Studies in the History of Statistics and Probability*, II (London 1977)

Kingston-Mann, E., 'Statistics, Social Science, and Social Justice: The Zemstvo Statisticians of Pre-Revolutionary Russia', in: S.P. McCaffray and M. Melancon (eds), *Russia in the European Context 1789–1914. A Member of the Family* (New York 2005), pp. 113–139

Kiss, C. E. and J. Stagl (eds), *Nation und Nationalismus in wissenschaftlichen Standardwerken Österreich-Ungarns, ca. 1867–1918* (Vienna 1997)

Klein, J.L., *Statistical Visions in Time: A History of Time Series Analysis, 1662–1938* (Cambridge 1997)

Klep, P. and I. Stamhuis (eds), *The Statistical Mind in a Pre-Statistical Era: The Netherlands, 1750–1850* (Amsterdam 2002)

Knapp, G.F., *Grundherrschaft und Rittergut. Vorträge nebst biographischen Beilagen* (Leipzig 1897)

Knies, C.G.A., *Die Statistik als selbständige Wissenschaft. Zur Lösung des Wirrsals in der Theorie und Praxis dieser Wissenschaft. Zugleich ein Beitrag zu einer kritischen Geschichte der Statistik seit Achenwall* (Kassel 1850)

Koren, J. (ed.), *The History of Statistics: Their Development and Progress in Many Countries* (New York 1918)

Körösi, J., *Statistique internationale des grandes villes. Première section: mouvement de la population*, I (Boedapest 1876)

Krüger, L., L.J. Daston and M. Heidelberger (eds), *The Probabilistic Revolution*, I, *Ideas in History* (Cambridge, MA and London 1987)

Krüger, L., G. Gigerenzer and M.S. Morgan (eds), *The Probabilistic Revolution*, II, *Ideas in Science* (Cambridge, MA and London 1987)

La Berge, A.F., *Mission and Method: The Early Nineteenth-Century French Public Health Movement* (Cambridge 1992)

Labbé, M., 'Le projet d'une statistique des nationalités discuté dans les sessions du Congrès International de Statistique (1853–1876)' in: H. le Bras, F. Ronsin, and E. Zucker-Rouvillois (eds), *Démographie et Politique* (Dijon 1997), pp. 127–142

Laspeyres, E., *Die Kathedersocialisten und die statistischen Congresse. Gedanken zur Begründung einer nationalökonomischen Statistik und einer statistischen Nationalökonomie* (Berlin 1875)

Le Mée, R., 'La statistique démographique officielle de 1815 à 1870 en France', *Annales de la démographie historique* 16 (1979), 251–279

Lécuyer, B.-P., 'The Statistician's Role in Society: the Institutional Establishment of Statistics in France', *Minerva. Review of Science, Learning and Policy* 25 (1987), 34–55

Legoyt, A., 'Du mouvement de la population en France', *Journal de la Société de Statistique de Paris*, 1 (1860), 131–143; 149–167

Legoyt, A., *La France et l'étranger. Études de statistique comparée* (2nd edition, Paris and Strasbourg 1865)

Legoyt, A., *La France statistique ou la France intellectuelle, morale, financière, industrielle, politique, judiciaire, militaire, physique, territoriale et agricole* (Paris 1843)

Levra, U., 'La "statistica morale" del Regno di Sardegna tra la Restaurazione e gli anni Trenta: da Napoleone a Carlo Alberto', *Clio* 28 (1992), 353–378

Lindenfeld, D.F., *The Practical Imagination: The German Sciences of State in the Nineteenth Century* (Chicago and London 1997)

Lottin, J., *Quetelet. Statisticien et sociologue* (Leuven and Paris 1912)

Lyons, F.S.L., *Internationalism in Europe 1815–1914* (Leiden 1963)

Maestri, P., *Annuario economico e politico dell'Italia per l'anno 1852* (Turin 1852)

Maestri, P., *Annuario economico- statistico dell'Italia per l'anno 1853* (Turin 1853)

Marucco, D., *L'amministrazione della statistica nell'Italia unita* (Rome and Bari 1996)

Marx, K. *Das Kapital. Kritik der politischen Ökonomie*, I (Berlin 1981)

Meaux, L. de (ed.), *Saint-Pétersbourg: histoire, promenades, anthologie et dictionnaire* (Paris 2003)

Moreau de Jonnès, A., *Eléments de statistique comprenant les principes généraux de cette science et un aperçu historique de ses progrès* (Paris 1847)

Mouat, F.J., 'Preliminary Report of the Ninth International Statistical Congress, held at Buda-Pesth, from 1st to 7th September 1876', *Journal of the Statistical Society of London* 39 (1876) no. 4, 628–647

Mouat, F.J., 'Second and Concluding Report of the Ninth International Statistical Congress, held in Buda-Pesth, in September 1876', *Journal of the Statistical Society of London* 40 (1877) no. 4, 531–556

Neumann-Spallart, F.X. von, *Die Erfolge der internationalen statistischen Congresse 1853–1876 und Vorschläge zur Gründung eines Institut International de Statistique. Bericht an die Jubiläums-Versammlung der Statistical Society in London, Juni 1885* (Vienna 1885)

Nietzsche, F., *Menschliches, Allzumenschliches* (original edition, Chemnitz 1878)

Nixon, J.W., *A History of the International Statistical Institute 1885–1960* (The Hague 1960)

Nordau, M., *Erinnerungen. Erzählt von ihm selbst und von der Gefährtin seines Lebens* (Leipzig and Vienna n.d.)

Orlovsky, D.T., *The Limits of Reform: The Ministry of Internal Affairs in Imperial Russia, 1802–1881* (Cambridge, MA and London 1981)

Palsky, G. *Des chiffres et des cartes. Naissance et développement de la cartographie quantitative française au XIXe siècle* (Paris 1996)

Pasquino, P., 'Politisches und historisches Interesse. "Statistik" und historische Staatslehre bei Gottfried Achenwall (1719–1772)' in: H.E. Bödeker, G.G. Iggers, J.B. Knudsen and P.H. Reill (eds), *Aufklärung und Geschichte. Studien zur deuschen Geschichtswissenschaft im 18. Jahrhundert* (Göttingen 1986), pp. 144–168

Patriarca, S., 'How Many Italies? Representing the South in Official Statistics' in: J. Schneider (ed.), *Italy's "Southern Question". Orientalism in One Country* (Oxford and New York 1998), pp. 77–97

Patriarca, S., *Numbers and Nationhood: Writing Statistics in Nineteenth-Century Italy* (Cambridge 1996)

Pelling, M., *Cholera, Fever and English Medicine 1825–1865* (Oxford 1978)

Perrot, M., 'Premières mesures des faits sociaux: les débuts de la statistique criminelle en France (1780–1830)' in: *Pour une histoire de la statistique*, I (Paris 1977), pp. 125–137

Pesci, U. *Firenze Capitale (1865–1870)* (Florence 1904)

Pflanze, O., *Bismarck and the Development of Germany*, I, *The Period of Unification, 1815–1871* (2nd edn, Princeton 1990)

Poovey, M. 'Figures of Arithmetic, Figures of Speech: The Discourse of Statistics in the 1830s' in: J. Chandler, A.I. Davidson and H. Harootunian (eds), *Questions of Evidence. Proof, Practice, and Persuasion across the Disciplines* (Chicago and London 1994), pp. 401–421

Poovey, M., *A History of the Modern Fact: Problems of Knowledge in the Sciences of Wealth and Society* (Chicago 1998)

Porter, T.M., *The Rise of Statistical Thinking: 1820–1900* (Princeton 1986)

Quack, H.P.G., 'De internationale statistieke congressen en dat van Pesth', *De Gids* 40 (1876) IV, 18–105

Quetelet, A., *Anthropométrie ou mesure des différentes facultés de l'homme* (Brussels 1870)

Quetelet, A., *Du système social et des lois qui le régissent* (Paris 1848)

Quetelet, A., *Lettres à S.A.R. le duc régnant de Saxe-Coburg et Gotha, sur la théorie des probabilités, appliquée aux sciences morales et politiques* (Brussels 1846)

Quetelet, A., *Physique sociale ou essai sur le développement des facultés de l'homme* [1869]. Réédition annotée par É. Vilquin et J.-P. Sanderson (Brussels 1997)

Quetelet, A., *Recherches statistiques sur le royaume des Pays-Bas* (Brussels 1829)

Quetelet, A., *Recherches sur la population, les naissances, les décès, les depôts de medicité, etc. dans le Royaume des Pays Bas* (Brussels 1827)

Quetelet, A., 'Résultats du recensement de la population. Rapport au Ministre de l'intérieur' (23 December 1846), *Bulletin de la Commission de Statistique* 3 (1847), 152–155

Quetelet, A., 'Sur le recensement de la population de Bruxelles en 1842', *Bulletin de la Commission de Statistique* 1 (1843), 27–163

Quetelet, A., *Sur l'homme et le développement de ses facultés, ou Essai de physique sociale* (Brussels 1836)

Randeraad, N., 'Negentiende-eeuwse bevolkingsregisters als statistische bron en middel tot sociale beheersing', *Tijdschrift voor Sociale Geschiedenis* 21 (1995), 319–342

Randeraad, N., 'The Dutch Path to Statistics (1815–1830)' in: P. Klep and I. Stamhuis (eds), *The Statistical Mind in a Pre-Statistical Era: The Netherlands, 1750–1850* (Amsterdam 2002), pp. 99–123

Ranke, L. von, *Das Briefwerk*, ed. W.P. Fuchs (Hamburg 1949)

Ranke, L. von, *Neue Briefe*, ed. B. Hoeft and H. Herzfeld (Hamburg 1949)

Rawson, W., 'An Inquiry into the Statistics of Crime in England and Wales', *Journal of the Statistical Society of London* 2 (1839), 316–344

Recherches statistiques sur la ville de Paris et le département de la Seine (4 vols, Paris 1821–1829)

Reden, F.W. von, *Allgemeine vergleichende Handels- und Gewerbs-Geographie und Statistik. Ein Handbuch für Kaufleute, Fabrikanten und Staatsmänner [...]* (Berlin 1844)

Reden, F.W. von, *Deutschland und das Uebrige Europa. Handbuch der Bodens-, Bevölkerungs-, Erwerbs- und Verkehrs-Statistik; des Staatshaushalts und der Streitmacht in vergleichender Darstellung* (Wiesbaden 1854)

Rümelin, G., *Zur Theorie der Statistik* (1863) in: G. Rümelin, *Reden und Aufsätze* (Freiburg i. B. 1875), pp. 208–264

Schaab, M., 'Die Herausbildung einer Bevölkerungsstatistik in Württemberg und in Baden wahrend der ersten Hälfte des 19. Jahrhunderts', *Zeitschrift für Württembergische Landesgeschichte* 30 (1971), 164–200

Schaer, F.-W., 'Die Mitwirkung der nationalökonomischen Disziplin bei der Neuorganisation des Preußischen Statistischen Büros im Jahre 1860', *Vierteljahrschrift für Sozial- und Wirtschaftsgeschichte* 56 (1969), 233–244

Schmal, H., *Den Haag of 's-Gravenhage. De 19de-eeuwse gordel, een zone gemodelleerd door zand en veen* (Utrecht 1995)

Schmidt, D., *Statistik und Staatlichkeit* (Wiesbaden 2005)

Schweber, L., 'Controverses et styles de raisonnement. Débats sur la statistique de population au XIXe siècle en France et en Angleterre', *Enquête* 5 (1997), 83–108

Schweber, L., *Disciplining Statistics. Demography and Vital Statistics in France and England, 1830-1885* (Durham and London 2006)

Schweber, L., 'L'échec de la démographie en France au XIXe siècle?', *Genèses* (1997), no. 29, 5–28

Schweber, L., 'Manipulation and Population Statistics in Nineteenth-Century France and England', *Social Research* 68 (2001), 547–582

Scott, J.W., 'Statistical Representations of Work: The Politics of the Chamber of Commerce's *Statistique de l'Industrie à Paris, 1847-48*', in: S.L. Kaplan and C.J. Koepp (eds), *Work in France: Representations, Meaning, Organization, and Practice* (Ithaca, NY and London 1986), pp. 335–363

Smits, É., *Nationale statistiek. Ontwikkeling der een-en-dertig tabellen uitgegeven door de commissie voor de statistiek en betrekkelijk tot de gesteldheid der bevolking in de Nederlanden sedert de oprigting van het Koninkrijk tot en met 1824. Memorie* (Brussels 1827)

Sofia, F., *Una scienza per l'amministrazione. Statistica e pubblici apparati tra età rivoluzionaria e restaurazione* (Rome 1988)

Sofia, F. and P. Garonna, *Statistica, storia e nazione: la statistica ufficiale tra passato e futuro. Annali di Statistica* 126, serie X, no. 14 (Rome 1997)

Soresina, M., *Conoscere per amministrare: Luigi Bodio. Statistica, economia e pubblica amministrazione* (Milan 2001)

Soresina, M., 'Economia politica e statistica in Luigi Bodio', *Storia in Lombardia* 20 (2000), 5–60

Stamhuis, I.H., *'Cijfers en Aequaties' en 'Kennis der Staatskrachten'. Statistiek in Nederland in de negentiende eeuw* (Amsterdam 1989)

Statistische Mittheilungen aus dem Königreich Sachsen (1851–1855)

Sterling, D., *The Making of an Afro-American: Martin Robison Delany 1812-1885* (New York 1971)

Stigler, S.M., 'Adolphe Quetelet: Statistician, Scientist, Builder of Intellectual Institutions', in: *Actualité et universalité de la pensée scientifique d'Adophe Quetelet. Actes du colloque organisé à l'occasion du bicentenaire de sa naissance. Palais des Académies 24–25 octobre 1996* (Brussels 1997), pp. 47–61

Stigler, S.M., *The History of Statistics: The Measurement of Uncertainty before 1900* (Cambridge, MA and London 1986)

Tóth, Z., 'Liberale Auffassung der Ethnizität in der "Ethnographie von Ungarn" von Pál Hunfalvy', in: C. Kiss, E. Kiss and J. Stagl (eds), *Nation und Nationalismus in wissenschaftlichen Standardwerken Österreich-Ungarns, ca. 1867–1918* (Vienna 1997), pp. 57–64

'Uit 's-Gravenhage', *Utrechtsch Provinciaal en Stedelijk Dagblad*, 7 and 9 September 1869

Valera, G., 'Statistik, Staatengeschichte, Geschichte im 18. Jahrhundert', in: H.E. Bödeker, G.G. Iggers, J.B. Knudsen and P.H. Reill (eds), *Aufklärung und Geschichte. Studien zur deuschen Geschichtswissenschaft im 18. Jahrhundert* (Göttingen 1986), pp. 119–143

Velle, K., 'Statistiek en sociale politiek: de medische statistiek en het gezondheidsbeleid in België in de 19de eeuw', *Belgisch Tijdschrift voor Nieuwste Geschiedenis* 16 (1985), 213–242

Verhandlungen der Permanenz-Commission des Internationalen Statistischen Congresses (Vienna 1873)

Vicinus M. and B. Niergaard (eds), *Ever Yours, Florence Nightingale: Selected Letters* (London 1989)

Vissering, S., 'De statistiek in Nederland', *De Gids* 13 (1849) II, 1–33

Vissering, S., *Herinneringen*, II, *Politische vertoogen* (Amsterdam 1863)

Wagner, A., 'Statistik', in: J.C. Bluntschli and K. Brater (eds), *Deutsches Staatswörterbuch*, X (Stuttgart-Leipzig 1867), pp. 400–480

Weintraub, S., *Albert: Uncrowned King* (London 1997)

Westergaard, H., *Contributions to the History of Statistics* (London 1932)

Woolf, S.J., *Napoleone e la conquista dell'Europa* (Rome and Bari 1990)

Woolf, S.J., 'Statistics and the Modern State', *Comparative Studies in Society and History* 31 (1989), 588–604

Woolf, S.J., 'Towards the History of the Origins of Statistics: France 1789–1815', in: J.-C. Perrot and S.J. Woolf, *State and Statistics in France 1789–1815* (London 1984), pp. 132–155

Woud, A. van der, *Waarheid en karakter. Het debat over de bouwkunst 1840–1900* (Rotterdam 1997)

Woude, F. van der, *Minister Mr. P.P. van Bosse en de fiscale wetgeving rond het midden van de 19e eeuw* (Ph.D. Rijksuniversiteit Groningen 1997)

Zeitschrift des Statistischen Bureaus des Königlich Sächsischen Ministeriums des Innern (1855–1904)

Index